Hartland de Montarville Molson
Man of Honour

Hartland de Montarville Molson

Hartland de Montarville Molson

Man of Honour

Karen Molson

FIREFLY BOOKS

A FIREFLY BOOK

Published by Firefly Books Ltd. 2006

First printing

Library and Archives Canada Cataloguing in Publication

Molson, Karen
    Hartland de Montarville Molson : man of honour / Karen Molson.

Includes bibliographical references and index.
ISBN-13: 978-1-55407-150-0
ISBN-10: 1-55407-150-X

    1. Molson, Hartland de Montarville, 1907-2002. 2. Canada. Parliament. Senate—Biography. 3. Molson Breweries—Biography. 4. Montreal Canadiens (Hockey team)--Presidents--Biography. 5. Directors of corporations-- Canada--Biography. 6. Businessmen--Canada--Biography. 7. Montréal (Québec)--Biography. I. Title.

FC601.M64M64 2006   971.06'092   C2006

Publisher Cataloging-in-Publication Data (U.S.)

Molson, Karen.
    Hartland de Montarville Molson : man of honour / Karen Molson.
[328] p. : photos. ; cm.
Includes bibliographical references and index.
ISBN-13: 978-1-55407-150-0 (pbk.)
ISBN-10: 1-55407-150-X (pbk.)
1. Molson, Hartland de Montarville, 1907-2002. 2. Canada. Parliament. Senate--Biography. 3. Molson Breweries--Biography. 4. Businessmen--Canada--Biography. I. Title.
971.0647/092 dc22   F1034.3.M64M65 2006

Published in Canada by
Firefly Books Ltd.
66 Leek Crescent
Richmond Hill, Ontario L4B 1H1

Published in the United States by
Firefly Books (U.S.) Inc.
P.O. Box 1338, Ellicott Station
Buffalo, New York 14205

Cover and interior design by George Walker

Printed in Canada

The publisher gratefully acknowledges the financial support for our publishing program by the Government of Canada through the Book Publishing Industry Development Program.

Photo credits: Front cover clockwise from left: Max Hardinge; CP/ Montreal Gazette; CP/ Montreal Gazette; Zoë Murray. Front flap: Department of History, DND, Ottawa. Back cover: Andrew Hardinge. Back flap: Nancy Drozd.

Dedicated to
Hartland's loving daughter Zoë,
his grandchildren Charles, Andrew and Max
and in loving memory of my father, Robin Molson.

Acknowledgements

In the course of working on this book, from the preparation and research to finding background information, relevant documents and photographs, from fact checking to editorial suggestions, I owe a debt of gratitude to many people.

First I would like to extend special thanks to all of those who consented to be interviewed, sharing their memories of Hartland, including his daughter Zoë Murray, his grandsons Charles, Andrew and Max Hardinge, his nephews Eric and Stephen Molson, Hartland Molson MacDougall, his niece Lorna Bethel and great-niece Elena Heard, his cousins Ian Molson, Pat Molson, Mary Iversen and Stuart Iversen, and Hartland's former sister-in-law, Celia Lafleur.

Of the above I am indebted particularly to Zoë Murray and her son Max Hardinge for generously lending me Hartland's private papers and photographs, answering myriad questions, giving me names and contact information for others and keeping in touch for updates on the manuscript's progress.

Others who were most helpful in enlightening me about Hartland's character and actions were his contemporaries and friends, including Steve Stevens, John and Helen Starnes, Joan McKim, Marjorie Buttrum and Betty Henderson Paul, the latter of whom I interviewed when she was 99 years old, and still quite spirited. In Knowlton, Quebec, I had the pleasure of meeting and interviewing the valiant Dal Russel, Hartland's good friend and the last living member of the No. 401 RCAF Squadron who flew in the Battle of Britain.

Professionals who were associated with Hartland and also became his friends were consistent resources of information and kindly helped me find any information I asked for. These included Dr. Douglas Kinnear, Bruce McNiven, Rolland Peloquin and William Stavert. I also enjoyed conversations with the gracious Jean Beliveau, who remembered Hartland with respect and affection.

Help was also generously extended to me by David Smith, Arthur Bishop, Dr. Barry Posner, James Patterson, Archdeacon Peter Hannen and Victor Suthren, former director of the Canadian War Museum. At the Forest and Stream Club in Dorval I had delightful conversations with Bob Hall and Dick Irvin. In Lennoxville I was treated to an extensive and impressive tour of Bishop's College School by headmaster Lewis Evans. There I was also accompanied by François de Sainte Marie, director of finance and operations; Charles de Sainte Marie, associate director of development and William Stavert, the latter kindly arranging the trip and tour.

For research at Library and Archives Canada in Ottawa, I would like to warmly thank Patti Mitton for her professional genealogical research and Ted Kelly for his parliamentary inquiries. Stephen Harris and William Rawling of the DND Department of History in Ottawa aided my research there. Royal Military College archivist Ross McKenzie was patient and thorough in answering all my questions and mailed me packages of photocopied archive papers. RCAF archivist Captain Doug Newman was enormously helpful with military research and proofreading wartime chapters, and his enthusiasm was warmly appreciated. Ottawa journalist Jeff Esau spent some time combing his contacts and resources in search of evidence of a flying stunt that was alleged to have taken place in June 1940. David McCall kindly mailed me information about Hartland's career in the air force, Christopher Marks spoke with me about the Montreal Racket Club and archivist France Belisle provided answers to questions dealing with the Senate.

I am grateful to my publisher Michael Worek at Firefly Books, for his vision, faith and patience, and to Jennifer Pinfold for her thorough and consistent efforts with regard to photo illustrations.

I would like to express my appreciation to Joanie Flynt, who devoted much of her time to help me with initial proofreading and fact checking, and I especially thank her for spontaneous insights and steadfast encouragement. I am grateful also for the assiduous efforts of many friends and family members who acted as proofreaders, some of whom read through several early drafts, unearthing my many errors. These include Robin and Carolyn Molson, as well as Stuart Iversen, Ian Molson, Max Hardinge, Zoë Murray and William Stavert. It is through their time and attention to detail that the final draft has been carefully screened; I take full responsibility and apologize for any errors that remain.

Contents

Introduction   10

Genealogical Reference   16

Preface   18

Milestones   22

Chapter

   One 25

   Two 41

   Three 61

   Four 82

   Five 102

   Six 121

   Seven 136

   Eight 158

   Nine 175

   Ten 192

   Eleven 211

   Twelve 233

   Thirteen 251

   Fourteen 275

   Fifteen 298

Select Bibliography   320

Index   322

Introduction

A man's life can be measured by what he does with his talents and other resources for the benefit of mankind. In this respect, Hartland Molson was a unique human being whose likeness may never be seen again. Born into a prominent Montreal family, he was equally proud to be a Canadian and a Quebecois, both at the same time. He was a self-confident man of wise judgement and the utmost integrity who charted his own way through life and rendered outstanding service to his country. He was a man of remarkable courage, leadership and generosity, rare in his own generation and a vanishing breed in ours. He left a fine example for us all to follow.

I feel very honoured to have been asked to write the Introduction to this biography of Hartland Molson. I hesitated at first to accept this invitation, inasmuch as I questioned whether Hartland would be altogether happy about a book being written on his life so soon after his death, or at any time at all for that matter. He was such a modest man that I am sure he never expected to be praised for all his accomplishments. However, Hartland's life was so important and touched so many people in so many ways that I think we can all benefit from reading Karen Molson's story about this magnificent man's life, honour and legacy.

Hartland reminds me of the young man described so eloquently in Kipling's famous poem "If." Hartland met the high standards of all the characteristics and qualities set out in every verse. I can just imagine one or other of his loving parents Herbert or Bessie Molson reading this poem to him:

> If you can keep your head when all about you
> Are losing theirs and blaming it on you …
> If you can meet with Triumph and Disaster
> And treat those two impostors just the same …

If you can talk with crowds and keep your virtue,
Or walk with kings – nor lose the common touch …
you'll be a Man, my son.

Hartland grew up to be a dignified and charming man. He may have been born to wealth and social eminence, but he returned to his community such enormous value in service and munificence that he deserves to be remembered as a truly outstanding person.

There are several interesting threads running through Hartland's life, of which the principal ones I think were sport, leadership and philanthropy. From his earliest days, Hartland played all the usual boyhood games at school at Charterhouse in England and in Canada at Bishop's College School and the Royal Military College. He was a keen athlete who loved his games and other sports such as track and field. His love of hockey stayed with him all his life and led to his purchase and re-purchase of the Canadiens hockey team when he was older.

Flying was also a sport that Hartland took up as a young man. This led to his military career as an air force officer and pilot during the Battle of Britain, when he became one of Churchill's "few," to whom so much was owed by so many, for fending off a German invasion of Great Britain in the Second World War. Another favourite sport of Hartland's that lasted into his advanced years was fishing. He was a member of the Bonaventure Club and every summer he went salmon fishing at the Club's property on the Bonaventure River. He was also a member of the Montreal Racket Club where he played rackets with several of his good friends who were also members. This club has the only racket court in Canada and he became a "double" honorary member of the Club in 1999, after seventy years of membership.

Another thread running through Hartland's life that I mentioned above is leadership. He learned the first principles of leadership in sports at school. He knew that to become a leader he first of all had to be a team player. This he developed without any difficulty as a child. I am sure that a great deal of his character and talents for leadership were learned on the playing fields of Charterhouse, Bishop's and the RMC. At the latter institution he was taught leadership and that helped him not only as a courageous pilot in his squadron of the Canadian Air Force during the war, but also in his subsequent military service in which he reached the high rank of Group Captain.

Hartland was a born leader and he had a natural air of authority. In his profession as an accountant and in business he was able to earn the respect and loyalty of others working with him or for him. He had a couple of business interests before joining the family brewery, including aviation transport and the cultivation of soy beans. In Molson's Brewery itself, he was employed for fifty years and rose to be president and chief executive officer. For the latter position he was chosen ahead of two other older members of the family. The brewing and sale of beer has reached into the seventh generation of the family since the original John Molson established Molson's Brewery in 1786, but Hartland was the last family member to be president. The Brewery prospered mightily during Hartland's watch. He led more by example than by command, and he often attributed the success of the business to the efforts and loyalty of the good people whom he hired as employees of the company. His leadership abilities are demonstrated by the record of his career; the facts speak for themselves.

A very popular person, Hartland was always impeccably dressed and immaculately groomed. People were attracted to him because of his pleasant personality and his active participation in community affairs, serving on boards of charities and canvassing in, or chairing, fundraising campaigns. At one time in his life, he seemed never to be at home and always at meetings or dinners and constantly involved in some way or other in almost every sort of benevolent organization.

Hartland made and kept friends very easily. He liked and was interested in other people, and he was always prepared to listen to friends' problems and help them if he could. This is all no doubt true because of his unfailing courtesy and good manners. He was also understanding and forgiving. I never knew him to take offence or bear a grudge, except perhaps on one occasion when his beloved hockey team was sold to strangers by other members of his extended family.

Hartland also had a very dry sense of humour. I remember that on one occasion when I visited him at his house on Rosemount Avenue, we sat in his study upstairs, next to the bar, and we had one or two drinks. On leaving, I said that he need not come downstairs, that I could easily find my way out. "Oh no," he said, "I will certainly come downstairs, I don't want you to take the silver."

The third thread in Hartland's life was philanthropy, and this set him quite apart from any of his peers. He was a very kind and generous man. He established the Molson Foundation with his brother Tom in 1958, and he donated to the foundation more than half of its contributed capital. In addition to the foundation, he also contributed substantial sums to other charities during his lifetime and on his death.

Towards the end of his life, Hartland decided that he wanted to make one more significant gift while he was still alive. This particular gift epitomized in many ways the nature of Hartland's philanthropy in giving for the benefit of others. His idea was to find an institution for which a gift of several million dollars would make a real difference and improve the services that it provided. He considered several different charities with this purpose in mind. The one he chose was Bishop's College School, which he had attended as a child. You can be sure that the directors of the school were overcome with joy that this large gift had come unsolicited and quite unexpectedly from a graduate.

Hartland did not attach any strings to this gift. He had complete confidence in the management of the school; all he said was "Be sure to do it right." Nevertheless, the school very sensibly decided to treat the gift as seed money for a capital campaign and to try to raise additional funds to improve its facilities. The school had to consider its needs, to determine what the objects of a campaign might be and how much it could raise from its supporters. There had been a campaign for funds at the school about ten years before. Not all the objectives of that campaign had been realized and other priorities had become apparent in the meantime. Accordingly, an exercise in strategic planning was undertaken before the gift was announced and more than twenty consultation dinners were held with a large cross-section of the school population, comprising students, teachers, staff, graduates and friends.

One of the key issues that had to be decided was what percentage of the funds to be raised should be applied to items of bricks and mortar and how much to scholarships and bursaries. There was a concern that donors would be more interested in giving if they knew that their money was going to be invested in buildings that they could see, rather than in intangible items such as endowments. However, the prevailing opinion of both the students and graduates was that although the construction of new facilities was important, more money should also go into helping deserving boys and girls to attend the school. This opinion was also supported by the foundations and key donors who were consulted in a feasibility study.

The result has been an outstanding success. The school entered upon a capital campaign for $15 million in the year 2000, and in less than three years they raised even more than they set out to get. They commenced immediately the renovation of old parts of the school and the construction of new parts, including the upgrading of the science classrooms and laboratories. They have also been able to set aside for endowments, comprising scholarships, bursaries and the funding of scholastic programs, about 40 percent of the proceeds of the campaign.

The most important and exciting element of the new school is a brand new building in the centre of the campus that houses the library, the students' common room, the theatre and the band room.

These features of the school were previously scattered around in different, inappropriate places within the complex, and now they are all together and much more accessible. This new building is called Hartland Molson Hall. It is situated between the school house and the sports centre and provides the third side of an open quadrangle, its outside architecture reflecting the style of the other buildings. The most significant result of the improvements of the school is the pleasure enjoyed by both the teachers and students in teaching and learning in such a magnificent setting.

The whole campaign for funds and the renovation and construction of the buildings was commenced at the end of Hartland's life and completed shortly after his death. He was kept abreast of the progress of the campaign and the building plans as they were developed. It is regrettable that he never saw the finished product, but there is no doubt that he would have been pleased with the result.

You must now read Karen's book, and as you do so you will come to know the splendid man about whom she is writing and all he did to improve the lives in so many ways of all of us who have survived him, and generations still to come.

William Stavert
Montreal, April 2006

William Stavert with Hartland Molson, October 2000. Photo: Courtesy David McCall.

Genealogical Reference

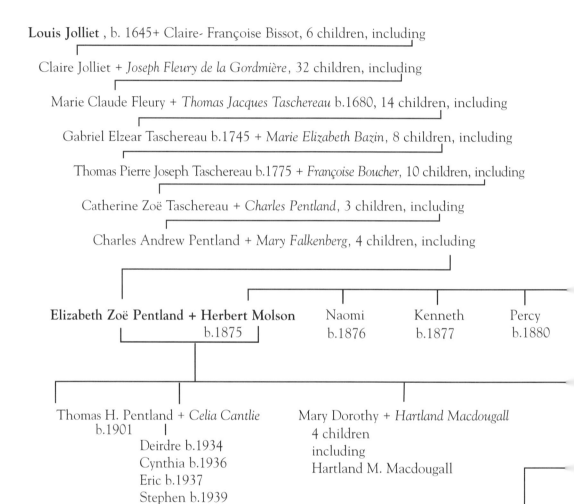

Louis Jolliet , b. 1645+ Claire- Françoise Bissot, 6 children, including

Claire Jolliet + *Joseph Fleury de la Gordmière*, 32 children, including

Marie Claude Fleury + *Thomas Jacques Taschereau* b.1680, 14 children, including

Gabriel Elzear Taschereau b.1745 + *Marie Elizabeth Bazin*, 8 children, including

Thomas Pierre Joseph Taschereau b.1775 + *Françoise Boucher*, 10 children, including

Catherine Zoë Taschereau + *Charles Pentland*, 3 children, including

Charles Andrew Pentland + *Mary Falkenberg*, 4 children, including

| **Elizabeth Zoë Pentland + Herbert Molson** b.1875 | Naomi b.1876 | Kenneth b.1877 | Percy b.1880 |

Thomas H. Pentland + *Celia Cantlie*
b.1901
Deirdre b.1934
Cynthia b.1936
Eric b.1937
Stephen b.1939

Mary Dorothy + *Hartland Macdougall*
4 children
including
Hartland M. Macdougall

The Honourable Senator Hartland de Montarville Molson, OBE , OC , DCL , FCA (May 29, 1907 - September 28, 2002) was an Anglo-Quebecer states-man, and a member of the prominent Molson family of brewers. His heritage can also be traced back to Louis Jolliet who was a Canadian explorer born in Quebec who is known for his explorations in North America. Jolliet and missionary Jacques Marquette were the first white men to map the Mississippi River.

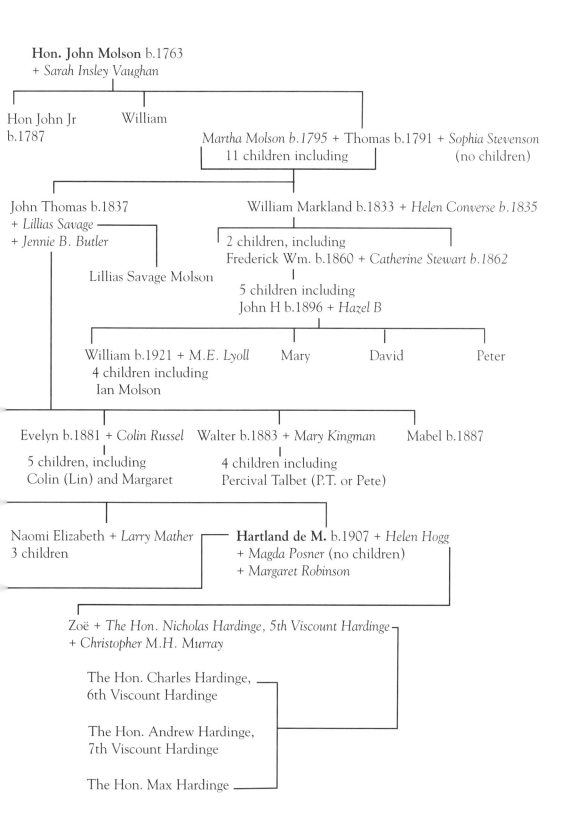

Hon. John Molson b.1763
+ *Sarah Insley Vaughan*

Hon John Jr
b.1787   William

Martha Molson b.1795 + Thomas b.1791 + Sophia Stevenson
11 children including   (no children)

John Thomas b.1837
+ *Lillias Savage*
+ *Jennie B. Butler*

William Markland b.1833 + *Helen Converse b.1835*

Lillias Savage Molson

2 children, including
Frederick Wm. b.1860 + *Catherine Stewart b.1862*

5 children including
John H b.1896 + *Hazel B*

William b.1921 + *M.E. Lyoll*   Mary   David   Peter
4 children including
Ian Molson

Evelyn b.1881 + *Colin Russel*   Walter b.1883 + *Mary Kingman*   Mabel b.1887

5 children, including   4 children including
Colin (Lin) and Margaret   Percival Talbet (P.T. or Pete)

Naomi Elizabeth + *Larry Mather*   **Hartland de M.** b.1907 + *Helen Hogg*
3 children   + *Magda Posner* (no children)
                                                            + *Margaret Robinson*

Zoë + *The Hon. Nicholas Hardinge, 5th Viscount Hardinge*
+ *Christopher M.H. Murray*

The Hon. Charles Hardinge,
6th Viscount Hardinge

The Hon. Andrew Hardinge,
7th Viscount Hardinge

The Hon. Max Hardinge

Preface

Aside from official introductions at family gatherings, the first time I properly met my cousin Hartland Molson was in 1997 at his office in the brewery, where he had agreed to be interviewed for my book *The Molsons – Their Lives and Times*. Some weeks prior to this interview I had mailed him a small packet of photographs of Molson family members, copies from a collection held at the National Archives in Ottawa. The people in the photos were not identified, though they appeared to be taken in the early 1900s, and I was hoping Hartland could tell me who they were. As I was shown into his office, he had the photos in his hand; he told me he had managed to identify them all. "I hope you didn't go to any trouble, Cousin Hartland," I said as I thanked him. "I assure you," he replied, "I went to a great *deal* of trouble."

I didn't know it at the time, but Hartland's sense of humour was legendary. It came naturally to him: he had an abundance of it and he wielded it expertly, whether offering it with affection to friends or using it pointedly to counter his detractors. His humour also served to deflect the feeling of awe many felt upon meeting him, which he likely sensed in my own demeanour. My grandparents and parents, who always referred to him as Cousin Hartland, had always spoken of him with the utmost respect and deference. I grew up knowing about some aspects of his career, more about his eminence as family patriarch, but relatively little about his character.

It was at this meeting in his office at the brewery that Hartland shared with me the story of his mother, Bessie, who, attempting to spank him at the age of 7, collapsed instead into giggles. Here I first heard about Hartland's father Herbert's stern countenance, and the funny chugging sound he made when he was trying to stifle laughter. Hartland told me about his own early ventures in the business world and how he came to be asked to join the brewery in 1938.

Hartland readily described his experience in the Second World War, and it was easy to tell that those years had been very meaningful to him. He was able to be philosophical about the decades he spent serving the Senate. His love of and dedication to the game of hockey, especially during the years he owned the Montreal Canadiens, was evident. But when I dared to ask him about how he and his cousins had resolved their differences over the sale of the team, his discomfort was palpable. "We never speak of it," he answered brusquely, and would not elaborate.

Even though I had the pleasure of other conversations with him after our initial meeting, Hartland remained very much an enigma to me, his modesty alone forming a screen between my questions and his answers. His valued privacy was also something I was loathe to violate, and as such posed my questions carefully, not wanting to appear disrespectful.

It was Stephen Molson, Hartland's nephew and president of the Molson Foundation, who first suggested to me shortly after Hartland's death that I write this biography. At the beginning, though I agreed it was a good idea, I was apprehensive that I might not be up to the task. Furthermore, as a writer, while I could see that human dramas, conflicts and resolutions were all present in Hartland's life, I worried about two things: one, how could I write his life story and not make it sound like a panegyric, and two, how could I, some fifty years his junior and having led a completely different life than he did, possibly interpret his myriad actions, let alone do justice to their impact?

In the end, my intention to give a full and balanced account of an extraordinary person was, as I suspected, no simple undertaking. After examining Hartland's public and private documents; questioning his acquaintances, friends and family members; reading copies of speeches spanning sixty years and a multitude of topics; poring over Hansard reports of Senate debates and reading through transcripts of interviews by others, there was still something elusive about him that was impossible to pin down.

It's not that the truth was hidden somewhere – on the contrary, the truth was everywhere, and the only surprises I discovered were ones that shed more light on his good qualities. It soon became evident that, unlike many others who have been as successful in business, as respected in politics, as admired in sports or as lauded in philanthropy, Hartland, while being all these things, had no ulterior motives. There was nothing concealed, no artifice to his character; in all respects and under every examination he came across as a man of integrity.

Some might point out that Hartland had a life without handicaps. It is true he never had to rally against a difficult upbringing, nor did he have to grapple with poverty, or even much bad luck. All the same, he rose above his circumstances: that is, he didn't allow his good fortune to corrupt his moral code, he didn't live as though there was one set of rules for himself and one for everyone else and he didn't lapse into laziness or self-indulgence.

Another person born under the same lustre of wealth and privilege as he was might have been settled in a much different life, might have been a dilettante, a professional socialite or established in a comfortable, predictable routine in some wood-panelled executive office. Instead, Hartland continually chose to take on any challenge to which he was able to rise and accepted the responsibility he felt was his, from childhood until long after he had reached the age when most people consider retirement. Dignified and resolute to the end, he used his gifts to better the lives of others, in near and wider communities.

One of the things that particularly struck me while researching and writing this book was the devotion of Hartland's friends, those who knew him best, a group that encompassed his elders, his peers and his closest associates. One of these friends was his principal private secretary for many years, Rolland Peloquin, who disclosed that Hartland always used to keep a letter from his father, Herbert, in a drawer of his desk. It was written in 1928, while Hartland was working in Paris apprenticing as a banker. Herbert's letter, a reply to Hartland's request for extra money, contained a soft admonishment, his attempt to teach his son not to be a spendthrift. However, Herbert sent the money his son requested anyway. Hartland not only kept the letter all those years, but took it out from time to time to read it. His father's words touched him, and he liked to be reminded of the meaningful and important values that he was raised to represent. This small private action – keeping this letter, and sharing its contents with Peloquin – may say as much or more than any public speech, business decision or legislative achievement, about what made Hartland the man he was.

Karen Molson
April 2006

Robert Nadon, La Presse

Hartland Molson poses with The John Molson, a 1971 replica of one of Canada's early steam engines, at the Canadian Railway Museum in Delson, St.-Constant, Quebec.

MILESTONES
HON. HARTLAND de M. MOLSON

1916–1918	Selwyn House School
1918–1921	Bishop's College School
1921–1923	Charterhouse School, England
1923–1924	Bishop's College School
1924–1928	Royal Military College – No. 1800
1928–1933	McDonald-Currie – C.A.
1933–1938	President – Dominion Skyways
1938–1939	Assistant Secretary-Treasurer – Molson's Brewery Limited
1938	Director – Jamaica Public Services
1939 (Sept.)	Enlisted RCAF and went overseas June 1940 with No. 1 Canadian Fighter Squadron (later 401). Wounded October 1940. Stayed in Air Force until 1946
1943–1946	Honorary Aide de Camp – Governor General
1945–1972	Director – Canadian Corporate Management – Vice President in 1965
1946	Awarded Order of British Empire
1946–1950	Secretary – Molson's Brewery Limited
1946–1947	President – The Canadian Club of Montreal
1948–1968	Governor – McGill University
1950	Fellow – Canadian Institute of Secretaries F.C.I.S.
1950–1953	Vice President – Molson's Brewery Limited
1951–1975	Elected Director – Canadian Industries Limited (C.I.L.) and re-elected to news company May 25, 1954. Retired April 1975
1951–1978	Elected Director in November – Bank of Montreal — Vice President in December 1964. Retired in January 1978
1953–1966	President – Molson's Brewery Limited
1955–1993	Appointed to the Senate of Canada – 28 July 1955 Resigned 31 May 1993
1955–1975	Elected Director in November – Sun Life Assurance Company. Resigned in 1975
1957–1968	President and then Chairman – Le Club de Hockey Canadien Inc. and Canadian Arena Company
1958	Commander Brother – Order of St. John
1958–1966	Director – Bank of London & Montreal
1959	Acquired Control – Sick's Breweries

1960	Honorary Degree (D. Sc. C.) – École des Hautes Études Commerciales – Université de Montréal
1964	Honorary Member – Montreal Racket Club
1966–1968	Chairman – Molson Breweries Limited
1968	Honorary Degree (D.C.L.) – University of Calgary
1968	Sold Canadian Arena Company to William, David and Peter Molson
1968	Acquisition of Anthes Imperial Limited
1968–1974	Chairman – Molson Industries Limited – and Director of Molson Breweries of Canada Limited
1970	Human Relations Award – Canadian Council of Christians and Jews
1973	Elected – Hockey Hall of Fame – Builders' Category
1974	Honorary Degree (LL.D.) – Royal Military College, Kingston
1974	Honorary Degree (D.C.L.) – Bishop's University
1974–1983	Honorary Chairman – The Molson Companies Limited
1982	Knight – Order of St. John
1982	Silver Wolf Award – Boy Scouts of Canada
1983	Honorary Degree (LL.D) – McGill University
1983–1988	Director – The Molson Companies Limited
1986	Honorary Associate Award – Conference Board of Canada
1988	Resigned as Director of the Molson Companies Limited – remained as Honorary Director
1991	Honorary Degree (D.Admin.) – Collège militaire royal de Saint-Jean (Quebec)
1993	Resigned from the Senate of Canada
1995	Order of Canada – Officer
1995	F.C.A. – Fellow Chartered Accountant – Ordre des Comptables agrées du Québec
1999	Double Honorary Member – Montreal Racket Club
2000	Officer – Ordre national du Québec

Chapter One

A T A MEETING of the Senate late on the evening of December 1, 1970, 63-year-old Hartland Molson stood up to deliver the most personal, heartfelt and impassioned speech of his career. An unprecedented major national crisis was playing itself out in Montreal – a series of crimes had terrorized the people; Prime Minister Trudeau had invoked the War Measures Act; and fear, anger and bitter debate dominated the streets and legislative chambers. Six weeks earlier, cabinet minister Pierre Laporte's body had been found in the trunk of a car, murdered by members of the Front de libération du Québec. Diplomat James Cross, kidnapped before Laporte, was still missing. Members of the armed forces had taken up guard positions in Montreal and Quebec, while privately hired security guards shadowed many members of parliament, cabinet ministers and senators. Though he'd been informed by the RCMP that his name was on the FLQ's list of potential targets, Molson was one of the few who refused their offer of protective escorts.

Long before Hartland Molson stood in the Senate chamber on this evening, his reputation as a man of courage and integrity was well established. His speeches always embodied common sense and elegant detachment, and while never imperious or commanding, he inspired others through words and actions. Molson's accomplishments, spread over a lifetime, included his brewing background, sports affiliations, philanthropy and his wartime air force experience in England. This time, the battleground was between nationalists and separatists over a crisis that had developed at home.

After fifteen years in the upper chamber, Molson may have been the best-known senator in the Canadian legislature. While others' opinions were predictable – liberals defending the War Measures Act ramifications, conservatives arguing against them – no one was sure with which camp Hartland would side. He sat as a political independent, with deeply ingrained beliefs, an aptitude for well-aimed reproofs and an instinct for *le bon mot*. He was able to go straight to the heart of a sensitive issue without wavering from conventional propriety.

Molson was the last to speak that evening; his words, underpinned with patriotism and modesty, found their way to the front pages of the country's major newspapers the next morning.

I am Quebecois. Although Anglophone, I have French blood in my veins and can claim to be truly, wholly, Quebecois. I say this not only because I am proud of it, but because I must point out that a Quebecer follows events in his province with an understanding and a sensitivity which at times seems to escape other good Canadians brought up in a less complex, unilingual part of the country.

We must hasten the changes necessary in our Constitution, and perhaps even more importantly, in our attitude, to reassure the French-speaking people of Canada that there will be no erosion of their cultural and linguistic heritage. It is up to all of us, French and English, to go beyond the old nagging arguments of history and rise to the realization that grace and sympathy, understanding and affection, surrounded by all the enormous gifts with which, in this country, we have been blessed, can and will bring the peace, prosperity and happiness which we all seek to establish for our children.

That Molson's name had been put on a hit list was an example of history repeating itself, echoing a long-ago incident in the summer of 1837. At that time, John Molson Junior had been singled out by Patriote leader Louis-Joseph Papineau, who declared his intention to have Molson kidnapped and be forced to give £80,000 to Les Fils de la Liberté. John Molson Junior felt compelled to have escape tunnels secretly dug under his Sherbrooke Street home, which fortunately he never had to use. Now, in December 1970, Hartland Molson did not appear to be practising caution; he was going about his usual routines: regularly showing up at his office at the brewery, having lunch at the Mount Royal Club, attending hockey games in Montreal and travelling to Ottawa for Senate sessions. Then, just as he did every winter, he left for a holiday in Jamaica.

The December 1970 speech was the first time Hartland Molson had voluntarily spoken about his matrilineal heritage in public. Modest though he was, he could scarcely avoid the subject, as his middle name, de Montarville, was an unusual appellation about which he was often asked. He'd become weary enough of the question that once he replied that his mother had chosen the name out of a book she was reading, and another time he joked that it was a "burden my mother saddled me with." In spite of this public bandy, however, most of those who knew (or knew of) him were unaware of its full significance. Reporters invariably referred to his paternal ancestry, and it was not Molson's inclination to enlighten them nor in his manner to speak about that which to him was obvious, both for the sake of economy of words and not wanting to appear arrogant or snobbish.

Hartland Molson was the son of Herbert Molson and Elizabeth Zoë Pentland. On his father's side of the family, Hartland was a fifth generation descendant of John Molson Senior who came to Canada in 1782 and established a brewery in 1786. On his mother's side, Hartland was a ninth generation descendant of Louis Jolliet, the legendary explorer. It was from this source that Hartland came to bear the name de Montarville. In a sense, his ancestors on his mother's side of the family were even more distinguished than those on his father's.

In tracing Hartland's maternal ancestors, we start with Louis Jolliet, whose life and remarkable accomplishments have been immortalized in Quebec's popular history. Born in 1645 in the town of Quebec, Jolliet attended the first Jesuit college there, where his musical talent and interest in philosophy came to light. He joined the Jesuits on their missionary travels during the summers; through his work with the natives, Jolliet developed a proficiency in indigenous languages. He went on to become a fur trader, and during his journeys through uncharted wilderness became intrigued with exploring.

Thus began the work by which he became best known, becoming the first white "discoverer" of the Mississippi River. Jolliet's geographical range was enormous: by foot, canoe and dogsled, depending on terrain and season, he steadfastly mapped much of the continent from Louisiana to Labrador. To his superiors, his records and cartographic skills were found to be thorough and groundbreaking. His work came to the attention of the governor and then the French king, who appointed him Royal Hydrographer and gave him a generous pension and finally the plum seigneury of the Île d'Orléans.

Louis Jolliet and his wife, Claire-Françoise Bissot, the daughter of a wealthy lieutenant in the provost corps, had six children.

Claire, one of his daughters, evidently inherited Jolliet's "courage, prowess, and robust health" for she, according to the parish register, after marrying Joseph Fleury de la Gordenière (seigneur of Deschambault), gave birth to thirty-two children. Their daughters all married into the *meilleurs partis de la colonie*, including one who wed the last governor of la Nouvelle-France, and another, Marie-Claire Fleury, who in 1728 married Thomas Jacques Taschereau. Of the latter's fourteen children (some died in infancy, two became nuns, some never married, one who married had no issue) only one – the thirteenth child, a son Gabriel-Elzéar – had children who would carry the Taschereau name.

Gabriel-Elzéar Taschereau, Hartland's great-great-great grandfather, was born in 1745. At the age of 14 he followed Montcalm into battle against General Wolfe at the Plains of Abraham. Terms of the French surrender stipulated that seigneurs' property, revenues and rights would remain intact as long as they laid down their arms, and young Taschereau, who inherited seigneuries in La Nouvelle Beauce, a district north of the Eastern Townships and bordered by the St. Lawrence River, swore allegiance to the new crown. Fifteen years later he voluntarily fought against Americans invading in 1775–76, and became a colonel in the 2nd Battalion of Militia in Quebec City. In 1776 he was named a justice of the peace in the civil district court in Montreal and in 1777 he was appointed as a judge.

In 1791, when the Constitutional Act divided the colony into Upper and Lower Canada, Taschereau was elected as one of the first members of the Legislative Assembly. A year later he was acting as deputy to Lord Dorchester and was called to the Legislative Council in 1798. By the time Taschereau died in 1809, he had amassed what the *Gazette* called "one of the most considerable fortunes in Canada."

Gabriel-Elzéar Taschereau and his wife, Marie-Louise-Elizabeth Bazin, had eight children, the eldest son of whom was Thomas

Pierre-Joseph Taschereau, who was born in 1775. Thomas Pierre-Joseph's career also began in the military, fighting for the British in the Royal Canadian Volunteers. In 1797, at age 21, he was a lieutenant stationed at Niagara. Ten years later he was back in Quebec, where he was appointed justice of the peace for the district; he commanded a battalion at Quebec during the War of 1812 and was appointed to the Legislative Council in 1818. Upon his father's death he inherited the seigneury of Sainte-Marie de la Beauce.

Thomas Pierre-Joseph Taschereau married Françoise Boucher, the daughter and heiress of Joseph Boucher de la Bruère de Boucherville, seigneur of Boucherville and de Montarville. Hartland's great-great grandmother Françoise was a direct descendant of Pierre Boucher, 1667 founder of Boucherville, and, as a "linguist, soldier, interpreter, ambassador, judge, governor, writer and seigneur," one of the most prominent figures of the early French colony and the second Canadian to be ennobled by Louis XIV. Behind the Boucherville lands, frontage and shoals lay the de Montarville seigneury, also granted to Pierre Boucher in 1710. These two neighbouring territories near the confluence of the St. Lawrence and Richelieu Rivers south of Montreal included all of the Boucherville Islands and were known as the wealthiest and finest seigneuries in the colony.

Thomas Pierre-Joseph Taschereau and Françoise Boucher had ten children, the eighth of whom was Catherine-Zoë Taschereau. (A close cousin of Catherine-Zoë's, Elzéar-Alexandre, became the first Canadian-born Cardinal, a position of great prestige, and his nephew, Louis-Alexandre Taschereau, was later to become premier of Quebec.) Hartland's great-grandmother Catherine-Zoë Taschereau appears to have been the first in her family to marry someone outside her faith and culture when she wed Anglican solicitor Charles Pentland. The couple, Hartland's great-grandparents, had three children; the eldest son, Charles Andrew Pentland, followed his father's career in law. As Hartland explained, in those days the girls followed their mother's religion and the boys their father's, thus Charles Andrew was raised Protestant. In 1872 he met and married Mary Falkenberg, who was the daughter of Baron Alfred Falkenberg, consul-general of Sweden and Norway in Canada, and his British wife, Elizabeth Kimball.

Charles and Mary Pentland had four children, of whom the eldest daughter was Elizabeth Zoë (called Bessie). Born in Quebec on June 17, 1875, Bessie narrowly escaped death at the age of 2 near Montmorency Falls while she, her mother and other relatives were on their way to enjoy a picnic in the Laurentide Hills. A covered carriage directly ahead of them suddenly broke through a decayed wooden bridge and plummeted into a steep gorge: Bessie's grandmother, Elizabeth Kimball Falkenberg, was killed instantly, together with "a pair of fine black horses."

At the age of 16 Bessie lost her mother to a long illness, and everything changed in her life. She became the head of the household, responsible for ordering meals and overseeing the staff and accounts. Throughout her life she remained close to her Falkenberg aunts and cousins, though most of them moved to New York City. Bessie shared a special bond with her father. Charles Pentland had a childhood friend from Ancien Lorette, a native chief with whom he went on hunting and fishing expeditions. While on these trips he would scrawl notes to his eldest daughter Bessie on scraps of birchbark, which she saved all her life. From time to time Bessie would travel to New York City with a chaperone friend, where they stayed with one of the Falkenberg aunts, and went "to see the nice things in the shops."

Bessie Pentland met Herbert Molson sometime in 1898, either in New York or Quebec City, though details of their first encounter have not been recorded. Charles Pentland may not have considered the match a good one for his daughter. The families were dissimilar in fundamental ways, the Pentlands never having been involved in trade and the Molsons never having left it. As a brewer Herbert was certain to be able to provide well for Bessie, though at the same time his profession may have been a drawback. Still, Herbert was a man cut from very solid cloth, and he had very high expectations of living up to the ancestral standards of integrity and success in his business and personal life. These qualities were sure to have influenced Charles Pentland when Herbert asked his permission for his daughter's hand.

Herbert was bound to and very proud of his family's history. Rigid and conservative in some areas yet progressive in others, Molsons had embraced British traditions and free enterprise as well as public service. Politics and directorships, fund-raising and philanthropy were paramount in the lives of many Molson men and women over the generations. John Molson the Elder and his sons were involved in military service in 1812 and 1837, and over the years the family maintained its close ties and loyalties to the mother country. Generations of Molsons travelled to England, visited relatives in Lincolnshire, toured breweries in London and sent children to be educated at British schools. Molson women in Montreal were industrious as volunteers, one – Anne Molson (1824–1899) – having played a major part in breaking the gender barrier at McGill University. It was considered essential that all the Molsons be fluent in French, but their social interactions were confined within English enclaves, and none had ever married a Francophone nor anyone outside the Anglican faith.

Herbert Molson was the eldest son and heir of industrialist-brewer John Thomas Molson, who himself was a grandson of the founder of Molson's Brewery. John Molson Senior, born in England in 1763, was orphaned at the age of 8 when his wealthy Lincolnshire landowner parents died. Thereafter raised by his grandfather, Molson came to Canada at the age of 18 in 1782, sold the paternal estate when he came of age three years later and used the proceeds to finance a small brewery in Montreal.

A veritable genius of industry, the Molson patriarch later built

Canada's first steamship in 1809, took part in the War of 1812, and over the next two decades owned and operated the St. Lawrence Steamboat Company. He became involved in private banking, bought properties, built hotels and a theatre, financed the country's first railway, was appointed to the Legislative Council of Lower Canada and was also an active philanthropist, all the while maintaining his first core business, brewing British beer for the inhabitants of Montreal.

John Molson Senior married his illiterate housekeeper Sarah Vaughan in 1801, having had four sons with her, one of whom died shortly after birth. The second surviving son, Thomas, would carry on the brewery line while the other sons maintained and expanded their father's other business initiatives.

Thomas Molson married his Lincolnshire cousin Martha Molson and brought her back to Montreal with him. There he branched into the distilling business, feuded with his brothers and moved to Kingston for ten years, where he started another brewery before coming back to Montreal upon the death of his father. From John Molson Senior he inherited real estate, bonds and shares, and parlayed all of it into an even bigger fortune, commissioned Molson Terrace, built his own church and petitioned Queen Victoria for a title, which he never received.

Thomas and Martha Molson had five daughters and three sons. When Thomas died in 1863, his eldest son John Henry Robinson Molson inherited the brewery. John H.R. Molson's two brothers, Markland and John Thomas, also grew up in the shadow of the brewery. John Thomas was the youngest of Thomas Molson's sons. His responsibilities at J.H.R. Molson & Brothers were less clear, and succession to the brewery less certain. He loved to travel, and particularly taken with sailing, the young man had a steam yacht built in Scotland in which he sailed around the world. After this extraordinary trip he came back to Montreal and married Jennie Baker Butler, the daughter of a doctor from the Eastern Townships, whose family had United Empire Loyalist origins. John Thomas and Jennie had seven children. After his eldest brother died child-less in 1897, John Thomas took over, bringing his nephew Fred and eldest son Herbert into the business as well.

Herbert had just graduated from McGill University with a degree in science when his uncle John died and his father inherited the brewery. But John Thomas' health had been eroded by Bright's dis-ease; his condition had seriously deteriorated by then and he rarely left the house. The responsibility fell upon Herbert and Fred to manage the business. As his father could not be left alone, Herbert was entrusted with sleeping in his room at night.

Serious beyond his years, Herbert had little time or inclination for leisure pursuits: even sports, considered an essential part of a gentleman's experience growing up, had been limited at university to cricket and the occasional canoe excursion. He had, however, taken dancing lessons and attended at least one historical ball, given by the Women's Antiquarian Society at the Windsor Hotel in Montreal. The fact that both Herbert and Bessie had been handed responsibilities at relatively young ages was significant common ground between them and likely contributed to their being attracted to each other.

Herbert and Bessie's wedding, dubbed "the society wedding of the year," took place on April 11, 1899. At the time, Queen Victoria was still on the throne and while English Canada remained ensconced in a colonial mentality, French Canada was bristling with nationalism. At the turn of the century many Canadians were ready for change, especially those who had expe-rienced the economic slump of the 1890s. Even at Molson's Brewery, the 1898 output of 14,000 barrels was the lowest it had been in twenty years. Tensions spilled into other arenas as well. In March 1900, Francophone students protested in a demonstration at McGill over Canadian participation in the Boer War. The war was particularly controversial in Quebec: at Britain's request,

Wilfrid Laurier, the first French-Canadian prime minister, had sent Canadian troops to South Africa, yet not even Liberals were all behind him, and Henri Bourassa publicly condemned Laurier's decision.

Prosperity was just waiting to be reawakened however, and mechanization was one development that was about to play a large part in boosting commerce. Herbert had travelled to New York City in 1898 for technical training in the science of brewing and was exposed to some of the industry's most modern practices. In the year 1900, which saw the first automobile in Montreal, brewery production was up to 20,000 barrels. Fred and Herbert evolved a long-range strategy for Molson's, incorporating caution in order to meet the approval of John Thomas Molson and the brewery's managing partner, Adam Skaife. Their plan involved the gradual installation of new equipment and directing accumulated profits toward a rebuilding scheme that would be executed in stages. Their goal was to introduce new methods that would keep quality consistent and incorporate the modernizations that would bring their brewery up to American standards.

For decades, the brewery had offered only three beverage brands: Mild Ale, India Pale Ale and Porter. The younger Molsons soon introduced Stock Ale and Export Ale, the latter the strongest in alcoholic content. They divided the responsibilities: Herbert looked after product change and quality maintenance while Fred looked after the modernization of the existing plant. As business historian Merrill Denison described it, "changes were made in the malt mill, hot water reservoirs, mash tub, brew kettle, fermenting vats, and water, steam, ammonia and beer lines; an automatic, mechanical grain-drier was constructed to handle the spent grains … and patent metal taps were introduced in place of the wooden bungs invented in Woden's day or earlier." By 1904, once the old machinery was replaced by new, more efficient equipment, the output had reached 27,000 barrels.

What Herbert and Fred had accomplished was unprecedented and daring, but ultimately successful. They were riding on the crest of a wave: Montreal was entering a new century and was surprised to find it a brave, happy, hopeful world. In spite of the tensions between French and English Canadians in Quebec, the whole country seemed to come alive with growth and expectation – Laurier was elected to a second consecutive majority government, immigration was filling up the west and investors were starting to make money in the railways and newer speculative ventures.

Herbert and Bessie's first child, Thomas Henry Pentland Molson, was born July 21, 1901. As the first grandchild for both the Molsons and the Pentlands, the boy was prized and doted on, and in the manner of other families of their era and privilege, a nanny was hired. Miss Dora Brockwell (soon called "Brockie"), joined the household and was given a room next to the nursery. A little over three years later on October 26, 1904, Dorothy was born. Called "Dosh" by young Tom, the name stuck throughout her childhood. A year and a half after that, on March 22, 1906, Bessie gave birth to a second daughter, Naomi Elizabeth, who was called Betty.

In the spring of 1907, Herbert Molson was at a comfortable point in his career. Beer sales were skyrocketing but his own work-load had eased, since he and his cousin Fred were able to take alternating time off. Their employees put in sixty-hour work weeks at a daily pay of between $1.25 and $1.50, which was fairer than most employers offered. Twelve quarts of beer still cost less than a dollar. Molson's, one of fifteen breweries in Montreal, already handled more than 20 percent of the market and was about to have its first million-gallon year.

Herbert's income was plentiful from investments alone. Occupied with directorships, he sat on the board of the family business as well as the Bank of Montreal and the Montreal General Hospital. In winter he and Bessie were able to travel in Europe and

England while Fred ran the brewery. Spring and fall he cruised in his luxurious steam yacht down the lower St. Lawrence in the company of male friends for salmon fishing. Long summers were for golfing and relaxing at Metis Beach with his wife and children. When in Montreal, Herbert made time to call on people, and entertained friends, family, neighbours and business associates at home. He played bridge nearly every afternoon at the Mount Royal Club.

On May 29, 1907, Bessie delivered her fourth and last child, a healthy boy. They called him Hartland after Hartland Brydges MacDougall, one of Herbert's closest friends, an avid sportsman and head of the Montreal Stock Exchange. Hartland MacDougall and Herbert's brother Percy, asked to be the baby's godparents, accompanied the family in November to Christ Church Cathedral, where the infant was baptized in the Molsons' heirloom christening gown.

Most of Hartland's early days were characteristically English, spent in the second-floor nursery next to his mother's bedroom. The nursery was fitted with toys most children dream of, including a fully furnished doll's house, a mechanical train set and a rocking horse with a leather bridle and a real horse-hair tail. Brockie had moved on to take care of Kenneth Molson's son Jack, so at first, hired nursery maids spent time with Hartland and took him out for walks in the pram.

Hartland's first family outings were short trips on Sundays in the motor-car, picnics and sailing on his father's yacht during the summers in Metis. One of these excursions provided his first cognizant memory: being taken out at age 4 in the *Curlew* on the lap of his Uncle Markland Molson and noticing his uncle's expansive girth "across which was draped a most impressive watch chain." He would not remember the sailing party's misfortune upon landing, however. The *Curlew* struck a rock near shore, and Hartland, his father, Uncle Mark and another guest were overturned into water up to Herbert's waist. Herbert's sister Evelyn heard about the mishap that afternoon. "Herbert grabbed Hartland," she wrote to her husband, "and I suppose the rest waded ashore! It is the dickens of a beach to land on, eh?"

The Pentland family had traditionally summered in Tadoussac on the north shore, but the Molsons had preferred the south shore communities in Cacouna and Metis. Hartland was taken to Metis first as an infant and thereafter every summer of his childhood, and many of his happiest memories were formed there. The family would board a steamer at Montreal's bustling port, engage a cabin on board in which they'd spend the night, and disembark the next evening 275 miles downriver at Rivière du Loup. They would unload their trunks and bags into a waiting buggy at the wharf and clamber up for the bumpy ride to Metis. There they would settle into their house, which had been cleaned, aired and fully stocked for them a few days earlier.

The Molsons' rented house on the main road of the village faced the beach and the river, with a view of the bay full of boats anchored offshore and three landmark rocks known as Cow Rock, Bull Rock and Calf Rock. In the calm of these post-Victorian halcyon summers the four children played there, bathing in the sea, fishing on the river and picking berries in the fields. They romped on the beach and played games at others' houses with their cousins Jack Molson, Lin and Margaret Russel and friends, while their parents invited neighbours and relatives for tea, bridge parties and sailing excursions. There were often dances and dinners at the Seaside Hotel. Sometimes Queenie, Adam Skaife's youngest child from Montreal, would be invited to stay with the Molson family, as her unfortunate mother had developed a debilitating disease of the lymphatic system and had been admitted permanently to a British sanatorium.

For years after motorized vehicles became popular in the city, the family still preferred horses and carriages to get around Metis and brought their coachmen with them, as well as some of the household staff from Montreal. Great-Uncle Markland Molson and Aunt Velina, simply called "the Marks," were frequent guests, as was Herbert's sister Naomi Molson. Every summer the family stretched the season into September, staying as long as they could, lighting fires in the wood stove in the kitchen when the weather turned cold.

Winters in Montreal were made memorable by brightly painted sleighs and sparkling snow piled high on the sides of the roads. Spangled Christmases were followed by dazzling balls and fancy dress parties in January. If Bessie was too occupied with the demands of domestic life and children to attend many entertainments, her mother-in-law Jennie Molson was not. At the annual Charity Ball in 1908, Jennie stayed until the end, close to 3 a.m. The following day she went to a luncheon at the Women's Club, and in the afternoon had thirty ladies over to tea in honour of her titled cousin Alice Pignatorre.

Many Molson families lived close to one another in Montreal, in an area that became known as "the Square Mile." Herbert's cousin Fred lived on Drummond Street, above Sherbrooke, with his wife Catherine and their children. John Thomas and Jennie Molson lived on University Street with their grown, unmarried children Lily, Mabel and Percy, and grandson Jack. The latter's father, Kenneth Molson, lived in a house on Pine Avenue, while Evelyn and her husband, Dr. Colin Russel, who married in 1909, lived on Bishop Street. Herbert and Bessie Molson and their children lived in a house south of Sherbrooke on Mountain Street.

When Hartland was 2½ years old, Scottish governess Margaret McCulloch joined the household and took over Brockie's old room. "Culloch" would take care of Hartland and guide young Tom through his primary education before he was sent to Bishop's College School in Lennoxville, Quebec. Though she looked uncompromising and stern, Culloch was in fact remembered as soft-hearted and wise, and she kept a benevolent eye on her young charges. Cheerfully joining in their hide-and-seek and other games, she very quickly became considered a part of the family. After Tom's departure, Culloch set up lessons in the nursery for the girls. In 1909, Miss Edgar and Miss Cramp's day school for young ladies opened on nearby Guy Street, and the girls were promptly enrolled there.

While privileged childhoods have often been described as lonely or loveless, Hartland's was neither. His father, though somewhat of an idealistic, distant figure, nevertheless found the ability to be affectionate to his children, frequently hugging them. They remembered his scent, a mixture of pipe tobacco and polished leather, and his laugh, which sounded like a chugging train. Hartland appears to have been his mother's favourite child, and when she wasn't spoiling or indulging him, he thrived under Culloch's gentle attention. The bedtime stories of Hartland's childhood, which Culloch read out loud to him, were peopled with heroes on courageous adventures and laden with moral and British patriotic messages.

Given the demanding social life of his parents and the presence of three older siblings at home during the holidays, Hartland experienced a full spectrum of stimulation, from quiet playtime to bustling activity around him. His mother ably managed a challenging household with the four children and up to eleven domestic staff members. However, there was no discord in the early years, and no traumas seemed to have scarred his childhood before the death of his Uncle Percy in 1917. The orderly, unwavering ideals of domestic order and select taste would become the standards Hartland would hold throughout his life.

CHAPTER TWO

D URING THE YEARS Herbert and Bessie's little family was growing, Molson's brewery was also developing and prospering. Cousins Herbert and Fred had finally introduced electricity to replace steam, which was now applied to drying grain and pumping liquids at various stages of the brewing process. Instead of being gravity-filtered, using charcoal and isinglass as filters, aged beer could now be mechanically filtered under pressure. But most important, electric power enabled refrigeration to be installed, becoming the single most revolutionary change ever to affect the brewery. Wort-cooling could now be controlled and consistent fermenting temperatures maintained, which meant not only that batches could be processed more quickly than ever before, but for the first time brewing could continue year-round.

As with all types of renovations, modernizations in one area inevitably led to the need for improvements in other areas. In 1907, the year of Hartland's birth, labels were still being attached by hand to the bottles with flour paste. Increased volumes now being turned out necessitated the mechanization of the bottling and labelling processes. All local deliveries were still made by horse-drawn drays, but within a few more seasons the first flatbed trucks would be purchased and put on the road. Before the year was out, demolition had begun in order to make way for the replacement of several old buildings located on the west side of the brewery courtyard.

Production and sales at Molson's Brewery experienced unprecedented growth in the first decade of the new century. In 1907, the output of 43,000 barrels, or one million gallons, was an occasion to celebrate. More amazingly, buildings constructed and equipment installed the following year would have such an effect that by 1909, output increased 100 percent to two million gallons.

That year National Breweries Limited was formed in Montreal. The company was an amalgamation of most of the principal breweries in Quebec – including the Dawes' family brewery, Dow & Co., Ekers, Union Brewery and Imperial Brewery. The Molsons had briefly considered joining the merger, but in the end Herbert, Fred, John Thomas and partner Adam Skaife chose to remain independent. While the other breweries gained by consolidating their prices and distribution, as a member of the merger Molson's would have had less to gain, having recently implemented major modernizations and already enjoying competitive success. Another factor, in business historian Merrill Denison's opinion, was that "the sense of history and pride of family ownership … [was] too strong to permit the thought of obliteration."

At least one person was not thrilled when the first motor-driven truck, a Galloway, was purchased by mail-order for Molson's in 1910. Henri Halde, who had been the driver of the horse-drawn dray-wagon for many years, was reluctant to learn to drive the new-fangled motor vehicle, which had a wooden body with brass fittings, spoked tires rimmed in solid rubber and kerosene lanterns for headlights.

On October 13, 1910, John Thomas died, leaving his partner Skaife, his nephew Fred and son Herbert as the remaining partners. He willed all the original Molson property to Herbert and Fred, including the brewery, the old St. Thomas's church and college properties. The old sugar refinery, cooperage and malt house were left to Fred's brother Harry.

Early in 1911 Herbert began to consider that if something happened to him, it would leave "an awkward situation to deal with by will." He decided to form a private limited joint-stock company, to be known as Molson's Brewery Limited. "This, I am sure," he wrote in a letter to Adam Skaife, on Hartland's fourth birthday, "would meet with the approval of my Uncle John and my father were they alive today."

The terms of Adam Skaife's partnership were limited to a share of the profits during his lifetime and did not include any interest in goodwill or the brewery premises. Now Herbert offered him a choice, to pay him out in full or to arrange an income from the business in proportion to his share of the profits "for the remainder of your life, whether you should wish to take as active a part in the work as you have done or not." Herbert knew that his uncle John HR Molson had also expressed a wish in his will that Fred and his family should enter the business. He also suggested that they invite Fred's son Bert to join the family team at the brewery, not initially as a partner but on a salaried basis. Bert, who had some years experience in Molson's Bank and a year in a broker's office, was qualified to become assistant treasurer and secretary, while Skaife could be offered the positions of honorary treasurer and director of the company.

Herbert's suggestions were accepted by all. To conform to the legal requirements of a limited company, the partners remodelled the account books and appointed themselves – Herbert, Fred and Adam Skaife – as directors of Molson's Brewery Limited, formally established on September 1, 1911.

Growing up, Hartland Molson was an observant, bright child, sure of himself and encouraged to be expressive of his opinions at a very early age. Though his first declarations were met with indulgence and amusement, his ideas as a maturing child were treated with more and more respect by adults. His sense of confidence and perspective was quite unusual for his age, emerging from a firm foundation of unconditional love and nurturing. He demonstrated a precocious assumption of responsibilities. In early 1913, when Hartland was 5½, Herbert and Bessie left on a trip to England, Europe and North Africa. Household staff took on a few more responsibilities while the parents were away, ensuring that the children were well cared for. Fred dropped in from time to time to confirm that all was well. In a letter to Herbert, Fred reported that Hartland "complained frequently that the table wasn't up to the standard that his mother furnished." Moreover, it was young Hartland who would call his father's secretary to order more supplies for the larder and report a malfunctioning doorbell.

At the end of May 1913, Bessie was preparing for another summer at the seaside. The day they left Montreal was Hartland's sixth birthday, and a few minutes before they climbed into the Packard that would take them to the steamer, a courier arrived with a wooden egg-crate for him. Inside, to his delight, was a puppy, a longed-for wire-haired terrier. In Metis seven weeks later, Tom's twelfth birthday was celebrated with a traditional bonfire on the beach and an impressive display of fireworks afterwards. Aunt Naomi and the Russels, Aunt Evelyn and her children Lin and Margaret joined them. Evelyn wrote to Colin, "The fireworks were splendid. Two fire-balloons went off sailing across the water till they looked like stars."

Hartland and his brother could not have been more unalike.

They did not spend much time together as children, even when at home. Tom was sent to Bishop's College School in Lennoxville when his brother was still very young, spending time with his family only on holidays. At age 6, Hartland began to attend Selwyn House, a small private day school for boys on MacKay Street. By the time Hartland was sent to Bishop's, Tom had graduated to another school. Tom resembled his mother in his countenance, but his character was more like his father's. His disposition was serious, and he kept many of his emotions to himself. Hartland was more like Herbert in appearance – yet the boy's fair features were more often smiling than stern, his blue, reflective eyes shining with mirth. From the earliest years the differences between the boys was noted by many, and no doubt instilled a lifelong distance between them. In contrast to Tom who appeared shy or even mildly indifferent, Hartland exuded vitality and inspired volleys of wit.

Next door to Herbert and Bessie on Mountain Street, in a house that was an architectural mirror of their own, lived the Cantlies. Beatrice Campbell Cantlie had been a great friend of Bessie's since their Quebec City childhoods, and now the two families, whose children were of compatible ages, spent a lot of time together. The Cantlie daughters particularly loved to be invited to "Mr. Moley's," where they would play with the Molson girls' magnificent dollhouse in the nursery. Colonel George Cantlie, a superintendent with the CPR, accompanied Herbert often at the Mount Royal Club and was a senior member of the 42nd Royal Highlanders – known as the Black Watch – the regiment in which Herbert would soon enlist.

As a child Hartland was introduced to some of the most respected and influential people in Montreal, some already well known and others soon to become so. His parents' friends included statesmen, philanthropists and industrialists. The likes of Montague Allan of the Allan Shipping Line; John McRae, McGill professor and soldier-poet and even Herbert Holt, a powerful financier known to be reclusive, dropped in occasionally. During his formative years Hartland became accustomed to fine things and refined company, and, quietly observant of these adults, very early on developed a keen sense of propriety.

Through the decade leading up to the war, Anglo Montreal was revelling in the new century, which was bringing some exciting transformations. It was an age of superlatives, yet also of decorum and chivalry. Society was riding on the wave of emancipation, reined in by tradition at the same time as it was galloping for change. The city was becoming a modern metropolis. Gentlemen purchased automobiles and retired their horses; for some years both cars and carriages shared the roads, with predictable results.

The once-sleepy Mountain Street was slowly becoming less residential and more commercial as the downtown area expanded. As traffic volume and noise picked up, Herbert began looking for a quieter neighbourhood for his family farther up the slope of Mount Royal. In the summer of 1912 he bought a property on Ontario Avenue from the estate of John Redpath and commissioned architect Robert Findlay to design and build a house that would suit his family. The plans were approved; the foundation was dug that fall and by the time Herbert and Bessie left for Europe early in 1913, construction was well underway.

The Molsons' majestic new home, rimmed in beige cut stone and wrapped in warm red brick, stood alone in its splendour at the top of the road. Below them were situated a range of stone and brick mansions with towers and gables, and where the street was so steep, horse-drawn vehicles had to climb it in a zig-zag manner. Lanes behind the houses led to horse and carriage stables – space soon to give way to automobiles – and sheds where coal and wood were stored. The Molsons' back garden was shadowed by elm trees, and partially surrounded by a high wall; the front was enclosed by a decorative black iron fence.

Herbert could not have chosen a more beautiful or a more stylish neighbourhood. "The elms … fashioned each street into a Gothic cathedral," wrote Stephen Leacock, then an economics professor at McGill. The leaders of all the great commercial dynasties gravitated there and hired the best architects and landscape gardeners. Picturesque Canada proclaimed, "Taken all in all, there is perhaps no wealthier city area in the world."

The Molsons' new house on Ontario Avenue was a signature work for Findlay, in his anglicized Beaux Arts style, the interior panelled walls and beamed ceilings echoing the symmetry and classicism of the exterior. There were three floors, five if you counted the attic and basement. The front vestibule was a room in itself; inside the inner door was a central hall with a split stairway and a huge fireplace on the opposite side. Pillars stood on either end of the hallway, one way which led to the drawing room, dining room and kitchen, and another to the library and conservatory in the wings. Next to the library, the billiard room became the music room upon the installation of a grand piano.

The bedrooms on the second floor were spacious and well proportioned. More bedrooms and the servants' quarters were on the third floor; servants could be summoned from any room in the house through a private in-house telephone system. The main-floor rooms were tastefully furnished with tightly upholstered chairs, oil portraits, Persian rugs and French silk drapes. In the library, leather chesterfields complemented walnut tables, a marble bust of Apollo on a small green marble stand and a bronze doorstop in the head of a lion.

The Molson family fit somewhere in the comfortable middle of the social terrain – they were neither leaders nor followers — drawing on a consciously balanced mix of wealth and frugality. Though they enjoyed fine foods and entertainments and gave their children travel opportunities and the best of educations, compared to some they were not ostentatious with their wealth. Adornments were considered frivolous. They gave time and money generously to public causes, yet were relatively careful with the household budget, recycled clothing for the children, and often the cooks prepared meals with the least expensive cuts of meat.

Hartland recalled growing up in the Ontario Avenue mansion where during the winter the snow on the edges of the road would be piled seven or eight feet high, and eight to ten feet wide at the ground. He and his friends would spend hours building fortresses and connecting tunnels in the snowbanks before horses and carts arrived to take the snow away.

Christmases on Ontario Avenue were always spectacular. All the extended family members were invited for the formal dinner, and all arrived dressed in their best. Names were propped up at each place setting. Herbert and Bessie sat in the main dining room with all the adults, and out in the large hall, extra tables and chairs accommodated children and young cousins grouped by ages. Every year a different event was planned: one time a full professional choir filled the staircase and gave a concert after dinner. Another year a magician entertained the company, and once there were elaborate charades in which costumes were procured and everyone participated. The most memorable of these was when Herbert abandoned his reserve and donned a King Canute costume and all the children crowded under large sheets, simulating waves.

In the spring and fall, a seamstress arrived to stay for two weeks, fitting everyone for new clothes. During the early summer, the whole family donned dusters and goggles and went for drives out to the lakeshore, to the Forest and Stream Club, or to enjoy Sunday lunches at the yacht club. The summer of 1914 was another enchanted holiday the family spent in Metis. At age 7, Hartland was permitted to use the punt and oars as long as he stayed close to shore, staying within sight of the adults on the beach. One day he ventured a little too far and slipped behind the far side of Bull Rock. Bessie hadn't seen the direction in which he'd vanished and became increasingly anxious. By the time he reappeared, her anger and relief were palpable. She hadn't spanked him in a long time, but once she had him in the house, she turned him over her knee and raised the flat side of her hairbrush. But the effort of putting the wriggling 7-year-old there had made her realize he had grown a little too big for spanking, and her hand stopped in mid-air; she had started laughing. Years later Hartland would tell this story and he would chuckle warmly every time.

Hartland, his friends and his cousins played contentedly together. On July 24, 1914, Evelyn wrote to Colin:

> I have just returned from a very happy excursion with the children to the woods to pick strawberries. Hartland [and] Tommy MacDougall … were building a tree house [with] dead branches. Lin wanted to join in but I told him he was too small & next year perhaps he could. [Hartland said,] 'He is not too small, Aunt Evelyn, he can come in on it now and help.' So Lin & Margaret set to work & Hartland was too sweet for words, praising their strength & exclaiming at the weight of the branches they brought. So when we left, Lin & Marg gave them the strawberries they had already picked & came away the happiest children in Metis.

Three days later, Evelyn recounted another incident to her husband:

> Yesterday was most entertaining at the children's service! I was to play the harmonium so Margaret sat between 'Cullah' [sic] and Dorothy Molson in row 2, while Lin had an aisle seat next Hartland in row 1 … Margaret got busy trying to catch flies and rippled with laughter when they escaped & of course commented out loud! Lin & Hartland blew out their cheeks & then Lin would make a swipe at Hartland. Luckily no noise ensued. I was bub-

*bling inside almost to the boiling over point. Singing was so suc-
cessful that we had three hymns instead of two and the clergyman
was delighted & very deeply grateful.*

The following day news from south-central Europe trickled to
Metis and the vacationers learned that the Austro-Hungarian
Empire had declared war on Serbia.

It was hard to conceive the horror of it in the context of that
lovely summer, impossible to believe that hostilities wouldn't all be
played out in a few short weeks. To many, it all seemed so far away.
Still, it was devastating news that the careful manipulations of civilian diplomacy had fallen apart. Some understood better than others that once military mobilization had started there was no slowing
or stopping its momentum. As battlefields were being drawn, the
well-worn map of social tradition was about to become history.

While distinct familial order defined life inside the Molson
home, military order had long provided much of the framework for
Montreal's social life. The high point of the social season, the
annual St. Andrew's Ball, where debutantes were presented, was
always supplied with an honour guard by the Black Watch
Regiment. The Victoria Rifles Orchestra provided the music for
prestigious public events. Military processions and parades were
events that the family watched or in which they participated in
some way. Men in senior positions wore their uniforms to all social
functions, and a strong code of honour was paramount in language
and behaviour. And on the world stage over which conversations
roamed, uniformed European monarchies were an ever-enduring
institution and British supremacy an incontrovertible fact.

Events in Europe did not seem so far away to Herbert and Bessie,
who had been abroad just the year before. They followed the news
with grave concern as Germany took its place as an ally of Austria,
and France and Russia aligned with Serbia. Before the summer was
over, Germany had invaded France and marched through neutral

Belgium, and Britain had joined in as allies. That summer and fall, France lost hundreds of thousands of men in battlefields. The horrific losses, coupled with stories of hostages taken and shot and accounts of cities burned, filled all the newspapers.

People coped with the horror the only way they knew how, by masking it with glamour and honour. The conflict on the ground was epitomized by the image of brave horsemen forming impenetrable flanks of bristling resistance; the conflict in the air infused with legends of dashing young men buzzing about in aeroplanes, using artillery to defend civilians from evil marauders. The attendant image of glamour pervaded the Allies' enthusiastic recruiting drive. Half a million young Britons joined the military that fall and winter. In Canada, the social pressure to enlist was also compelling. Peace Year banners at the Montreal Exhibition were torn down and replaced with recruitment posters. Evening Protestant services and moving-picture theatres were requisitioned for Red Cross meetings. Sir Wilfrid Laurier, by then leader of the opposition, came to address crowds at rallies in Montreal. Recruiting officers visited young men at work, and newspapers printed lists of those who signed up.

Until war came, the seasons of Hartland's childhood were dotted with lessons, family dinner parties, garden parties, snowshoeing, skating and sleighing. The difference in his daily life after war was declared was at first subtle: while all the members of his family were still around him, the tones of their conversations had changed. Nationalism was creeping into the social consciousness. Even riding his new pony, Lady Grafton, purchased for Hartland from the Fairbanks family, was but brief distraction from the new mood. There were no more entertainments solely for the sake of amusement. When the Molsons returned from Metis at the beginning of

September, an invitation came for Bessie and her mother-in-law to join Lady Allan and others for a ladies' bridge party "in support of the war effort" in the ballroom at Ravenscrag.

Although he was 40 years old, an age most considered too advanced to join the armed forces, Herbert signed up in a training program in order to qualify as a lieutenant. He had no military experience, but according to biographer Merrill Denison, he was "a happy warrior whose temperament responded whole-heartedly to the order and discipline of army life." On October 3, 1914, Canada's first contingent left for overseas, filling thirty-one ships, and sailing for England under a British Royal Navy escort. Charles Pentland wrote to Herbert two weeks later to ask him if he intended enlisting. Herbert's reply was dated October 19, 1914.

> I received yours of Saturday and to relieve your anxiety I may say that I have not volunteered for the front and do not intend to until the time comes when I consider it my duty to do so.
>
> For that time I am preparing, for I cannot sit still at a time like this and feel that I am not doing something to fit myself to fight for my country if she needs me. It is, of course, the privilege of the younger & unmarried men to go first but examples of men like myself has (sic) stirred up the younger fellows and I have been thanked and congratulated by many for showing an example. I am working night and day to pass the examinations which come off in a fortnight and although it seems a large undertaking to do this in five weeks drill and study I believe I can do it and qualify as a lieutenant when I may have to take a company with a provisional captain's rank. As you know, I never took our militia seriously but now I see the necessity and am glad to be able to do something.
>
> In any case, if we shall all be needed as many think, Bessie and the children will be well provided for and I could be spared far more easily than many a bread-winner. However there are more men in this country willing to go than our government can equip, I believe.

Herbert added a postscript that he thought might reassure his father-in-law, "I will try to keep Bessie from worrying about it as much as possible." He did this by not dwelling on the subject at home, yet he did not try to keep the truth from her or the children, for they needed to be prepared for the eventuality of his going overseas. Already the German army had "dug in." New expressions were introduced in the press: the latest manifestation of hostilities was described as "trench warfare" and machine guns were arranged in "nests" as fierce battles tracked through northern France and back into Belgium. New trenches were built and old ones extended. By the end of October, conflicts were reported near Ypres in Flanders; six months later the first gas attack would be launched there.

On December 14, a second active service battalion for the Royal Highlanders of Canada was formally announced. The new unit of the Black Watch, to be known as the 42nd Battalion, would be under the command of Colonel George Cantlie. The unit was organized in February 1915, and Herbert joined the ranks as a lieutenant. In early April, after several more weeks of training, he was promoted to Captain. News of developments in Europe continued to come every day as the first Canadian brigades were making their way to the front. As casualties mounted overseas, supportive efforts continued in Canada.

On May 8, ocean liner R.M.S. *Lusitania* was torpedoed by a German U-boat and sank off the Irish coast. Allied spirits were shaken; over a thousand civilian lives had been lost. The event held a particular horror for the Molson family – their friends Lady Allan and her daughters Gwen and Anna, on their way to England to set up a hospital for Canadian troops, had been on board. Lady Allan was thrown into the sea and broke both her legs; her daughters drowned. One week later in Montreal, a sober recruiting meeting in Victoria Hall drew a standing-room-only crowd of men; Herbert Molson was one of the speakers at the event. Later that month Herbert's battalion underwent a formal inspection by the

Governor General the Duke of Connaught on the Champs de Mars, for which thousands of Montrealers turned out to watch.

On June 5, Evelyn borrowed Percy's car and driver, and took her two children to Sherbrooke Street for the Boy Scout Parade on Fletcher's Field. Bessie, her children and her mother-in-law came in the Packard to watch Herbert's Black Watch unit also parading there. It was to be the battalion's last public appearance before it was scheduled to leave for England. Like many other young sons of officers, Hartland was keen to be involved and proudly wore a replica of his father's uniform. Five days later he wore it again, as the 42nd Highlanders made their way through the dense, cheering crowds of women and children. Some were openly weeping. Evelyn observed "little Hartland marching beside his Daddy from the barracks to the docks – the dearest little soldier lad imaginable!"

To the skirl of bagpipes Herbert and his company embarked on the S.S. *Hesperian* to sail for Plymouth, with Colonel George Cantlie in command, and "a considerable number of barrels of Molson's Ale" aboard. Bessie and the children clambered aboard the Allans' tug boat to follow Herbert's ship out of the harbour. Evelyn had Percy's driver take her to the brewery and, in spite of being six weeks away from expecting her third child, climbed stairs to the roof to see the ship go by. Jennie, dry-eyed but with a "deep nervous flush" left with her maid, Miss Schneider, for Metis that night, to stay for the week.

Before the month was over, the second of Jennie's four sons had left for Europe. A favourite uncle and godfather to Hartland, Percy had joined the 2nd University company reinforcement unit for the Princess Patricia's Canadian Light Infantry. He left on the *Northland* after making arrangements with his brother Kenneth to look after his financial affairs. Kenneth would have given "worlds"

to go, reported Evelyn. "[His wife] Isabel's health is his great obstacle, though she says she would not hold him back." Walter, the youngest son, "restless and upset," also joined the Black Watch and prepared to go in the autumn.

Within days, letters began arriving from Herbert and Percy to various members of the family. Each was read out loud, and passed around to be shared and re-read. Cables and telegrams, called "Marconigrams," would be delivered for birthdays and anniversaries. At the end of September Evelyn, Bessie and their children went up to their chalet at Ivry for a week with Culloch. (Ivry, 62 miles north by road, involved an hour and a half's "difficult and dusty" drive.) Most housemaids and nurses had left their employers either to go home to England and Scotland or to work in munitions factories. Many families, including the Russels, had to make do without help. Hartland, his siblings and cousins were pressed into the war effort, earnestly making and rolling cloth bandages for the Purple Cross.

Other families hearing from their husbands and brothers shared news as well. Hartland learned there were many reasons to be proud of his father. Again, Evelyn wrote to Colin:

> Reports keep coming to us of what a wonderful officer Herbert is making. One of his regiment writing home said he was the best musketry instructor in the British Army! Allowing for some enthusiasm he still must be pretty good! Mother says there was talk of his being held permanently in England as instructor. He is such a clear thinker & so thorough in every detail, I can perfectly understand his developing a big talent in instruction lines.

His family learned that upon arriving in England, Herbert and his men were stationed in Shorncliffe where they lived in canvas tents, undergoing musketry training on the Hythe ranges. More intensive advanced training followed later in the summer; at the beginning of September, King George V inspected the Canadians at their camp. They proceeded to Boulogne, France, at the beginning of October, and arrived in Flanders mid-month. For two months Herbert's unit was attached to the headquarters of the 1st Canadian Division, supplying working parties to build a secondary defence line. While they lived in huts and tents along the Neuville Egile-Romarin Road, much of the time the men were under fire and slogging through mud and rain.

Herbert wrote from Belgium at the end of November:

We are once more under canvas in a muddy hole. The officers have bell tents built around with sand bags for warmth and the men are in small dug outs covered with canvas (3 or 4 to a dug-out). Stoves of a kind are improvised of biscuit-tins and oil cans but fuel is scarce and has to be rustled. The last 48 hours it was very cold. It must have been at least 20 Fahr. The mud was frozen solid but to-day it is pouring again and the mud is softening up. Half my company are on a working party under 1 officer & the rest are sticking to their shelter as I try to save them all I can.

Herbert's tailored letters to the children were lighter in tone and more engaging:

The camp is nearly all little bivouacs or dug-outs holding 3 or 4 men each and it looks like a lot of muskrat or beaver houses. They are dug down in the ground and then walls are made of sandbags filled with earth and a canvas roof is put over … Uncle Percy walked in to-day and told me that he was only about 6 or 8 miles away from me and from what I hear our regiments are to be put in the same brigade so that we will be close together all winter. Percy looks very well and so did Major Hamilton Gault who was with him. There is a big observation balloon just over us. It goes

up every morning and is tied to the ground and the man in it
watches the Germans and telephones what he sees. I was told that
I can go up in it. Wouldn't Tom like that. I wish he was here to
see it. He would enjoy watching the German airplanes too.

On December 22, the 7th Canadian Infantry Brigade was
formed, incorporating the Royal Canadian Regiment, the PPCLI,
the 42nd Highlanders and the 49th Edmonton battalion. Herbert
would now see more of Percy. By Christmas they were installed in
billets near Fletre, Belgium, where they spent the holidays. In
January and February 1916, Herbert's company was moved in and
out of front line trenches, usually on four-day "tours" in and four
days out. He wrote to Bessie and his mother Jennie every other day;
the two women and his children wrote him cheerful letters. The
letters reveal that as a father, Herbert was more involved and
demonstrative than most men of his generation. Just before
Christmas 1915 Herbert admitted to Bessie how much he missed
his children. "I wish I had them all here for a few minutes," he
wrote wistfully, "I'd hug them to death."

At the end of March Bessie, Jennie and his sisters sent Herbert
cables wishing him a happy birthday, and Bessie also sent him
cakes and maple sugar, which he shared with his men. Herbert's
letters continued to be spirited and full of detail.

I finished my 4 days in battalion reserve without incident and moved
up to the front line last night. This is quite a lively spot in a wood
the trees being mostly broken down, with shell fire. The weather is
beautiful although still cool and quite cold at night. My dug-out here
is tiny and only holds one …The quarters are not very commodious
but they might be much worse …While I write, a family of mice are
playing over my head, squeaking and throwing down earth so you
see that I have plenty company even in a dug-out holding only one.

Herbert tried to send Tom an unexploded German grenade in the mail, addressed to him at Bishop's College School in Lennoxville.

There has been sent you from London, the rifle grenade that I promised you. Let me know if you get it safely. This is a German rifle grenade which fell in my trench but didn't explode. All the explosive has been taken out and it is a perfect specimen of its kind. The rod screws into the head and is dropped into the barrel of a rifle which is fixed in a stand. Then a blank cartridge sends it up in the air and it will go about 175 yards and when it drops on its head the spring on the end is compressed and the firing pin hits a cap like on a cartridge, ignites the detonator, which explodes the [amonal] contained in the grenade. The explosion is very big and the pieces fly every way and will knock out anybody within about 15 yards. I have sent Hartland a shell nose like yours as he was anxious to get one.

Three days later, however, Herbert learned there was a problem with the shipment. He wrote his sister Naomi, "Tom's rifle grenade is stopped at Liverpool by the censor, so I do not know whether I will be able to get it to him owing to some absurd rule about the export of munitions."

Some days his news ranged from leisurely pursuits to sober reality:

We rode across fields by paths and had some fine gallops, our horses jumping the ditches in fine shape. My horse is the picture of health and is like a kitten so frisky, he wants to go all the time. I haven't ridden much since I returned from London but I think I will ride more. It is such a change, and good fun to pick one's way about the paths off the main roads. The country is looking beautiful, all the leaves out and blossoms on all the shrubs …Things over here drag along, day by day, with no appreciable change in the situation.

Gas attacks are frequently threatened and I suppose we will get a dose some day but I hope will be prepared. We are constantly drilling our men in the use of the helmet so that every man will be ready when the time comes.

The children listened raptly to his read-aloud descriptions of action.

One of our aeroplanes flying overhead with another of ours had a fight with two German planes and the former fell close to our camp. It hit a tree & fell into a ditch. One aviator was killed and the other wounded, we believe that they were shot before falling. Last night a German aeroplane came over the camp and dropped a couple of bombs not very far away. I got up and tried to see it but it didn't show in the dark. Later I heard four more bombs drop some distance off.

In May Herbert related that everyone had been roused to put on gas helmets when a gas alarm had gone off at 1 a.m., but it had turned out to be a false alarm. When news reached him that both Walter and Kenneth were planning to go overseas, he tried to reassure his mother by telling her that these new battalions that were forming would be "extremely unlikely" to be dispatched to the front "unless the war should drag on very much longer than anybody can imagine."

"Just think," Herbert wrote on May 24, "today is Victoria Day, the funniest holiday I have ever known. I am sitting in the doorway of my dug-out writing. If I remember rightly I spent last May 24th in hospital [having a vein removed] but all the other years I went yachting or golfing. How time slips away."

Near the end of May the 1st Canadian Division was moved into the front line of the Hooge sector, then came out in the Ypres Ramparts on May 30. In an effort to take Ypres, the Germans attacked on June 2 at Sanctuary Wood, Mount Sorrel. This battle was to be the first major operation of Herbert's 42nd Highlanders battalion; his company was ordered forward to support Percy's PPCLI unit, which was in the firing line. The men of the 42nd, who had been equipped with Ross rifles, found their weapons clogged and jammed, and none could fire properly. Although the battle would later be called "an unqualified Canadian victory," the Canadian Corps sustained 8000 casualties that day. Herbert and Percy were wounded within hours of each other – Percy shot through the jaw, and Herbert suffering a skull fracture.

CHAPTER THREE

THE CABLE THAT described Herbert's injury was grim: "Gunshot wound head, depressed fracture, serious." The family rallied around the children; friends came over to "comfort and distract" them. Their Aunt Lily, Herbert's elder sister, observed that "Tom was rather a pitiful object & Hartland very serious, while the girls were keeping a brave face." Everyone did their best to be solicitous to Jennie who, prone to depression, now had to cope with the reality that two of her sons had been seriously wounded. While the family understood within a short time that Percy's jaws would have to be wired and an operation was imminent, the extent of Herbert's head injury remained unclear. Writing to his mother, he minimized his own situation. "I have nothing but a swell crack on the head," he insisted. "They have decided I should go into hospital and have a few weeks' rest … [Percy and I] are out of trouble for a few weeks anyway."

Herbert had first been held at No. 7 British Stationary Hospital, in Boulogne, but after a week he was put on a hospital ship and brought to the officers' wing in the Royal Free Hospital in London, as, he explained, "the hospitals in France may be kept empty enough to receive fresh casualties from day to day." Before her husband's injury Bessie had been planning to visit him in London during his leave that summer. Now she booked herself on the first available transatlantic ship, but before leaving, travelled to Lennoxville with Mabel and Naomi for Tom's school closing ceremonies and then saw the other children off safely to Metis with Culloch. So it was in Metis that Hartland and his siblings learned that Herbert's operation on the last day of June had gone well.

Bessie spent every afternoon with her husband at the London hospital. Quite a few friends, including wives of officers who were in London that summer, dropped in to visit Herbert. Among these visitors were Edith MacDougall, Grace Ogilvie and Elsie Reford. Elsie and her husband, Robert Reford, Canadian representative of Cunard Steamship Lines, were close friends and neighbours of the Molsons both in Montreal and Metis.

Both Herbert and Bessie wrote to Jennie and the children at home, his letters continuing cheerful, "My room is full of beautiful flowers and you would think that I was seriously ill," and positive about getting back to his unit. Her letters were more pragmatic. "If by any chance the Dr won't let him go back [to his unit] for some months I imagine we may get Herbert to come back [to Canada]. It will be hard work because he won't give up what he has undertaken unless it is absolutely necessary – he has no idea of such a thing & we must not tell him because he would worry about his men – but we'll just have to wait for a couple of weeks – then we shall know all." Bessie was certain his convalescence would last much longer than Herbert anticipated. She cautioned her mother-in-law, "It would be better not to breathe a word about a possibility of H coming home as it some way might get back to him & he would worry if he thought he was leaving his men for a time. He's not a quitter like many others – he is anxious to know where to go after he is better & [when] I said, 'If you get 6 weeks leave we may go home,' his answer was 'Don't be absurd.'"

Hartland's Aunt Evelyn dropped by the house one day near the end of July to say she'd just received a Marconigram announcing that Bessie, Herbert and Percy would all be home by the end of the first week in August. The family was together again to enjoy the remainder of the summer in Metis; though Herbert had been instructed to rest, Percy played golf "in moderation." Hartland and the other children were transfixed to see Percy, who had lost much weight and whose jaws had been wired shut, and who had to suck soft foods through a straw for nourishment. They tried to make the most of their time together, which passed quickly. "Meatless Mondays" and "Fuelless Sundays" marked every week. In September, while newspapers and war bulletins were bringing home stories of the Canadians' offensive in the Somme, the family returned to Montreal and Tom went back to Lennoxville to school.

Herbert left again for Europe in October, while Percy stayed until March for follow-up surgery at the Montreal General Hospital. Once again the family waited for letters from Herbert. Cousin Fred was dealing with problems that had been developing at the brewery. Notwithstanding the new equipment and mechanization, output had plummeted since the war began, partly because of labour shortages and scarcity of raw material, but also because of the absence of so many men. The Molsons kept their spirits up even though the conflict was dragging on much longer than anyone had anticipated.

Most of Herbert's letters were addressed to Bessie; he wrote almost as frequently to his mother, and less so to Tom and "the kiddies." In these early years and later, of the four children it would be Tom who received the greater share of his father's time and attention, for like other fathers Herbert singled out his eldest son for expectations of succession. This fact did not appear to bother Hartland, who enjoyed copious amounts of affection from his mother and Culloch, as well as from members of his extended family.

The idea that he might not live through the war was obviously on Herbert's mind when he wrote to Tom early in 1917 to give him some fatherly advice.

> *I'm pleased at your report and glad to see you doing so well in your classes but don't neglect athletics & other accomplishments that go to make a real man and gentleman. Remember what I have often told you, try to be proficient in all manly sports and accomplishments such as dancing, music, etc. are most useful & necessary in after life if you wish to take your proper place in the world & command the respect of men & women who count. Above all things, though, it is character that counts & the more one sees of life the more one realizes this. Be generous with your money, whatever you have, but not wasteful and always be ready & willing to help a friend who needs such help whether it be advice, service of some kind or financial. On the other hand do not let yourself be imposed upon & if you feel that you are being drawn into things that are not right, put your foot down and say no! You'll be respected all the more & will not be looked upon as a softy. Do not stand bullying & remember that manners count for much in the world.*

Walter, the youngest of Herbert's three brothers, embarked for the front in March. His departure left only his brother Kenneth at home in Montreal, where for the next three months family members shared packets of letters with each other. Devastating news came in the first week of July. Percy had been instantly killed in France on the night of July 4 by a trench mortar. Hartland MacDougall sent a cable to Herbert, who wired Bessie to ask her to break the news to Jennie as gently as possible. "It is ever thus," Herbert wrote sadly to his mother five days later, "that the best are taken and many of the useless and craven-hearted left." But, he added, he would do his best to "look upon his death as an inspiration and while mourning him not give way to unavailing regrets but remain steadfast, doing our duty as we see it, and carry on."

Herbert asked his mother to "spare a thought of poor Lady Allan." He had contacted them by telephone at their country home just outside London to tell them about Percy, and Montagu Allan had said, "I suppose you know that I have lost my boy." In fact Herbert hadn't heard about the death of the Allans' only son. They had invited Herbert to lunch the following Saturday. "I dread going," Herbert confessed to Jennie, "but I don't see how I can refuse. [Montagu] says his wife will like it and that it will do her good. He is very composed but it is a terrible blow after losing his two little girls."

That summer Herbert took a staff course at Cambridge University, where, reported Walter, he "headed the Canadians … as the most striking success they had had at the school." Afterwards Herbert was posted to the staff at Argyll House, but his letters reveal that he would rather have been elsewhere. "There isn't a day goes by that I don't loathe and detest the fact that I am safely here in England rather than back with the battalion again [in] France." The following year he would get his wish, for he was transferred as chief staff officer of the Canadian section of General Headquarters in France, where he coordinated the flow of reinforcements. At the time General Sir Arthur Currie was commander of the Canadian Forces and became friends with Herbert while there, a friendship that would endure until Currie's death in 1933.

The two members of the family who were most grieved by Percy's death were his younger sister Mabel and his nephew Hartland, who were both in Metis when the news came. Mabel had always been the closest sibling to Percy, and his death left her distraught, visibly aging her features. As for Hartland, Percy had been his godfather, his favourite uncle, and he would miss him terribly. When he received Percy's bloodstone signet ring as a legacy, "still caked with mud from Sanctuary Wood," he cherished it and wore it for the rest of his life.

Anti-conscription rallies carried on in Montreal throughout the summer of 1917. Francophones in particular didn't feel that Britain's war had anything to do with them. When the Conservative government in power revoked an election promise not to introduce the conscription bill, angry and bitter crowds marched in the streets shouting, "Down With Borden!" In spite of all opposition, the bill was passed on July 24. Afterwards, demonstrators resorted to violence: store windows were smashed, tram rails were ripped up and police had to be called in to disperse crowds.

In the meantime, Fred Molson, his eldest son Bert and the old brewmaster John Hyde were still battling problems at the brewery. Not only was production still falling drastically, but by early 1917 the wave of prohibition that had been gathering all over North America had begun to lap at the borders of Quebec. Brewers in the province were required by law to brew only low-alcohol "temperance beer" during the later war years. Fred had kept experimenting to improve the taste, introducing a Temperance Porter, and mild ale in draught form. However he found that if the latter wasn't kept at extremely low temperatures before shipping then its shelf life was limited, as the alcohol content would increase after only a few days.

At first it had not seemed possible that prohibition could come to Quebec, as the Francophone majority who were Roman Catholic were traditionally opposed to temperance. Nevertheless the campaign took hold there as well, and region after region (who had local options) capitulated until in the early summer of 1917, 90 percent of the province was dry. When Quebec City voted in favour of eliminating alcohol, Montreal brewers began a vigorous publicity campaign to bring pressure on the government to modify its stand. The Quebec Brewers Association, led by Ekers, Dawes,

Dow, Boswell and Molson, sponsored newspaper articles and took out advertisements in favour of their cause.

Late in 1917, a rumour circulated that premier Sir Jean-Lomer Gouin was about to introduce a prohibition bill that would exclude beer and wine. However when the bill was introduced, it included beer and wine after all, and following the requisite three readings, it was passed in February 1918 to become law May 1, 1919. The outraged Brewers Association formed a "Beer and Wine Committee" and redoubled their efforts to sway the government. Fred organized a group called the Moderation Committee, and with Norman Dawes of National Breweries, directed a publicity campaign that built up a series of twenty-seven advertisements, the first of which read, "IS THE OLDEST MANUFACTURING BUSINESS IN CANADA TO BE LEGISLATED OUT OF EXIS-TENCE?"

Tom, in his final year at Bishop's College School, wrote an anxious letter to his father asking if, given the likelihood of the brewery's closure, he would still be able to attend Royal Military College as he had planned. Herbert's reply reveals that his priorities as a father were to ensure that his sons were given educations and that they did not take their privileges for granted. "Don't worry about going to college; Daddy has enough to educate his children and take care of them even if the brewery closes but we may not be able to do all that we like to do, and if the business was closed we would have to decide what to do with you and Hartland after the war as you have to work and can't be idle."

Herbert was discouraged to hear about events in Montreal, and even he, once so proud and positive a soldier, had also become disillusioned and weary of the conflict in Europe. He wrote to Bessie in October 1917:

> *The more this war goes on the more stupendous it seems and one wonders what the end will be and whether anybody will be safe &*

whether the world will be bankrupt when it does end. Who could have imagined such a condition of affairs as exists today with cities being bombed from the air & ships being sunk from below the water. The latest Italian news is very serious and coupled with the Russian affair does not look well. I wonder what the situation will be a year hence. Our fellows are plugging along grimly and the fighting is very fierce on the Western Front. There have not been many casualties lately amongst our friends but I fear for the next few weeks.

The war would continue for another year. By then Walter too had been seriously injured, but had been operated on, shipped home and was expected to recover. By the summer of 1918 resolution was visible, and the armistice was signed on November 11.

The end of the war brought joy; the celebrations and familial reunions were gratifying for all, but the time was also tempered by grave circumstances at home. To give all the brewery employees their jobs back, Fred and Herbert had to shorten the work week and increase wages to almost double. This was at a time when due to imminent prohibition, production was about to be suspended, the brewery was facing closure and industrial strikes affected many related trades. As if that weren't enough to dampen the spirits of victory, the Spanish flu swept through the city and struck a quarter of the population. During the weeks of November and December 1918, processions of hearses crawled through the streets, while schools, shops, libraries, factories, courthouses, theatres, churches, restaurants and dance halls closed their doors.

Having passed the entrance exam for the Royal Military College in Kingston, Tom left Montreal again in September. Hartland had completed his second year at nearby MacCauley's School, later known as Selwyn House. Bessie and Herbert had wanted to send Tom to Charterhouse, one of the oldest and most respected schools for boys in England, but as long as the war was on they kept the children in Quebec. Bessie had also located a suitable boarding school for her daughters at the historic Bentley Priory in Middlesex, which had recently been converted to a Girls' School. Now that the war was over, Hartland would have a chance to attend Charterhouse after prep school. In the fall of 1918 Betty and Dosh were sent to England while 11-year-old Hartland was enrolled at Bishop's in Lennoxville.

Hartland entered Bishop's College School as one of twenty new boys that fall. The preparatory school consisted of two buildings, one containing dormitories and classrooms, and the other the dining and assembly halls. Among Hartland's schoolmates there were Weir Davis, who would become a lawyer and lifelong friend, and William Mitchell, who later became a prominent Quebec judge. At BCS Hartland was a member of the debating society and was noted for his polished and compelling speeches. He also joined the Cadet Corps, played quarterback on the football team and centre on the school hockey team. The Spanish flu swept through the school and thirty-two of the forty-eight boys there became seriously ill. Hartland was one of sixteen pupils who remained healthy; they called themselves the "Lucky 16" and spent most of their time skiing. None of the boys died but, Hartland remembered, a few "hovered near death."

That winter, Herbert put all his time and effort into fighting the impending prohibition legislation, to prove that to ban the sale of beer would be in direct opposition to the wishes of the public. He researched and published all the information he could find that would be favourably relevant to allowing the sale of beer and wine in Quebec. Its disappearance, he argued, would affect jobs, provincial revenues and invested capital. He gathered and quoted opinions of respected prominent leaders such as physicians and educators. He stressed the wholesome nature and nutritious content of beer, while highlighting the old and honourable character of the brewing industry in Quebec:

For more than a century brewers have promoted temperance in its truest form. They have given the public a pure, wholesome, delicious beverage, healthful and nutritious in winter, refreshing and thirst-quenching in summer. The men who founded these breweries played important parts in the affairs of the early history of Canada. And their successors (their sons and grandsons and great-grandsons) became among the leading public men of the Dominion, giving their time and their ability to fostering the financial, commercial and charitable institutions of their city and their province.

A poll conducted by Fred's moderation committee in Montreal revealed what the brewers long suspected: that 75 percent of the population were in favour of the sale and manufacture of beer and wine. Still, Molson's was obligated by law to suspend all production in February 1919. Finally to their relief, the provincial government agreed to have a referendum on the matter, and in March 1919, the announcement was made that the polls would be open on April 10 for a final decision. On April 9, a Yes torchlight parade lit up the streets in downtown Montreal, and the following day 78 percent of voters agreed to except beer and wine from the restrictive legislation. Molson's Brewery was reopened the next day. Since the federal order-in-council restricting beer to 2.5 percent alcohol by weight still applied for one year after the end of the war, it wasn't until November that full-strength beer was back on the shelves.

Hartland described Bessie as a very good mother, "intelligent, firm, a woman who had definite ideas," but, he added, "she was not tough." She did, it was said, spoil her youngest son. Although some others who remembered her described her as "bossy," they were quick to add that this trait likely came from the loss of her mother at such a young age and her assumed burden of responsibility for her younger siblings. Bessie had a keen sense of humour and a host of devoted friends and family who loved her. Certainly her relationship with young Hartland was marked by indulgence on her part and familiarity on his. Hartland's letters to her from BCS attest to the liberty he felt in addressing her, which he did in a manner that ranged from mild scolding to mock-disparagement.

Three letters survive from the spring of 1919, one of which warrants quoting in full.

Monday May 6, 1919

Dear Mother,

I am up in the sick-room with a little cough, a little sickness at the stomach.

Do not worry, I am alright. Feeling fine most of the time. Will you please have my bed moved down to the little spare bed-room? You promised that I could have a room to myself these holidays. Also do you think it possible for us to have marrow-bones for lunch?

We get from the 31st to the 12th. Perhaps I can get a few days extra. I hinted gently at that to Wilkie this forenoon. I asked him if it would matter very much if I missed a couple of days. He was telling us fellows in the sick-room that any fellow that did not come back on time this time would get it hot. When I asked him about myself he said in a confidential way that it did not matter for fellows forward in their class so much. But I advise you strongly to write to him this week asking his permission for a few days extra for me.

For goodness sake don't get him sore at you! One time a man telephoned up and said to him, "Mr Wilkinson, kindly send down my boy right away with a master." It was 7:00 a.m. Wilkie spoke to the whole school saying that some parents had no manners, as only one parent was out here in the middle of the term we all knew

*who it was. I don't mean to insinuate you would do a thing like
that asking him as if he were just here to be ordered about as a ser-
vant, but if you did not mention it beforehand he might get sore and
you'd lose the power over him you* UNDERLINE*THINK* *you have. You [know]
Wilkie's a wily old bird; he keeps you ladies on the good side.
Don't be cross at me for telling you this.
No offense meant, old dear.
From your loving son,
Hartland*

Four days later, still in the sick-room, Hartland wrote again,
plaintively this time, "If Daddy has gone up to see Tom because he
was in hospital, why can't he AND YOU come up and see me? ...
Too bad about Tom!"

Hartland reminded his mother that a coupon on his Victory
Bond had come due, and asked her if she had remembered to cut it
off and take it to the bank. When she failed to mention the bond
in her reply, he repeated sternly, "Did you take the slip off my victory bond? I've asked you that 3 times & received no answer!!
Also, mother, I asked for a little cash & some stamps with no result.
But I do not mind your slight slip & do send them."

If Hartland was confident and willful at age 5, ordering supplies
for the household when his parents were in Europe, he was no less
so at age 11, dictating birthday cake instructions. He described his
wishes for his upcoming birthday, May 29 (which his family would
celebrate that year on the 30th):

*Please get me a birthday cake (for the 30th) made as follows –
white icing with pink frills. NO ALMOND ICING. 12 walnuts
'round the edge, with spaces for ditto candles. Make it as big as
you like but only one story high. On it have:*

— *Hartland Molson
On his 12th birthday
May 30th 1919*

Hartland's letters during this time reveal his happiness, security and confidence. His relationship with Bessie would grow away from being somewhat disparaging to become more affectionate and teasing. As a boy his sense of mischief ranged from subtle to complex, often expressed in barbs tempered with self-mockery. It was hard to distinguish the cavalier from the ironic, but clearly the ambiguity was deliberate. On one of his letters he drew a female figure seated at a dressing table, facing a mirror, lifting a round powder puff to her face, the word "powdering" printed underneath. "Here is a little picture of you 99 times per day, mother. (Next time you offend me I will send or draw worse things!)"

His birthday was celebrated at school; writing that evening, Hartland thanked his mother, "Dad, the girls & Culloch for their good wishes." His parents had given him a rifle, and he asked to be sent:

> … any little present that I could read, eat or use such as books, $ & knife. Mother, dear, I am rather afraid to confess that many afternoons I have been almost frantic with lust for some fruit or candies. Out here we only get down to buy things twice a week. And as I only have had 1 grub box this term I have got so that I could eat tacks. Would it be asking TOO much to ask you to order a grub box with about 1 dozen oranges, ½ dozen grapefruit & a few apples?

Hartland's particular way with words and the manner with which he handled humour developed into a personal trademark, with his droll delivery always tempered with an expression of mirth spilling from twinkling eyes. But he could also be serious. "Mother," he wrote at the end of one of his letters, "speaking honestly, I don't think I'll come 1st in the exams. I'll do my best & keep my end up."

When Hartland was 13 years old his parents decided he was ready to be sent to Charterhouse School in England where he stayed for two years, coming home only for the summer holidays. The prestigious school was founded in London in 1611, but moved in 1872 to a Regency stone estate on twenty acres in the Surrey countryside near Godalming. The school encompassed 750 boys divided into ten "houses," each house competing with the others for sports. The students, who went to chapel every morning, took their studies and sports seriously, wore academic gowns to classes and donned uniforms for cricket, soccer and compulsory military drill.

Hartland slept in an extensive dormitory, where each boy was assigned his own cubicle. Before going to bed they were each required to say their prayers in Latin, for which they were presided over by an Anglican schoolmaster-priest. Compared to life at BCS, conditions were rudimentary. The boys slept on iron beds with coarse blankets and they had to bring water in for washing, which they did using basins and jugs.

According to Charterhouse classmate Steve Stevens, who was also from Montreal, Hartland was a well-groomed young gentle-man, who was "very smart and sporting." Although compared to other boarding schools Charterhouse had an impersonal environ-ment, the classes were stimulating and academic competition was encouraged; Hartland continued to come first or second in his class. "He finds work easy and does it well," reported one master. "He is a very good boy in every way," wrote another. The July 1922 House Master's report reads, "Much of his work is good – He is a manly boy, with honesty and character which should bring him through well. He knows what we expect of him: it is up to him to justify our confidence."

At Charterhouse Hartland played cricket, made trips to Godalming on weekends to the pharmacist to purchase tooth powder; to the cobbler for boots and the tailor for blazer, ties, braces, breeches, white flannel trousers and collar pins; to the athletic outfitter for cricket uniforms; and to the local bookseller for schoolbooks. On the grounds of the school they ran an Officers Training Corps, for which uniforms were also required and where the boys set up camp on the expansive grounds.

For the month of December in 1921 Herbert and Bessie rented a house in the Swiss resort town of Murren. The whole family was able to join them there for Christmas and to watch an annual hockey match between Cambridge and Oxford, in which both Tom (who was one of two Canadians on the Cambridge team) and Herbert (who acted as referee) participated. Among the members of the Oxford team, who were predominantly Canadians, were future Governor General Roland "Roly" Michener and future Prime Minister Lester "Mike" Pearson. Hartland and others noticed Pearson's spectacular stick-handling skill, reportedly so impressive that the Swiss press nicknamed him "Herr Zigzag." It was here that Hartland, at age 14, and Pearson, at age 24, met for the first time, neither one realizing that this encounter would be the beginning of a significant friendship.

The Oxford team soundly defeated Cambridge; the game was stopped at the end of the second period because Oxford was leading with a score of 27 to 0. The following winter Tom would play again for the Cambridge team, also in Murren, and nine years later Hartland (though not as a student) would join the Oxford Canadians and have his turn.

In 1923 Hartland returned to Canada and was enrolled for another year at Bishop's. He persuaded his father that it would be wise for him to "get back to Canadian sports and also to have a few friends" before undertaking the "rather rigorous life" imposed at the Royal Military College in Kingston. Tom, also a Bishop's graduate, had just completed his RMC training and was headed to England to register in a chemistry program at Cambridge. After Cambridge he would enroll in a brewing course at Birmingham University before joining the family brewery.

Hartland's final year at Bishop's was very successful. In sports he played hockey and football, and also excelled in track. His proudest achievement was creating a record for the 100-yard dash, which would stand for the next thirty-three years. He also came first academically in his form, excelling particularly at Latin, French, geometry, trigonometry, algebra and chemistry. "Conduct excellent," wrote the housemaster succinctly at Michaelmas term. At the end of the year he was awarded the top student's prize, which was the Governor General's Medal, as well as several form prizes including the Old Boy's Prize, the Latin, French, Science and English prizes, and "Mrs. [Herbert] Holt's Essay Prize."

"Dear Family," Hartland wrote just after his seventeenth birthday in the spring of 1924, "(all of you, including Culloch), Many thanks again for your letters, food, money, and anything else I may have omitted." He enthused about the hockey games he'd played in, mentioned his own scoring record and asked Herbert if he would consider giving a cup to be competed for annually by schools in the hockey league. Having taken on the responsibility for selling advertising space in the school yearbook, Hartland asked his father to ask Mr. Dawes if he would purchase a half-page ad for National Breweries.

Before enrolling at the Royal Military College in Kingston in September of 1924, like other students Hartland had to provide a certificate signed by the headmaster of BCS attesting to his good moral character, pass a physical fitness test and write an entrance exam. On his first day the recruits swore allegiance to the King before a police magistrate, promising to serve as Cadets of the Royal Military College for four years and be subject to militia regulations.

The college, which was founded in 1876 just outside Kingston on a peninsula across Navy Bay from Fort Henry, was considered the best in Canada for educating young men who wished to pursue careers as officers in the armed forces. It was organized on a military basis and subject to military law. There were 150 cadets in 1924, formed into a battalion of two companies, each with two platoons, each cadet enrolled in a curriculum of subjects both military and academic. Discipline and physical fitness were high priority, making sports very important. Initiation rituals included an obstacle course directed by the seniors, which took some recruits "from sunset to dawn" to complete – after which they earned the name Gentleman Cadet. A booklet outlining the "standing orders" for guidance and observance of cadets filled sixty-seven pages.

Like every student in the first year, Hartland had a room to himself, which was plainly furnished with an iron military cot, a chest of drawers, a writing table, two chairs and a bookshelf. Every morning the students rose at 5:30 a.m., then prepared for a daily room inspection and joined a parade, which was followed by a uniform inspection in the gym after breakfast. Precision was required in everything, even bed-making: Hartland had to learn how to give his bed knife-edge creases, how to properly fold his uniforms and how to clean all his equipment including belts and rifle slings. The Junior cadets were expected to clean the Seniors' gym shoes and all their equipment, as well as attend them at meals, taking away dirty plates and replacing them with clean ones, passing them everything they needed and carving their roasts.

Hartland took to the military life with characteristic enthusiasm. While the clock in the tower of Kingston struck the hours and pealed across the harbour, the cadets were forced to exercise while the sergeants bellowed commands and insults at them, such as "You're not dead yet!" and "Show your guts!" While they marched to church they were shouted at to improve their attitude and appearance. Hartland and the other recruits learned to appreciate little things, such as small portions of informal free time (known as "lids-off" time), ice cream sent in from town and sing-songs on campus.

Most cadets at RMC were culled from the professional or upper classes, so it came as no surprise to Hartland to find himself there with other young men from his neighbourhood in Montreal, many of whom were sons of his parents' friends, including Andrew Holt, Jack Cushing, Bart Ogilvie, Tommy MacDougall and Larry Mather. One summer Larry Mather was invited to be a guest of Hartland's aboard his father's new yacht, where he met Hartland's sister Betty and fell in love with her. Upon their return to college that fall, Bessie had pressed Hartland to bring photographs of his sisters with him. Hartland, indifferent to the photographs, agreed promptly when Larry asked to "rent" Betty's photo from him for a dollar per term.

Other cadets who were enrolled at the college became lifelong friends, such as (football team captain) Walter Gordon, later to become finance minister in the 1960s, and classmate Dwight Ross, who would become air commodore. Governors general always took an interest in the college and would visit to present medals at sports events and annual closing ceremonies. Sport was a favourite activity; Hartland joined the school's rugby, ice hockey and track teams. In December 1925 the RMC hockey team travelled to Madison Square Gardens in New York City to play the team from Princeton University, and defeated the prestigious American team 3 to 1 in front of a crowd of 6,000 spectators. Hartland must have been pleased to read an article in the *RMC Review*, which read, in part:

R.M.C. led by 1 goal to 0 at the end of the first period. This was due to a very clever shot on the part of Molson, playing center at the time, after he and Clarke had carried the puck three-quarters the length of the ice and through the Princeton defense with as clever a bit of passing as one would care to see. Clarke took a long shot from the extreme left side of the ice. Colebrook stopped it with

his shin guard, but before he could sweep it out of danger Molson
pounced in on the rubber and flicked it into the webbing.

In the fall of 1926, heats for field sports and football occupied all his spare time. That year his team beat the West Point Cadets in hockey and went on to win the Canadian Intercollegiate championship. Hartland won a spot in the Kingston Junior Hockey Club team, made up of the best players from RMC, Queen's and Kingston, and participated in the Dominion Championship for the Memorial Cup Finals in Winnipeg. He also became a member of the RMC football team, which won the Dominion Intermediate Championship in the same year.

In mid-September 1926, letters came from Culloch, Tom and Betty at home in Montreal; to save time Hartland wrote back one letter to the whole family. In it he managed to remonstrate with Tom and make a joke at the same time: "Tom wrote me a nasty letter full of shaving-brushes, and bitterly blamed me for sneaking up on the gears of the car and wrenching their teeth out when they weren't looking. I didn't do it. They are just making way for the second teeth same as we did when young."

On the football field, in a game against Queen's University, Hartland said he found himself frequently opposite "a Brockville steam-fitter, imported from the Ottawa Roughriders, called 'Irish' Monahan. He has a curly nose & cauliflower ears, & when I came off the field I thought a truck had run over me – twice." Later he added, "Football's a wonderful game, all right, & I sometimes wish I could make some people I dislike take it up seriously!"

On October 11, 1926, during a practice of the RMC football teams after classes, Hartland was inadvertently involved in the fatal injury to another cadet. Tommy Smart, a young man in his graduating year who had been one of Hartland's closest friends in Montreal as well as Kingston, was acting as a substitute centre in the game. "At one point in the game the ball was kicked to Cadet

Molson who was playing quarterback for the first team," recalled (Colonel) Reg Sawyer. "Molson attempted to carry the ball up the field, and two players of the second team set out to tackle him unsuccessfully. Tommy Smart, who had broken through centre, approached Molson at full running pace."

"In those days flying tackles were the big thing in football," Sawyer explained. "They were usually pretty hard on a fellow, but he had to master them to stay on the team." One morning, the coach had rebuked team members about the lack of "drive" in their tackling. Hartland, who found it extremely difficult to talk about at the time, vividly remembered the event nearly forty years later: "Smart took the coach's tongue-lashing and instructions very much to heart and when he ran down to tackle me, after I had received the kick, he took off in a flying tackle rather like a dive made at the start of a swimming race, with his head down and in a horizontal attitude. His helmet hit my thigh pad as I was in full stride." It was an exceptionally rough tackle; Hartland scrambled up immediately but Smart was unmoving, unconscious. With two broken vertebrae and a crushed spinal cord, he died the following morning at the Kingston General Hospital.

Hartland called upon his friend's father after the funeral, which must have been a very emotional and difficult meeting. Molson's way of dealing with the grief and horror of Smart's death was to will himself not to brood or dwell on the tragic event, but to apply himself even more arduously to his studies. Though reluctant to play football again, he finished the sports season out of a sense of duty. At the end of the final term that year he ranked second in his class in Military Engineering and he was described in a report as "exemplary, keen, smart, and dependable." He also did well in equitation, tactics, math and mechanics. The following year, he came first in both French and Military Organization and Law. In 1928 he was the top student in Tactics and won a competition with an essay entitled "The Forest Wealth of Canada."

At the end of his final year, the time when a minstrel show was traditionally put on by cadets, the students organized a "Pill Box Review" instead, in which they lampooned staff and seniors. Friends and family were invited to the show; Betty Henderson sat with Dosh and Betty Molson in the audience. For decades afterwards she would remember a farce called "The Bathroom Door," in which Hartland dressed up as a Cockney housemaid named "Boots," gamely singing over hoots of laughter, "Take me in your arms again, and kiss me once or twice, for kissing you is awfully nice …"

CHAPTER FOUR

URING HIS LAST TWO years at RMC, Hartland attended two weddings as an usher. The first was for his cousin Jack, who had married Doris Carington Smith in Quebec City in 1926, with Tom as best man. Home in Montreal in 1928 Dorothy married Tommy MacDougall, Herbert's best friend's son. Hartland's sister Betty was engaged to Larry Mather, but their wedding wouldn't take place until 1931.

For each wedding Hartland appeared in his immaculate scarlet cadet uniform. He was a very dashing young man who had numerous female admirers; the glamorous uniform with its polished brass buttons only added to his natural charisma. For the most part, however, he was uninterested in young female attention. His precociousness, so often expressed in early manifestations of mature wit, would endear him more to the company of older male and female friends. For the entire span of his life, his closest friends would be significantly older than he was.

Hartland appeared to pay little attention to the brewery in those days. The family had, as he would point out later, little need of him. By the time he graduated from RMC, five Molsons were active in the family business. Fred's sons Bert and John Henry had joined the administrative team after the lifting of temperance restrictions late in 1919. In 1921, a five million gallon year, Fred was installed as president and Herbert became chairman. Tom had been hired as an assistant in 1922, having completed his brewing course in England. At this time the team realized they needed, once again, to replace all existing equipment, expand their processing space and install a new brew kettle. They agreed they had to tear down the buildings on the west side of the brewery, including the old Molson Terrace and St. Thomas's Church, and replace both with a $2.5 million four-storey building dedicated to administrative use.

In January 1926, Evelyn and Colin Russel left for an eight-week trip to Jamaica, prescribed for Colin to recover from a respiratory infection. At the same time Jennie left for her annual trip to Atlantic City, New Jersey, where she had been going each winter since at least 1916, upon her doctor's advice. Herbert and Bessie left Montreal in mid-February heading for Gibraltar, planning to overtake the Empress of France there and enjoy a Mediterranean cruise. When Jennie died, "easily and quickly" in Atlantic City, neither Herbert, Bessie nor the Russels were able to return on time for her funeral, which Hartland, Tom and their sisters attended.

The economic depression that had marked the first half of the decade was lifting by the mid-1920s. Consumer confidence climbed; more jobs became available for better pay and shorter working hours. New products, such as electric stoves, refrigerators, improved cars and talking pictures were a few manifestations of staggering technological changes. Radios, it seemed, became ubiquitous (even though good ones cost as much as cars), and soon they became the hub around which people gathered to hear the latest entertainment, news and sports. American politics and jazz drifted into Canadian living rooms and sports heroes were lifted to a height larger than life in people's imaginations.

As Hartland found himself growing closer to the anticipated day of graduation, likewise grew his awareness of what an enviable position he occupied in his family and in the community. No obligations or pressures were put on him to follow in the family business; matters at the brewery were ably looked after by other Molsons. Now that prohibition had been lifted in Ontario and the market in that province had opened up, the expanded brewery's production had risen to seven and a half million gallons. Hartland's financial stability would be secure, thanks to his father's lifetime gifts and his own education, now making his skills marketable.

Luxurious holidays were assured: in 1925 his parents purchased a commodious summer house next to Fred's in Metis, which they renovated, enlarged and transformed into an elegant villa of airy proportions and surrounded with hedges and perennial gardens. Hartland's appreciation of elegant comfort did not extend to traditional summer pastimes such as picnicking on the beach. Twenty years later, turning down an invitation to a picnic in Chester, Nova Scotia, he mockingly protested to his niece Elena Mather, "I don't like picnics. I don't want to go on a picnic. I'd rather stay at home in the billiard room and throw ants and sand in my food!"

The young man continued to be invited on annual fishing trips with his father and Uncle Walter on the Bonaventure River. In 1926 Herbert and Fred had the steam yacht *Curlew* built in Southampton and sailed to Montreal the following year, replacing Herbert's yawl by the same name. The new *Curlew* was 189 tons, 117 feet long and accommodated seven passengers and a crew of ten.

It was an extremely exciting time to be 19 years old and celebrating one's graduation. To Hartland, life must have seemed like an endless banquet of stimulating possibilities. A crowd of young people provided a round of social activities. Although his parents introduced Hartland to some coy debutantes, the company he preferred to keep included male friends in the "fast" crowd, and progressive, modern women in loose flapper dresses and bobbed hair who dared to smoke cigarettes. He too liked to be fashionable, wearing the latest styles in suits and ties, and keeping his hair slicked back and parted in the middle. Hartland's experience was typical of the youngest sons of privileged families, though unlike many of the others he didn't drink, was not aimless, could never be accused of being irresponsible nor did he seem to indulge in excesses of any kind.

Hartland's sense of responsibility was not universally recognized, however. In the opinion of some members of his family, including his father and brother, Hartland was self-indulgent and easily led. Compared to Tom, who had "settled down" immediately into the brewery, and his sisters, who completed secondary school, attended finishing school in Paris, made their social debuts and promptly married, their younger brother wasn't behaving in the way his elders expected him to. They interpreted his manner of dress as evidence of affectation, his choice of friends as unwise and his love of music and dancing as an expression of disdain for tradition. On many occasions Hartland found himself rallying against this impression, and trying to prove, particularly to his father, that his character had positive qualities. "Dad does not think I have much determination or will," he complained in one letter to his mother. Writing to Herbert, he said "I have a real lack of effusiveness which sometimes makes the family think that I take everything for granted and don't realize how lucky I am, & how good you are to me. That is my nature, but I do appreciate your great generosity."

Upon graduation in the spring of 1928, Hartland and his fellow cadets were offered commissions; his was as a Lieutenant with the 27th Field Battery, 2nd Field Brigade, Canadian Artillery. He was gratified to have had the training and the qualifications to join the militia when it might become necessary but had no immediate desire to make a career in the military.

In the fall of 1928, Herbert offered Hartland a trip to Europe as a graduation gift, as he had done for Tom. Herbert wanted his sons to have the opportunity to extend their physical and cultural boundaries, as well as become more comfortable in conversational French. He gave Hartland a list of names of friends and associates on whom he could call, including General Robert Britnell in Paris, the president of the Banque Adam, who declared it was "impossible for a foreigner to break into French society without a shove." Herbert arranged for him to travel with Bartlett Ogilvie, 19, who had known Hartland in Montreal and was also a graduate of the Royal Military College. (Bart was a descendant of Archibald Ogilvie, who had come to Canada from Scotland in the early 19th century and established a very successful flour milling and exporting business.)

Hartland and Bart left on September 7, 1928, aboard the CP Steamship *Duchess of Bedford*. They did not travel lightly: between them they had four trunks, six suitcases and two hatboxes, and would purchase many more clothes and accoutrements while in Europe. "Leaving wasn't so awfully good," Hartland admitted in his first letter to his mother, "but as soon as we'd left we began to feel like a million."

In London, the chums shared rooms at the Mayfair Hotel, where Hartland described the service as "splendid – valet unpacked, lays out everything, presses suits every time, shines shoes etc." He noted that he didn't have any appropriate clothes for calling on his father's acquaintances, so they visited a haberdashery where he ordered a dinner jacket, tails, waistcoats, dress shirts, day shirts, suits, evening ties, an overcoat and a morning coat, which "seemed really extravagant." That evening they went to the pictures and saw Norma Shearer in the newly released melodrama of New York life *The Trial of Mary Dugan*.

Hartland and Bart stayed a month in London sightseeing and socializing, flew to Paris for five days then carried on to Amsterdam where they had reservations in the Grand Hotel Victoria. Hartland wrote voluble letters home, his first one interspersed with French.

We started to fly here after 5 days in Paris, et parblue! Il faisait si mauvais temps que nous étions forces de nous retourner et de nous aterrir encore au Bourget! Nous n'étions que vingt minutes dans l'avion. How's that after 5 days? (I'll bite how is it?) Anyway we had to wait for 2¼ hours for better weather reports before we even started, & then ended up in the train at 1:35 from the Gare du Nord. We have now changed our plans and go to Copenhagen tomorrow (Thurs) by KLM & to Berlin by Lufthansa on Sat., & probably back to Paris Tuesday & London Saturday. None of our traveling will be done by Air Union planes, all by KLM., Lufthansa, or Imperial Airways. KLM use very nice Fokkers, & Luft. Junkers. The latter we have seen but not been in yet.

Hartland was clearly enamoured with planes and flying. He sent a postcard to his mother with a photo of a Fokker monoplane in which he and Bart had flown to Amsterdam with ten other passengers. The slogan on the Royal Dutch Air Lines read "world wide reputation for regularity, speed and comfort." They spent a few days in Copenhagen before flying to Berlin, which Hartland described as "the most enjoyable journey we have yet had."

The first 2 hours to Travenmunde was by Rohrbach flying boat, marvelous big thing, & we flew at about 95 m.p.h. only about 10 ft above the water. Never felt anything go so fast. Then we changed to all-metal plane of Lufthansa & came here in 2 hrs. Very steady plane & sunshine. Inside was leather, up to windows, & then grey cloth like Rolls. Adjustable long cane chairs, little cushion for head, wireless operator, & heating. Berlin has the finest airport in the world. Dozens of planes all over the place, & excellent buildings. I believe the Lufthansa fly 30,000 miles a day – Imperial Airways only 2,500.

In Berlin the young men went to nightclubs to dance, saw operas including *Carmen and Tannhauser* and stayed up until two or three in the morning taking in cabarets. One time, as Hartland recalled, they were "just going to bed after a spectacular round of Berlin nightclubs, about two or three o'clock in the morning," when they heard the sound of horses passing their hotel.

> *Looking out, we watched what must have been at least a whole divi-sion of Cavalry with supporting services, going by for what seemed like hours. We were surprised, because rearmament was complete-ly prohibited under the Treaty of Versailles. Later we went out to an airfield to see the Graf Zeppelin just returned triumphantly from South America. The crowds were enormous, and controlling them were the federal police called the "Green Police." We were really shaken by the thousands of these police on duty. We learned later that all were qualified N.C.O. instructors in the German army. They were hidden as police to get around the treaty.*

After a week they boarded a train to Potsdam on their way to Dresden, where a similar experience at the Old Imperial Life Guard Barracks convinced them they had to report their observations to the war office in London upon their return. However, in retrospect Hartland noted that their warnings – just as Winston Churchill's and others' would be some years later – were ignored. The travellers returned to Paris, where Hartland met General Britnell. Herbert's old friend immediately stepped in as a generous mentor and urged Hartland to make the most of his opportunity in France.

> *He was awfully nice – couldn't do enough & after talking it all over he thought that Paris was as good as anywhere. He is going to put me up at the Sporting & Racing Clubs for tennis, squash & swimming, etc., & is getting me invitations to a dance on December 8, where I will be in a totally French atmosphere …*

[He] thinks mixing one of the best ways to learn. I said rather timidly that I had thought of looking for a job, because one would talk more than by being alone on the streets and at lectures. He asked me what I'd like to do & I said I was going into Accountancy eventually. He just said, "I'll tell you what you shall do – if you like it."

Britnell explained to Hartland that he had a staff working on restructuring a bank, which he had done once before on behalf of the Banque Adam. He suggested that Hartland join his team and help with the organization work, which would give him an insight into every department including the trust company work that the French banks did. It had to be an apprentice's job, Britnell cautioned, because foreigners couldn't work in France without difficulty, and therefore he couldn't pay him anything. Nevertheless Hartland was keen to comply, anticipating the double benefit of learning banking and becoming proficient in French. "I'm sure it will be quite fascinating & I will be working with Frenchmen all day. There will also be reading & writing to be done." However Hartland soon had qualms. The general invited him out to dinner to join four of his Paris friends, and Hartland realized that "the thought of starting in that crowd terrifies me. They talk too quickly, & use trick phrases, they dance badly, & love dancing, they know too much about operas & music for me, & they don't take enough baths. However I think it will be bearable after, say, a month."

Hartland wasn't the only young Canadian in France on an extended trip. A hockey team made up of expatriate Canadians visiting or working in France was being organized by an old acquaintance named Rosie Patton, also staying in Paris. Familiar with Hartland's hockey record in Kingston, Rosie had offered him a spot with the "Paris Canadians" who were scheduled to participate in the Swiss National Winter Games, and Hartland had agreed to go. The team was scheduled to play their first game in

London in late December and their last in Switzerland in early January. However, now that Hartland had a job arranged by Britnell at the bank he didn't think it would be fair to ask for time off at Christmas to play hockey. He wrote to Patton and conveyed his regrets.

Meanwhile, for the few weeks that he had left before his job began (and before Bart had to return to Montreal), the friends accepted an invitation to stay with the Gaults just outside Taunton, Somerset, in England's west country region. Hamilton Gault, another friend of Herbert's, had also been a great friend of Percy Molson's through their connections with the Princess Patricia Canadian Light Infantry (PPCLI) during the war. Staying at the estate with Hamilton and his wife Dorothy was a welcome change for Hartland who protested that he was tired of going to dance clubs every evening. Even so, the young men's "splendid evenings" at the Gaults' included dinner parties, "gramophone dances" at the house and a fancy ball held in the village.

> We are extremely comfy here & treated as if it were home. We are very glad to be in a house even like home again, and staying about 10 days. We are going to have a pretty busy time shooting & hunting etc. & will be rather interesting to the country folk as we are not horsey. Tonight we were 11 for dinner & had quite a jolly eve. We are ... being treated wonderfully by Col. Gault & Dorothy, and all their friends ... are extremely kind and having us to lunch, shooting, and dinner before a dance, on different days. The people here are not snooty a bit – even hunting, and when Bart & I appeared in brown boots, golf-suit coats and bowlers, no one even smiled. We expected a barrage of asides and sneers.

After his sojourn with the Gaults, Hartland returned to Paris, found more permanent accommodations with a French host family and began working at the Banque Adam. As eager as he was to step

into the working world, to test and prove himself, at first he wondered if he had made a terrible mistake. "Going into this bank is
about the worst thing I've done yet. I don't even know my way up
to my office in the building & have 6 other Frenchmen in the room
who shoot off about 88 mph much to my confusion." Fortunately
he liked the family he was living with, which helped him cope with
his disappointment at work and his ambivalence about Paris.

> I really hate Paris at present – very different staying here from in
> a hotel, but I'm sure I will get used to it in a little while. My office
> hours are 8:45–12:15 & 2:15–6:45 – really quite a long day,
> but I don't see how I can help learning French when I am with the
> natives all that time … I shall breakfast with a French family,
> work all day with real Frenchmen, and return in the evening to a
> French family, & I don't know what more I could do.

Hartland had begun to despair at the thought of spending his
first Christmas away from Montreal and his family. "I … sincerely
wish I were home," he wrote his mother. "I find (as I suspected)
that I really am a great home-loving laddie, and miss you all a great
deal. Even all the bright lights do not appeal." One day General
Britnell told Hartland that the three weeks which encompassed
the Christmas and New Year period were spotted with thirteen
days of public holiday and advised him to take the opportunity. To
Hartland's joy, he found he was able to join the hockey team and
go to Switzerland after all. It was the perfect antidote to homesickness.

The first game – the only one in the series they would lose – took
place December 22 in London, following which the team left for
their next three scheduled playoffs – in Davos, St. Moritz and
Chamonix. He wrote to Bessie the day after Christmas, from
Davos:

We have played one game here so far & won 1–0. We have a smart team, but have run into a fuss about playing Bobby Bell late of McGill, Soo & Vics, because he is coaching a team here. We also have Dempsay, erstwhile star defenceman of McGill. The rest are French-Canadians, and pretty good. Roncarelli was playing on the Milan team we beat this morning. As usual he got a trifle crude … Dempsay is a tower of strength and quite clean, but if anybody starts anything he gives 'em the body and ends things. If we are allowed Bell we should win the Spengler Cup for which we are playing, and without him we have a good chance. We don't quite know our programme yet but I think Chamonix & Budapest are pretty certain. The other teams here include Berlin, Munich, Davos, Oxford & Milan.

Hartland found he loved Switzerland. "We all feel frightfully pleased to be in the snow and quiet after Paris, – it's so like home." Over the following three days his team played against the Berlin, Paris and Chamonix teams. They travelled to Chamonix on January 7 and then returned to Davos for the Swiss National Winter Games where they played against Germany, Poland, Switzerland and England. Teams were formed out of the pick of all the players to set up exhibition games against each other, and Hartland was asked to join the "European Canadian" team.

One of the players chosen from Oxford to be on Hartland's team was Clarence Campbell, whose acquaintance would mark the beginning of a long friendship with Hartland. Campbell would later stand for many years as president of the National Hockey League, during which time Hartland owned the Montreal Canadiens team.

So that his father didn't think he was only there for the sport, Hartland pointed out that his hockey experience was very good for his language practice.

It is completely French, and there are few foreigners … One cer-
tainly gets more "conversational" French here than in Paris …
The French fellows on our team say I speak v. well, & my accent
is good, but it is in the matter of vocabulary that all my difficulty
comes in. That is a very slow matter, & I can quite readily see
that one might spend 5 years in France & still be stuck for words
every now & again.

When the team moved on to Geneva to play their last games,
the secretary of the Chamonix hockey club approached Hartland
and asked him if he would be interested in coaching hockey there
for a month. As he was obliged to General Britnell in Paris,
Hartland thought he should write and ask him his advice first. His
response must have been positive, for Hartland's next letter to his
parents was from Chamonix at the end of January. Herbert meanwhile had wired his disapproval, but the telegram arrived too late
for Hartland to alter his plans.

I wrote Culloch all the details of my coming here, which I am sure
will have displeased you since you wired disapproval. As a matter
of fact it is a success, and I don't regret it. My French is coming
on, and it's so much more pleasant and healthy being outdoors than
in the bank, where I was learning French, but little or nothing of
banking. I will leave here in 10 days & go back to dirty Paris.

Hartland loved coaching the young hockey players, and wrote
about the experience in an animated way.

You should see me with the little schoolboys I teach to play hockey!
You'd laugh for months. They are very tiny, very respectful, & try
so hard while I yell "Vite! Vite!" at them & explain why they
mustn't hit each other over the head. To teach them to skate bet-
ter I make them play "Follow my leader" [sic] after me, twisting

*around the rink. For permanent results I have insisted on the kids
starting & playing a lot, so now they are excused Gym or something & I get them every day except Monday.*

However, he found it hard to get through the evenings, which
he found very empty.

*I don't know which is lonelier, Paris or here. For the first time in
my life I am living alone in a big hotel, & eating alone which I
hate. On the rink of course is OK & in the evenings I often go to
the casino. I hardly dance nowadays because the music is the fast
French variety, & such girls as I know don't dance well. I make
no excuses – if they don't want me on their parties they needn't
ask me – I like reading anyway.*

By the end of February, Hartland was back in Paris and working
again at the bank. His father had written again and gave his permission for his son to stay there until May, on the condition that
he was making "real progress." Hartland wasn't sure how to
respond to this. He replied:

*I must say, it leaves a rather funny decision to me. Undoubtedly I
have made progress, & cannot help continuing to do so, but you
must understand that a language is necessarily slow to pick up. It
is not a course or "exact science." What I am doing is this – I am
attending very conscientiously to my hours in the bank
(8:45–6:45, 2 hours for lunch) talking as much as possible, writing occasionally, and reading French books in my spare time. I
don't think I can do more.*

In the end Hartland and his father decided he would return to
Montreal in July. He had learned enough French to have developed
some insight into the way banks operated in France. His last letter

home summarized his experience. "The only thing I'm not learning here is banking but it's either French or banking, & I'm worrying about the French. Anyhow the system of French banking is so devious that it seems stupid to learn it when they try to copy ours."

When Hartland returned to Canada in the summer of 1929 he found his father had arranged a place for him as a Junior for Molson's Brewery's local accounting firm, McDonald Currie. Hartland had expressed his intention of acquiring his Certified Accountant certificate, and here, his father reasoned, his son could learn accounting theory, auditing techniques and how to go about a financial investigation.

Walter Gordon, another of Hartland's friends from RMC, was studying for his CA certificate at the same time at another firm. According to Gordon, "Learning to be an auditor in those days was dull and monotonous. But if a student showed interest and was lucky, there were opportunities to get away from the auditing routine for extended periods and to spend one's time on investigations and special assignments of one kind or another. I found this a fascinating way of learning what goes on behind the scenes and also of how to make individual businesses more profitable and efficient."

At less than $100 a month, Hartland's wages were not generous, but because he continued to live at home with his parents, he was able to invest all of it in the stock market. Many young people were doing well on small salaries and investing in shares, which had been booming throughout the late 1920s. Mining stocks, particularly gold and copper, yielded unprecedented profits. Exchanges were dealing with record volumes as the value of hitherto untapped natural resources continued to rise, and investors benefited handsomely.

Some voices of caution were raised, the *Financial Post* calling the trend, in 1927, "an orgy of speculation." And by early 1929, many partners at McDonald Currie and other firms believed the market was overpriced and that a crash was coming. One standard among accounting firms of the time prohibited members of staff from buying shares in any company for which the firm acted as auditors, and no members of staff were permitted to buy stocks on margin. Hartland confined his investments to utilities and well-established local industries. The first stocks he bought, in July 1929, were from Home Oil and Dominion Bridge, and to diversify, in September he purchased more stocks in Dominion Engineering Company, Bell Telephone and Shawinigan Water and Power.

The stock market dipped on September 3. During the days and weeks that followed, the market corrected itself, faltered once more, appeared to recover and lurched again. In October, Hartland would later recall, he was working on an audit of a brokerage house on Wall Street. On the morning of October 29, the day later referred to as "Black Tuesday," the market opened low, plummeted further and in the ensuing chaos the damage was calamitous. Many people who had used stocks as collateral for homes and businesses were financially devastated. The public was aghast; long faces were encountered everywhere and voices on news reports sounded heavy with disbelief. It was to be the worst collapse ever experienced in Canadian financial history.

But while others were lining up in an increasing frenzy of selling, Hartland persevered with his previous methodical pattern of buying stocks. The prices of those he preferred, and which he continued to purchase even on the day of October 29, had not in fact risen or fallen significantly in the wake of the disastrous slide of the others and carried on trading at their pre-crash volume. Throughout October and early November Hartland continued to build his portfolio, which by then included Victory Bonds, Western Steel Products, American Superpower, Anaconda and

Associated Oil and Gas.

The stock market continued falling in November. Squeezed by creditors demands, many brokerage houses and accounting firms went into receivership, some under clouds of scandal around highly publicized trials as the public looked for men to blame. There had been little legislation to control stock market fraud in those days and some brokers and bankers had been guilty of pretending that stocks were worth more than their market value. In later years Hartland would remember this as an "interesting time," a curious comment that seems to reflect his sense of being detached from it all, insulated by his privileged environment and innate sense of caution. His father, who maintained a belief in the Victorian principle of self-help, certainly had no sympathy for the men who found themselves in the unemployment lines. In Herbert's opinion, the crash was a direct consequence of the actions of foolish speculators and considered those suffering to have engineered their own downfall though unsound planning, even referring to them as having "made an unholy mess of things."

Although for many individuals and businesses it was a sobering end to a decade of excesses, McDonald Currie not only held fast but also steadily flourished. Between 1925 and 1932, the staff increased considerably, and the firm's business multiplied five times in volume. Audit work reached a plateau, trusteeships increased and insolvency practice (whereby companies were reorganized and reconstructed, "nursed" to become profitable again) became a mainstay.

Fortuitous choices and financial acuity were on Hartland's side. Still (in spite of the stability of McDonald Currie), immediate prospects for advancement in accounting fields were not encouraging in the aftermath of the Depression. Many businesses were following a trend to sell out to American corporations, and many of Hartland's friends headed to New York. Though, like Canada, the United States was coping with the economic fallout of the market crash, the cities of New York and Detroit seemed to contain, if not all the answers, then surely all the great events and ideas of the time.

One American who personified the industrialist success story was multi-millionaire entrepreneur Henry Ford, founder and owner of the Ford Motor Company. At the 1933 World's Fair in Chicago, Ford introduced his newest entrepreneurial dream, a unique processing system for agricultural crops for which a market had yet to be established. He was interested in developing the potential of legumes not only as good sources of easily grown protein, but also as the raw material – the source of oils and fibres – for useful industrial products.

Hartland was attracted to the principle, to products and to the idealism with which Ford promoted his system. The aging inventor maintained that society created far too much waste and that proper management could eliminate waste altogether. He carried his philosophy to the point of belief that if mass production of goods, specialization and the service ideal were all developed properly, they would harmonize relations not only between men but also between man and nature. He had long kept an experimental farm near his automobile plant, turning farm crops into new foods and industrial goods. In 1932 Ford had determined that soy beans – rich in versatile oil, high in protein and having a residual fibre that could be applied to myriad uses – showed the most promise of all other crops. Numerous parts of Ford cars were already being made from soybean-derived materials, including paint, door handles, accelerator pedals and timing gears.

In the summer of 1933 Hartland made a trip to Dearborn, Michigan, to meet Henry Ford. He remembered spending a day with "that interesting and brilliant old man," being shown around his plant and farms. Following this meeting Hartland became convinced that Ford's idea was viable, and Ford thought he would be just the right person to promote the new business in Canada. The benefits of soy food had been well known in China since "time immemorial," but the bean was relatively unknown in North America. While Ford was looking to manufacture plastic-like products, Hartland thought he could begin by marketing soy beans to the Canadian food and restaurant industry. He was sure the idea would catch on, for soy meal, flour and oil were less expensive and healthier than their wheat and corn-based counterparts. Moreover, if he started a processing and extraction plant, once that part of the business was well established he would be able to introduce other industrial derivatives of this "wonder bean."

Hartland approached his family for financial help but neither his father nor his brother Tom, who had just married Celia Cantlie that spring, was interested. However, among friends in Montreal and New York he found a few interested in supporting his venture, including Hunt Dickinson and Charles Douglas of New York. Encouraged, he purchased the machinery known as the "Ford Processor" and had it shipped to Montreal for assembly. He drew diagrams and wrote descriptions of his plans for his soy business's operation and efficiency, incorporating Ford's elements of mass production, recycling and elimination of waste. By December 1933 he had acquired a plant and had a list of clients and orders lined up. He set up an administrative office on St. James Street, tacked a sign on the door, "Dominion Soya Industries," and his first business was launched.

In spite of all his research, effort and seemingly thorough planning, problems dogged Hartland from the beginning. Long before the machinery could be started, first there were delays in consulting with technical chemists from the National Research Council, then mechanical difficulties that pushed product delivery dates forward again and again. As Hartland would explain later, "At the time of taking over Ford's Process it was thought that it could be operated at once on a commercial basis, but as it happened we had to experiment at considerable expense to ourselves in order to turn it into a commercial plant."

Delays led to dwindling finances, and Hartland approached his investors again for more capital, just to buy the time needed before they could go into production. He wrote to one friend, "At times I find it extremely depressing. Delays are so numerous and the task of finding money so disagreeable and difficult that sometimes the outlook is bleak. I think these periods are purely mental and I do feel that we will muddle through in the near future … We have a few interesting possibilities for money which are taking a long time. One never knows, they might solve our problem."

Testing, inspections and mechanical problems finally behind them, Hartland's soy processing plant operated for three weeks in March 1935 on a commercial basis. A maximum output per day of three and a half tons of beans was reached, but the average was recorded at approximately two and a third tons per day. He hoped that eventually, with his equipment properly tuned up, an average output of three tons per day could be maintained. As he said to one investor, "On this basis of output and sale, at the present spread of prices between the beans and products, a profit is anticipated."

Then Hartland learned that Ford had developed a faster and cheaper method of processing soy beans that rendered the equipment he had purchased obsolete. Charles Douglas wrote:

> There is no need for me to tell you how frightfully sorry I am that all the interesting work which we have put into the Soya business during the last eighteen months looks like it is vanishing into thin air and has in fact apparently vanished as far as D[ominion] S[oya] I[ndustries] is concerned … It is most inconsiderate of Henry Ford to butt in with a new and excessively cheap yet satisfactory process, but I can perfectly well see your position in the matter and I quite understand that under the circumstances you do not see that you have any alternative but to shut down. I can imagine how serious a disappointment it is.

Difficult as his experience was with Dominion Soya Industries, Hartland became philosophical about it fairly quickly and moved on to other ventures. Forty years later, when soy products were re-introduced into the Canadian market, they were widely accepted by the public. "The lowly bean was a wonder creation," Hartland would say wistfully in 1975. "However, we were a little before our time in this development."

CHAPTER FIVE

I N THE MONTHS following the closure of Dominion Soya Industries, Hartland was able to pay back his investors with his own savings. He turned his focus once again towards his studies to acquire his Chartered Accountant's certificate and passed the exam at McGill University with the highest marks in the province. For a while he "toyed with the idea of getting a law degree as well, and then," he explained to interviewer Peter Stursberg in 1974, "I decided I'd done enough midnight oiling on the educational process and I decided I'd just rather work."

Hartland continued to take part in Montreal's vibrant social whirl. Although he'd given up dancing and clubbing, he still enjoyed dinner parties and the company of "swish" friends, listened to swing music and smoked Gold Flakes, cigarettes advertised in *Canadian Aviation* magazine "for men and women of distinction." Weekend trips to New York, summer vacations in Metis and

salmon fishing holidays off Anticosti Island provided opportunities
to discuss possibilities of future endeavours with other business-
minded friends, but also to mix, mingle and fall in love.

At Metis in the summer of 1930, Hartland was introduced to
Helen Kerr Hogg, known as Babbie, a young woman from
Montreal who had been living in New York City and recently
divorced there. She was the youngest daughter of Annie Laing and
her husband William Hogg, a grain and feed dealer who had a residence in Montreal and a farm property in Longue Pointe, and who
had for many years done business with Molson's Brewery. Her
uncle George Hogg was mayor of Westmount and the founder of
the prosperous Guaranteed Pure Milk company downtown.

Babbie was three and a half years older than Hartland, quite
petite and very pretty, clever and captivating, and described by one
who knew her in 1930 as "a pet of Hartland's friends." She sang
very well, played the piano and took part animatedly in drawing-
room charades and skits. Like many of her Anglo upper-crust contemporaries, she was a member of a charity organization called the
Junior League, which put on a play or a musical every year for
fundraising. Babbie was always an enthusiastic participant in the
plays. For a debutante and society girl, this flouted the conventions
of the social register: both her acting and the fact of her divorce
earned disapproval in select circles. She had what one Molson
described archly as a "Hollywood look."

Babbie was as charmed by Hartland as he was by her, and the
couple married quietly on February 7, 1931. They lived in a rented
house in Chelsea Place while Hartland continued working at
McDonald Currie. At least twice a year they spent long holidays at
various resort hotels in Kingston and Montego Bay, Jamaica.

At the time of Hartland and Babbie's marriage, Herbert was
working in the brewery every day, Fred having died of a stroke in
February 1929. Herbert's days of leisure and long vacations were
over. Now president of the brewery at age 55, he turned all his

attention to the administration of the family business and lost no time taking over direction of the latest major expansion.

In addition to his duties at Molson's Brewery, Herbert continued to attend frequent board meetings of institutions of which he was a director. In 1934 these included the Bank of Montreal, the City and District Savings Bank, the Montreal General Hospital and McGill University. The Depression had affected all of them to some extent, from unpaid loans at the banks to net fiscal losses faced by the university. McGill's governors appointed a Survey Committee to assess the situation and formulate a plan to put the university's finances back in a healthy position. Herbert, as chairman of the committee, commissioned Hartland as a chartered accountant to help investigate and propose a reorganization of financial operations at McGill. Some months later Hartland and an engineering consultant hired at the same time submitted a report to the Survey Committee, identifying where expenses could be cut and services maintained on a smaller budget. This plan was later credited with enabling McGill to carry on through the Depression.

In the early 1930s Herbert began to be troubled by the possibility of his future succession duties becoming a problem for his children. Fred's death had been followed by that of his wife Catherine six months later, meaning that estate duties had to be paid twice on the same estate that year. By 1934 Herbert may have had a sense that something was amiss with his own health. He began to whittle at his estate in favour of his children, giving them generous cheques at Christmas time and for their birthdays. When in 1935 doctors at the Montreal General Hospital discovered he had lung cancer, they operated and hoped for a full recovery. Herbert would not speak about it afterwards, but continued to distribute portions of his estate to his children.

To Hartland, he wrote:

It is unnecessary for me to enlarge on the importance of its wise

*investment by you as it will probably be increasingly difficult and
expensive for me to give substantial sums to my children at my
death; the succession duties will make a huge hole in the results of
a lifetime of work ... This amount of money is what, I believe,
you call in accounting circles "non-recurring profits" and must
not be counted upon in future years or as a precedent. The till
wouldn't stand it. So invest it wisely if you can and do not disap-
point me.*

It is questionable whether or not Herbert would have considered
all of Hartland's "investments" wise. In January 1935 he bought a
"fancy" cashmere suit, grey flannel trousers and poplin shirts. He
hired maids and a cook. In February he bought shares in a gold
mine and more in a natural gas company. Then he bought a four-
year-old used Cadillac convertible and hired a chauffeur. In May of
1935 a minor accident involving his Cadillac and a tram car on St.
James Street was another expense. But in Herbert's opinion, the
most objectionable of Hartland's extravagances was taking up flying lessons.

Hartland learned to fly in a de Havilland Gipsy Moth at the
Montreal Light Aeroplane Club in the summer of 1934. Small and
stable, ideal for training, the open cockpit single-engine biplane
was one of four assorted aircraft owned and operated by the
Montreal club. Behind the cloth-covered steel fuselage was room
for two: the instructor sat in the front and demonstrated to the student, behind him, the various points of flying, beginning with take-
off, circling the airfield and landing.

The Montreal Light Aeroplane Club, which had recently
expanded and moved to St. Hubert airfield from Cartierville, was
one of a string of Canadian flying clubs that benefited from a gov-

ernment grant program established in 1928. Club directors and key figures in the federal defence department had foreseen a bright future for military and civil aviation at a time when most looked upon flying as a spectator sport. The "flying club scheme" had enabled these private clubs to purchase aircraft, hire pilots (former First World War fliers), engineers and mechanics, and to stay solvent during lean times. Still, the tuition fee of $250 for ground school lectures and flying instruction was out of reach of all but the privileged few in the mid-1930s.

Like most student pilots at the time, Hartland took up flying as a hobby. His sister-in-law Celia remembers that even as a student at RMC, the young man had a fascination with flying. Like many boys who wanted to grow up to become aviators, Hartland's interest in this exciting new field stemmed from the perception that the dashing and daring leaders in this dangerous sport were considered heroes to the public. Pilots and their rescue missions commanded so much attention and praise in the press that newspaper readers followed the exploits of bush pilots they knew by nicknames, like "Punch" Dickins, "Spike" Miller and "Duke" Schiller, making exploratory flights over Canada's northern territories. Whether bringing medicines to the sick in remote communities or delivering mail to isolated areas, pilots and their aircraft were opening up the northern frontier, which in previous years had only been accessible by canoe or dogsled.

While travelling in Europe and England in 1928, Hartland's admiration for various aircraft on which he had flown was evident from his letters home. While staying with Hamilton Gault in December of that year he had been introduced to "an awfully nice, quiet little man" named Robert Reeve, a 25-year-old visiting American pilot who was, Hartland pointed out, "the finest flying instructor in the world, and a friend of all the well-known airmen." The latter included Charles Lindbergh and also the writer Antoine de Saint-Exupéry, who was, along with Reeve, establishing the first routes for airmail service in South America at the time. (As a brilliant pilot and entrepreneur, Reeve's career was only beginning. He would later fly thousands of flights over Alaska, distinguish himself as a pilot in the Second World War, and by the 1960s, would be a millionaire airline owner.)

Meeting Robert Reeve was memorable for Hartland. But it was a chance encounter two years later with the Great War's flying ace Billy Bishop that had an even more profound influence on him. Hartland had met Bishop in 1931 at a board of directors meeting of McColl Frontenac Oil Company, later to become Texaco, in which Hartland owned shares. Bishop had recently moved to Montreal from England to fill an executive position at the company and lived on Drummond Street, opposite the Ritz Hotel where he and Hartland began to meet for lunch. In spite of the difference in their ages (Bishop was thirteen years older than Hartland) the two men and their wives – Babbie Hogg and Margaret Burden – became fast friends. They visited each other's homes frequently, and Hartland remarked particularly on how "happy and cheerful" Bishop's family seemed. The couples began to spend summer weekends on the Molson yacht. In the winter of 1933–34, Bishop's son Arthur recalls, "my father persuaded Hartland to learn to fly."

Born in 1894, Billy Bishop had attended Royal Military College from 1911 until 1914 before enlisting in the war. He had entered in the Canadian cavalry, but transferred to the Royal Flying Corps in 1915 as an observer. Posted to 60 Squadron as a pilot, he soon made a name for himself flying Nieuport 17 Scouts in France. He survived against all odds and developed an extraordinary skill in attacking enemy aircraft, mostly while flying solo. Over two years of combat he claimed a record number of destroyed enemy aircraft and was the first Canadian to be awarded the Victoria Cross. Since the end of the war he had been engaged in various aeronautic activities. In the early 1920s he ran a barn-storming business with fellow RAF pilot Billy Barker, putting on aerobatic exhibitions and giving passengers joy-rides. Following Barker's death in a flying accident, Bishop continued buying and selling aircraft and began to work on behalf of the Royal Canadian Air Force.

Since the onset of the Depression, the RCAF's role was confined to minimal, mostly civilian activities. Bishop's work in England had been related to his position as Honorary Group Captain of the RCAF, a responsibility he retained after he moved to Montreal and began working full time for the oil company. Elevated to Honorary Air Vice-Marshal in 1934, Bishop became determined to rouse the Canadian government to expand its role. When Hartland took him up on his suggestion and began his flying instruction, it had been nearly ten years since Bishop had piloted an aircraft. And as much as he looked forward to steering the administration towards a stronger RCAF, Bishop also yearned to get back in a cockpit again. The first thing he did upon his return to Montreal was to join Hartland at the flying club.

Hartland enjoyed his flying lessons immensely. With his instructor, who early on encouraged him to handle the controls, he learned to become familiar with the element of air and observed how the aircraft responded to different movements of the controls for the ailerons, elevators, rudders and flaps. The Gipsy Moth was equipped with the basics – a compass, an altimeter and a turn-and-bank indicator – but it had neither navigational instruments nor a radio. After a few hours of instruction he began to feel familiar with the aircraft, learning the rudiments of take-off, turning, banking, climbing, stalling and landing. He discovered how, when turned in one direction, the craft could right itself again in the air. He began to spend all his spare time at the club.

To boost membership in their organization, the Montreal Light Aeroplane Club offered a wide range of events and activities in the summer of 1934. They hosted a Royal Air Force display and club members entertained the officers afterwards. They welcomed visiting aircraft and pilots from New York City and organized civic receptions for the visiting airmen. They sponsored trophy events. The publicity gained the club several new members by the end of the year and an unprecedented demand for flying time, for which they charged $10 per hour.

As he worked toward obtaining his private pilot's licence, Hartland enjoyed not only the experience of flying but also the company of other rich sportsmen. Though he was young, he was welcomed into the fold of the older men. This was made easier not only through his friendship with Bishop but also by the fact that his cousin, Stuart Molson (son of Fred Molson), had been one of the club's first members, and his father Herbert was a well-known businessman and philanthropist in Montreal. Because both Stuart and Herbert were members of the 42nd Battalion of the Royal Highlanders, or the Black Watch, and Hartland himself had military training at RMC, it must have occurred to other airmen that as a pilot, Hartland would be a prime applicant for the RCAF.

Flying was a pursuit that groomed paragons like Charles Lindbergh, and that all over the world attracted the elite, including members of the British royal family, titled gentlemen and others who had courage, ambition, time and money to spare. The Montreal club drew Sir Herbert Holt – then president of the Royal Bank of Canada – one of the most prominent (though unpopular) people in the Montreal business community. The club was delighted when Bishop decided to join as well.

"Colonel Bishop soon got back the 'feel' of the controls and went off solo very quickly," reported the club to *Canadian Aviation* magazine that fall. "It is a great boost for aviation in Montreal to have Colonel Bishop flying again and a great help to the club to have him as an active member."

Then 40 years old, Bishop was stout and his hair was completely grey. Although he was considered too old to fly actively for the air force, his was still a commanding presence, his opinions carried great weight and the prestige of his fame and position was a great advantage to the club. Bishop accepted a position as honorary president of the club in September, the same month Hartland agreed to become a director.

Another member of the MLAC that summer was "Tim" Sims, an aero-engine expert and career pilot who had received his commercial licence in 1930. Sims and Peter Troup, a demonstrator pilot for Bellanca Aircraft (who had also been flying for Fairchild Aviation), had formed a partnership in 1932. Sims and Troup owned a Bellanca Pacemaker and a Fokker Super Universal, both sturdy single-engine bush planes. With these two aircraft they operated a flying business "on a shoestring" in northern Quebec which they called Northern Skyways.

Hartland had no expectations of becoming a commercial pilot. However, the business of bush-flying interested him very much. The aviation industry seemed untouched by the financial gloom paralyzing the rest of the country. Commercial aviation, though not subsidized by government, had a bright place in the Canadian economy. With experienced pilots, sound aircraft and solid business principles, a bush-flying company could make some handsome profits. It didn't take long for Hartland to raise the subject of going into business with Sims, Troup and Bishop one afternoon at the club.

Since the demise of his earlier venture, Dominion Soya Industries, Hartland didn't want to make the same mistake again. This time he would minimize the risks: he would do more research, be more prepared, more realistic. This time he would invest in a proven business, with partners who were as informed – or more so – than he was.

Aviation was a boon to the entire North American economy, but particularly in Canada, where there seemed to be no limits to this new frontier. Airships, zeppelins and auto-gyros competed along with the comparatively stable and conservative bush planes over the northern skies. Canada led the world in tons of freight carried by air. Although landing facilities were crude or non-existent (and drums of fuel had to be cached) pilots were doggedly transporting prospectors, trappers, officials, the sick and injured, and thousands of tons of supplies in and out of northern Quebec, Ontario, Labrador and the Northwest Territories.

Ever since Hartland had returned to Montreal in 1929 to work at McDonald Currie, he had continued to pay close attention to the aviation industry. In the months following the failure of the stock market, he could not fail to note that the aeronautics business was one of the few where a modest investment continued to promise rich rewards. Though the stocks that had seen the greatest losses were mining stocks, they were the first to recover. Discoveries of gold continued to pique intense interest. While many companies – large and small firms representing everything from textiles and foods to lumber and printing – were struggling, the air transportation industry continued to make legends and fortunes.

From the beginning, Sims, Troup and Bishop were positive and keen about forming a partnership with Hartland. But when Hartland asked his brother, Tom, and his father, Herbert, to put up some of the capital, they resisted. They had disapproved of Hartland flying at all, considering the hobby foolhardy and ostentatious. Herbert and Tom were unimpressed when Hartland flew with Tim Sims to the Molson compound at Ivry one weekend for a surprise visit, calling attention to themselves by landing noisily on the lake. To finance an airline business seemed at first absurd to them. Nevertheless Hartland, who was used to getting his own way, persisted. Bishop's endorsement lent Hartland's argument a lot of credibility. Sims prepared a summary of commercial flying activities in Canada that illustrated how steadily the industry was expanding. Within weeks Hartland was able to persuade his father and brother that – whatever they thought of his character – as a venture capital business, this one was secure.

By December, Hartland was ready to make Sims and Troup an initial offer: $25,000 capital to the company, in return for majority shares and administrative control. The partners agreed that the pilots would stay in the company and own minority shares. Bishop would be an advisor; as "Honorary Chairman" his name would appear with Hartland's on the letterhead. Hartland would guarantee the funds required for expansion, and he would become president of the re-formed organization called Dominion Skyways.

Two secretaries and a treasurer were hired to work in the small office rented by Hartland on St. James Street. One of the secretaries, Marjorie Buttram, remembered that her boss's arrival would always be heralded by that of the butler/chauffeur, James Lowther, and that Hartland would come into the office looking "exceptionally handsome, and always immaculately dressed." The rumour in the office was that Dominion Skyways was completely financed by Molson money.

In fact, Hartland was backed in this venture by a strong partnership that maximized capital, experience and expertise. His father Herbert and brother Tom would remain as silent partners, while John David Eaton, a cousin of Bishop's wife Margaret (who likely introduced Eaton to Hartland), would complete the partnership.

Two years younger than Hartland, John David Eaton was another young man from a powerful, old-money family. Like the Molsons, the Eatons ran their financial affairs conservatively and were fundamentally unaffected by the Depression. John David's grandfather was Timothy Eaton, founder of the retail company that bore his name. Schooled first at Upper Canada College, John David continued his education in England before returning to Canada. He worked in Toronto before moving, in February 1931, to Winnipeg, where he learned to fly twin-engine aircraft. By 1934 John David had returned to Toronto, having been made a director of Eaton's. Working in the areas of business development, manufacturing and merchandising, Eaton had no time to take an active role in Dominion Skyways. Motivated and single-minded, in two years he would become vice-president at Eaton's, and by 1937, president.

In early 1935 Dominion Skyways had only two aircraft, the Bellanca and the Fokker single-engine bush planes. Reliable and sturdy, they could each carry almost a ton of cargo and fly vast distances without having to refuel. For two years the pilots operated their business delivering prospectors, miners and supplies in and out of northern Ontario and Quebec, large tracts of which remained unmapped. But two aircraft weren't enough to meet the growing demand.

Hartland and Bishop discussed the benefits of purchasing an Auto-gyro for their new company. Another flying club member, Don Marcuse, had travelled to England the previous summer and, while there, flew aboard one of these aircraft, the predecessor to the modern helicopter. He returned to Montreal convinced there was a great future in store for this type of machine, talking it up to anyone who would listen. Hartland made a list of considerations that included engine performance, the costs of importing parts, maximum payload and insurance costs. He and Bishop concluded it was unwise, being unproven and financially unsound, and eventually decided to purchase more conventional bush planes to build up a small fleet.

The first new aircraft bought by the company was a high-winged monoplane known as a Fairchild freighter. Able to carry seven passengers and 6,000 pounds of freight, this most popular bush plane of the 1930s was designed so it could be outfitted with skis, floats or wheels. Soon after, Dominion Skyways acquired a Waco 3-passenger biplane and another Bellanca. Though their first customers had to sit on sacks of potatoes and crates of dynamite, the new aircraft enabled them to compete with other airline companies.

Dominion Skyways had a base already established at Rouyn, in northern Quebec; following the purchase of new aircraft, other bases soon added to their service included one in Haileybury, in northern Ontario, and another in Senneterre, Quebec. A typical bush-plane crew would be a pilot and a mechanic. Conditions were harsh and primitive, and instruments minimal: to see the terrain and assess the weather, all the flying was done in daylight. The pilots and mechanics were responsible for keeping their aircraft serviceable, generating business, making up tickets and bills, collecting money and keeping the books, as well as loading, flying and navigating the aircraft to destinations which often they'd never seen before. Astonishingly, they managed to maintain an accident-free record.

"I have gone into the flying business and since last December have rather enjoyed it," Hartland wrote his friend Jack Keeling in the spring of 1935.

> *This is a private company in which my brother, Tom, Dad, Billy Bishop and myself are interested in conjunction with the pilots whose business we took over. We are operating in the far North carrying mostly mining, prospecting and survey parties, supplies and equipment with some daily and some tri-weekly services. The fleet at the present time consists of only four machines but we are increasing it quietly. I imagine the end of this year should see us with six at least.*

In a letter to Charles Douglas (in London, England) in April 1935, Hartland wrote about being actively engaged as president of the company:

> *It is an extremely absorbing activity … Our "new North" is entirely dependent on the airplane now, in fact in another few years I think there will be a breed of man there who would be at a loss had he to get about by canoe or dog team. In addition wages are high, opportunities of spending few and therefore the population has no objection to paying well for a trip of a couple of hours which would otherwise require a couple of weeks.*

At the end of the letter, Hartland added: "The two great difficulties with this industry in Canada are the lack of government support and the high price of aircraft suitable for the task."

Hartland had effectively summarized the advantages and disadvantages of being involved in the air transportation industry. Unlike other countries, such as the United States and Great Britain, Canada offered no support system of any kind for commercial flying companies. Independent contractors had to take all the risks and remain profitable, or go out of business. Although a federal "Trans-Canada Airways" plan had been undertaken to build a string of airports across the country (constructed by men who'd lost their jobs in the Depression), no such landing facilities existed for the northern regions. Nevertheless, Canada was leading the world with the amount of freight carried and for miles of flight over uncharted territories. And with seemingly infinite natural resources to be tapped, this elite profession was bound to keep growing in importance.

With their new planes and plans to acquire more, Dominion Skyways was able to compete with other companies, including James Richardson's Canadian Airways. In 1936, with more capital put forward by his silent partners, Hartland bought two more Fairchilds. He hired more pilots and mechanics. He also bought the first prototype of the Noorduyn Norseman, the first airplane to be entirely designed, owned and built in Canada for commercial bush flying. A high-winged cabin monoplane, the Norseman was built specifically for the northern climate; it was rugged, versatile and could be converted from a nine-passenger aircraft to accommodate up to 3,000 pounds of freight.

Hartland's involvement with the company went beyond administration duties and buying aircraft. He personally flew in the geologist Dr. Joe Retty to investigate iron ore deposits in Labrador, and later brought in his prospecting party and all the needed supplies and equipment. Molson flew up to visit other prospecting parties and on one occasion invited Jules Timmins, president of Hollinger

Gold Mines, to go to Sandgirt Lake with him. Timmins, though protesting that he was interested in gold, not iron, made the flight with Hartland, which led to his company later undertaking vast developments in Labrador.

Hartland recalled, years later:

> *I used to go up [north] quite a lot and I remember Rouyn on a winter morning in the pitch black going over the base, and here would be these mechanics with the nose-cover hood, canvas things, and our four planes that were in Rouyn, blow torches under all of them, all cooking like hell and all waiting to take the oil – you'd rush out and put the oil in, and, you know, long before first light, and about 30 below, and oh boy!*

The primitive conditions in which bush pilots and engineers made their flights in the early to mid-1930s are hard to imagine. In the winter, engine oil had to be drained every night to prevent it from freezing and warmed again in the morning. Pilots had to draw their observations, making rough pencil-sketches of lakes and rivers to use as a guide for return flights. In addition to the hazards of the harsh environment, landing facilities were non-existent. No navigational aids or radio equipment were available and weather had to be assessed visually. Compasses became unreliable as one flew further north. Sometimes engineers would have to improvise when the plane needed repairs. If one became marooned, in order to attract the attention of searchers one would have to light a fire; in the winter, some would tramp out the word "HELP" in large letters in the snow. On one memorable occasion, Dominion Skyways pilot "Babe" Woollett, who after waiting six days was still confident of rescue, but increasingly impatient, stamped a new message in letters twenty feet high: "LAND HERE YOU BASTARDS."

Though it seemed like a paradox (the stocks that had seen the greatest losses were mining stocks), there seemed no less interest in

prospecting and there was a constant stream of miners and survey-
ors who needed to get up north. Besides prospecting and mining,
the need for aerial mapping, forest surveillance, airmail delivery
and provincial survey parties continued to create demand for flight
time. Freight rates for equipment carried on board an aircraft, at
five cents per pound, were cheaper than typical overland rates. Of
course an even greater advantage to flight was speed. A trip that
would normally have taken prospectors several days or even weeks
might be reduced to an hour, giving the men more time to work,
stake and collect their samples.

In 1935, pilot Frank Young flew Dominion Skyways' first scheduled air service linking Montreal, Val d'Or and Rouyn, a service
that would become known as the "Goldfields Express." In the fall
of 1936 Hartland formed a subsidiary company called
Newfoundland Skyways, and set up a base at Moisie, near Sept Isles
on the St. Lawrence River. Earlier that year, Mackay Exploration
Company geologists had discovered huge iron ore deposits near
Schefferville in Labrador. The company bought mineral rights
from the Newfoundland government and contracted with
Dominion Skyways to transport geological and prospecting personnel in and out of Labrador during the summer season. Hartland
bought two second-hand bush planes called Bellanca Skyrockets
from the United States and registered them directly in
Newfoundland, avoiding the necessity of paying import duty on
the aircraft.

In 1935 and 1936 Hartland hired his cousin, Kenneth Meredith
Molson, age 20, to join the summer maintenance staff. Meredith,
who had been single-mindedly passionate about aircraft since he
was a small child, had naturally developed a bond with his older
cousin. He worked for Hartland for two summers, learning all he
could about aeronautical mechanics and engineering. At the end
of the second year, Hartland would enable Meredith's dream to
come true by sending him to the Boeing School of Aeronautics in

California for flying instruction.

Dominion Skyways pilots had their share of adventures. One time, Tim Sims was contacted by U.S. newspaper executive Ralph Pulitzer, who needed to get to Romaine River after his boat had broken down. The pilot agreed to fly Pulitzer and his friends to their camp in return for half their provisions – "frozen steaks, lettuce, fresh vegetables, and a bottle of Bourbon." Sims also recalled that he and other pilots sometimes transported "ladies of the evening" who offered a form of payment "other than cash" – but, he added, these customers were always excellent credit risks, who paid their fares cheerfully on their return from pay-day at the lumber camps and mines.

Business remained brisk in the bush. Advances in the airline industry in 1936 and 1937 included base radio stations installed and operated to provide weather reports for aircraft, which now had 2-way radios. "Blind" instruments for night flying were being more widely used. Dominion Skyways pilots (though still paid half what Canadian Airways pilots earned) now wore smart uniforms. One enterprising pilot with a sense of humour had a chauffeur's cap with three interchangeable labels, reading "Pilot," "Ticket Agent" and "Baggage Handler."

Competition would be relentless and fierce throughout the years that preceded the establishment of a federal department of transport and its related policies. As long as the business remained unregulated, the battle for customers was cutthroat. Once bases were equipped with air-ground equipment to guide aircraft to pickup points, operators from rival airlines started eavesdropping on others' frequencies so they could swoop in and steal traffic. This was not only problematic for the pilots and owners but also for their clients, especially prospectors who needed to stake their claims privately. To mislead the competition, operators began giving false information over the air. This and other instances of price-cutting, overloading aircraft and other practices that compromised safety continued to affect the integrity of the business. The competition between Canadian airline companies was spiralling into an uncontrolled battle, placing the whole industry in a chaotic state.

When Mackenzie King was elected prime minister again in 1935, he made plans to establish a federal department of transportation, "to bring order out of transportation confusion." Aviation was added to C.D. Howe's former portfolio of railways and canals; the new department's minister began forming and implementing plans for a national airline. At a July 1936 dinner in London, Ontario, celebrating the centenary of Canada's first railway (which had been established by Hartland's great-great grandfather, John Molson), Howe stated, "I believe that within a few years aviation will be a serious competitor for the transportation business of this country."

Howe invited companies to submit reports outlining their suggestions and concerns about a sanctioned national airline. Post office delegates, railroad companies and civil aviation representatives presented briefs. The country's largest and most experienced airline, Canadian Airways, was seen by many (particularly owner James Richardson) as the main contender for the prize. Hearing that Canadian Airways was about to become Canada's national airline, Hartland got together with several other owners of bush flying companies and made an appointment to see Howe in August. Details of this meeting have not been preserved, but as Hartland recalled, "All bush-line operators from coast to coast met in the Fort Garry Hotel to try to develop a common front to present to Mr. Howe. The objective was to persuade him that their combined flying skills were quite sufficient to form the proposed Trans-Canada Airlines. After three days of deliberation it became apparent that common ground couldn't be reached, largely because of the competitive fear of each regional air operator."

After months of equivocating, Howe brought in Philip Johnson from Boeing in Seattle to organize the airline. Hartland acknowledged that Johnson "did a great job in forming TCA, but it could well have been done by Canadians had we been successful in setting aside our petty regional parochialism." Howe later announced that Trans-Canada Airlines would be jointly owned and operated by Canadian National Railway, Canadian Pacific Railway and certain private interests. When the latter minority control was offered to Canadian Airways, James Richardson refused.

Trans-Canada Airlines inaugural flight took place in the summer of 1937, in a successful, much-publicized dusk-till-dawn flight from Montreal to Vancouver. Later in 1938, licensing was introduced for TCA's branch lines to private air carrier operators. Richardson's Canadian Airways was able to establish many of these routes. Soon after, smaller airline companies including Dominion Skyways would start consolidating.

Hartland had a meeting with Richardson in the fall of 1937. Richardson wrote that Molson was disturbed about the competition. "[He] wants to get our help in regard to zoning, and generally wants us to tell him how he can carry on his airways successfully, by co-operation or otherwise, or how he can extricate himself from his airways investment without losing whatever he has put up." Richardson did not record whether or not the subject of selling Dominion Skyways to Canadian Airways was raised in their conversation, but that eventuality was soon to come.

CHAPTER SIX

SOMETIME IN 1936, Hartland crossed paths with an ambitious young inventor with a penchant for adventure named Grettir Algarsson. Born in 1900 of Icelandic parentage, Algarsson was raised by an adoptive family in Montreal. His enthusiasm for aviation and exploration had inspired him to dream of being the first person to fly to the North Pole, which he hoped to do in an airship, or dirigible, in 1925. But plans for this trip fell through. Described by one journalist as "an enthusiastic young idealist of engaging personality with a talent for organization," Algarsson would participate in a major Arctic expedition by ship instead. But his interest in aircraft and flight never waned, and by the early 1930s he had developed a variable-pitch aircraft propeller, which he called the Algarsson Automatic Supercharger.

Algarsson's invention allowed automatic pitch adjustments to be made to propellers in flight, so that the air-screw could give optimum thrust for all conditions of flying. He needed financial backing so he could develop his idea, build and test it, and obtain a patent. Hartland agreed to help, and with partners Jackson Ogilvie Rae and M. Lawson Williams, set up a fund to test and patent Algarsson's invention.

Early in 1937 Hartland and his new partners sent prototypes and copies of the plans to Alexander Klemin, an aeronautical engineer in New York City, and to the National Research Council in Ottawa. Klemin, who was an excellent choice as a well-known lecturer, editor and expert in aeronautics, was asked to report back to them on the principles and design of Algarsson's propeller. Klemin's answer was prompt and positive. "The introduction of the sliding weights and weight spacer in combination with the gear train is one of the most subtle, ingenious yet simple, mechanical devices which I have ever been privileged to see, and two of my colleagues fully share this admiration." His four-page report concluded, "I believe that the development and experimental construction of the device is fully warranted from every possible point of view."

In mid-February 1937 Hartland had an agreement drawn up between three partners and Grettir Algarsson, in which he agreed to fund the patent in Canada and retain an interest in the invention of 32 percent, while Algarsson's share would also be 32 percent, and Rae's and Williams' each 18 percent. A few days later he wrote to Sherman Fairchild, the aircraft manufacturer in New York City. "I expect to be in NY on Thursday next, the twenty-fifth, and would like to have a few minutes with you if possible to discuss a new automatic variable pitch propeller." Fairchild, however, was skeptical and wanted to see more proof.

Williams wrote Hartland in May 1937 from New York, where he, Rae and Algarsson had been working all week on improvements to the blade, gears and the casing, "finishing in one sitting all the aerodynamic, inherent and inertia movement calculations," concluding, "I do believe the little bastard is really working." In June, the partners had hopes of selling the propeller to the U.S. army.

Throughout the summer, they set up meetings and presentations for interested parties in the U.S., including a captain in the navy, the navy headquarters, McCauley Propeller Co., Wesley Smith and the Engineering Division at Wright Field in Ohio. An application for a U.S. patent was prepared and filed by November 1937.

However, by then numerous delays in testing procedures had rendered Algarsson insolvent. He began staying at Montreal's YMCA and was receiving overdue notices on his account there by July 1938. In September, Hartland provided start-up financing for Algarsson to establish Algarsson Engineering Co. to enable the development of new products including a Super-Charger Automatic Pressure Control (for high-altitude cabins) and an Automatic Synchronizer (for aircraft engines). A new partnership was formed, with ten individuals including R.J. Moffett of the aircraft manufacturer Canadian Vickers Ltd., who accepted 2 percent of the company in return for hangar space and the use of an aircraft suitable for testing.

Hartland had agreed to continue paying all the expenses, on the understanding that he would receive fair remuneration from the sale of Algarsson's invention, to reimburse himself for his prior expenses, and then disburse percentages to his partners. Hartland's outlay included fees to Klemin for preparing his report, draughtsmen work time, patent fees and travel expenses for the partners.

The Vickers company would manufacture the first Algarsson variable-pitch propeller in October 1938. But it was an anti-climactic triumph. Wallace Rupert Turnbull from New Brunswick had patented a more practical version some years earlier, and many others in England and the United States had introduced and flight-tested similar versions; the competition weakened the market for Algarsson's invention.

By then Hartland had other things on his mind. His wife Babbie was struggling with problems which Hartland referred to as "nerves"; the birth of their daughter Zoë in 1935 had been the one high point in an increasingly troubled marriage. The strain was such that for two consecutive summers they had elected to stay at Seaside House, one of the local hotels in Metis, instead of Hartland's family's house. Zoë became the sole focus of Hartland's attention and happiness at home, and he lavished her with trinkets and affection. By early 1938 Hartland and Babbie had separated and a future together looked unlikely.

Meanwhile Herbert's health had seriously deteriorated in the fall of 1937 and he was admitted to the Montreal General Hospital for the last time. When Hartland went to visit him, to his surprise his father stated that he hoped he would enter the brewery, but that he didn't think his youngest son was cut out for the work. Herbert was thinking about future succession but he still had misgivings about Hartland's character. Could he apply himself to working there? He feared his son was too frivolous, too busy disgracefully flaunting his wealth. Could he commit himself, follow through, give up his wild outside interests, direct all his talents and efforts into the family business? Hartland protested that he could, and would. He reminded his father that in his senior years at RMC, when he'd been asked to choose between an emphasis on engineering or chemistry, he'd chosen the chemistry option specifically because of its relevance to possible future work in the brewery.

Hartland had already begun winding down his outside interests so he found himself ready and willing to direct his career into the family business. Final details were completed for selling Dominion Skyways to James Richardson. The sale netted approximately $30,000.00, the value of the fleet of aircraft, plus stock in Richardson's company, Canadian Airways Limited (later Canadian Pacific or CP Air) which was destined to become Trans-Canada Airlines' (later Air Canada's) main competitor.

In a few short months Hartland's life had completely changed. Separated and soon to be divorced, he was working six days a week at the brewery, and there was a new woman in his life. He had no time for flying. In less than a year, war would be declared and everything would change once again.

On March 10, 1938, Herbert's niece Jane Molson wrote to her sister Winnifred, "Uncle Herbert … grows weaker every day & only his immediate family can see him & only one at a time – but he is not suffering very much which is a blessing." Herbert died eleven days later, at his home on Ontario Avenue. He was 63 years old. His funeral service at Christ Church Cathedral, presided over by two Anglican bishops and two archdeacons, attracted hundreds of mourners, overfilling the cathedral; those outside stood in the snow and joined in the singing of the hymns, including Herbert's favourite, "Fight the Good Fight." Opposite the church, across Phillips Square, Eaton's, Birks' and Morgan's stores closed for the day. McGill University cancelled all its classes for the afternoon.

So many people flanked the funeral procession along St. Catherine Street that extra police were stationed at intersections to direct traffic away from the mourners. Floral arrangements filled seven open limousines. Glowing tributes filled the newspapers, and the *Gazette* and the *Daily Star* devoted full pages to the event. Letters of condolence piled up in the foyer at Ontario Avenue. Hamilton Gault wrote, "To us all, he ever stood – *sans peur et sans reproche* – for everything that was fine, and great, and true – the very best that Canada produces."

Herbert's death marked the end of an era for Molson's Brewery and a turning point for his family. Though he continued to travel to New York City from time to time, Hartland had turned away from entrepreneurship, dinner parties and leisure flying. His work as assistant secretary and treasurer called upon his accounting and organizing skills and he focused on the benefits of feeling needed and useful. Fred's son Bert had moved into the presidency of Molson's upon Herbert's death, and more changes were about to be incorporated into the production facilities.

Divorce at first did not seem to be an option for Hartland. In those days, divorce and marriage were in the realm of the federal government, and the only way to end a marriage was to apply to the Canadian Senate, where a special committee had to undertake an investigation, and if in their opinion the request had merit, the marriage would be dissolved by an act of parliament. The legal hurdle was only part of the problem, social ostracism was another. But Hartland had been persevering and hoping for the best for a long time, and now that his father had died the way might have seemed easier. His mother was certainly understanding of his unhappiness and didn't stand in the way when he broached the subject of divorcing Helen. Bessie offered to take care of Zoë for as long as needed; she would, in fact, welcome the company now that Herbert was gone. Zoë, who called her grandmother "Gaga," dates her earliest childhood recollections to that time. Her cousins Christine and Margaret Pentland came to stay as well, and Marg, who was a composer, used to play the piano rather often and badly. Zoë ate her meals in the breakfast room overlooking the garden and recalls being very happy during her time in that house.

New York continued to lure Hartland and his friends, where the vastness and awesome wealth, skyscrapers, rapid transit system, musical extravaganzas, celebrities and the display of style were intoxicating to them. They would drive down to Peekskill, forty miles outside New York and take a train in, considered "the only way to go," with its comfortable leather armchairs, monogrammed china and cut flowers. They would either book themselves into one of the extravagant hotels such as the Ritz on Fifth Avenue, where Fred Molson had always stayed, or rent a service flat at the Mayflower. They visited the Museum of Art, walked through Central Park and dined at the city's best restaurants. R.C.A. Studios and Broadway advertised Rudy Vallee on stage, as well as the Goldwyn Follies with Edgar Bergen and Charlie McCarthy. Dinner at the Commodore or the Biltmore might be followed by dancing at the Rainbow Grill.

The attitude of New Yorkers was cosmopolitan and open-minded, current and savvy. During and after the Depression the city was still a holiday goal of thousands of Canadians. Young people especially were drawn to the centre of North America, the city of King Kong and Fay Wray, to shop, eat and be endlessly entertained. It was an ideal destination both for those looking for a fast, noisy and expensive life and for those content to buy a ten-cent sightseeing tour via the Fifth Avenue bus. It was a city of romance and adventure, endlessly exciting.

In New York City, as in Montreal, events in Europe at the time were viewed with growing concern and alarm. The rising power of Germany and the influence of its new Nazi leader Adolf Hitler, had menacing overtones. In 1936 and 1937, anti-Jewish actions and legislation had spread in Germany, Hungary, Austria and Poland; Jews became the favoured scapegoats for all economic and political ills and dangers; anti-Jewish riots broke out in widespread urban centres. One quarter of New York's population was Jewish, and the numbers continued to grow through the 1930s as one in every three refugees escaping the increasingly intolerable restrictions in Eastern Europe headed to the United States. Such was the feeling of empathy in New York City that in November 1938, two weeks after *Kristallnacht*, a mass demonstration was held against the violence perpetrated by Hitler and his followers, at which protestors burned swastika flags.

One young woman named Magda Posner escaped with her family earlier that year from Budapest, Hungary, and sailed to New York to join relatives in the city. Hungary, which had over the last two decades survived a series of brutal dictatorships, revolutions and counter-revolutions, was ruled by a clique of industrialists and police bullies. Its political neutrality was unsustainable; by 1938, unable to resist the economic pressures from Germany, Hungary had begun isolating its three-quarters of a million Jews and imposing ever-increasing numbers of anti-Jewish laws. Capitulating to the Fuhrer's demands, in May 1938 Hungary passed a law restricting to 20 per-cent the number of Jews allowed to hold jobs in commerce, industry and administration, and soon thereafter forbade Jews from becoming judges, lawyers, schoolteachers or members of parliament.

Like tens of thousands of others, the Posner family found itself marginalized, harassed and living in fear. Magda, who had an excellent education, was told she had to look for work as a seam-stress, but was refused at seamstress shops, told she had to graduate from a course – yet the course was never offered or available. At great personal expense and risk, and forced to leave all his posses-sions and savings behind, her brother obtained a visa and booked passage on a steamer bound for New York. Some months later, he was able to send for his sister and their mother to join him.

Hartland met Magda Posner at the swank speakeasy 21 Club in New York City in early 1938. To young socialites in the 1930s, the West 52nd Street restaurant was known as "the place to see and be seen," where an attendant at the door screened gangsters and drunks from its preferred clientele, a strict dress code was enforced and the décor gave it a private, club-like atmosphere. Hartland was attracted to the graceful blonde woman with green eyes, who was animated and talkative. Notwithstanding her distinctive Hungarian accent she had a good command of English vocabulary, and, in spite of all she'd been through, downplayed her own expe-rience and spoke about the plight of her family and friends and how help might be found.

The couple began to spend more and more time together, and as their relationship deepened in the fall of 1938, Hartland made his first inquiries about obtaining a divorce from Babbie Hogg in Montreal. The only grounds for divorce were desertion or adultery, and it was necessary to prove either. Hartland took what was con-sidered the most honourable course under the circumstances – he offered his wife a financial settlement, then hired a lawyer who arranged to procure credible evidence of a tryst between Hartland

and another woman. As the plaintiff, Babbie travelled to Ottawa and presented the requisite petition to the Senate for a divorce, which would be granted in the spring. Meanwhile, Tom suggested to his wife Celia that she write to a friend of hers in Budapest to ask if she could find out any information about Magda's family. However, because the state of affairs in Hungary had deteriorated, and the friend did not know that the Posners were Jewish, information was next to impossible to locate.

As early as December 1938, war seemed imminent. In October, Hartland wrote to his friend Jack Keeling in London: "I must say that … we … [are] waiting from moment to moment for developments and almost all of us had thoroughly decided that we would be shining our buttons within a week." He had already proposed to Magda. Hartland had introduced the new lady in his life to his family, but Bessie was the only one who was supportive of him and kind to Magda. To the others, including his brother and sisters, aunts and uncles, Magda was not only a foreigner, but also a non-Anglican – though no one seemed to have guessed she had Jewish heritage.

Since separating from Babbie, Hartland had been continuing to live in rented accommodations and now considered buying his own house. Not only would he need a home for Magda, but he also knew that before war broke out would be the better time to buy, as war would inevitably be followed by inflation. Bart Ogilvie had told Hartland about a house on Redpath Street above McGregor Avenue, owned by an aunt of his who wanted to sell it. It was a stone, well proportioned, 10,000-square-foot home on a 30,000-square-foot lot, which from the outside resembled a small apartment block. Hartland liked it immediately and made an offer; when it was accepted, he and Magda went shopping for furniture to fill it.

The home had nine bedrooms, four bathrooms, seven fireplaces, a library, dining room, living room and two kitchens. A sound system was installed in several key rooms, including the 45-foot by

23-foot dining room, where a tap on the pedal in the floor by the hostess's feet would summon the servants when needed. A garage large enough for three limousines extended from the back of the house, and a small cottage behind the large garden completed the property.

In May, King George VI and Queen Elizabeth undertook a Canadian tour and came to Montreal. King George VI had been on the throne less than two years, following the abdication of his brother Edward VIII under the cloud of his scandalous liaison with the American divorcée Mrs. Simpson. The tour, described in one journal as "a conquest of peace, goodwill and loyalty in a surge of enthusiasm from ocean to ocean," was the first visit of any reigning monarch to North America. While obviously intended to stir up support for England in the event of war, the tour had this effect and more. The royal presence lifted Anglo people's spirits, infused them with a surge of national pride and solidarity and helped them believe they could move out from under the shadows of a decade of depression.

By the morning of May 18, Montreal had decked itself out in British flags and bunting and hung patriotic banners from building windows. A million people who crowded the twenty-five mile route as the royal train entered the city on the approach to Windsor Station were rewarded by the sight of the king and queen standing at the end of the caboose, waving. Later in the morning they were hailed by 45,000 Catholic schoolchildren who stood in the circular stands at the Delormier Baseball Stadium, a thousand of whom formed a huge Union Jack with red, white and blue clothing, all chanting "Vive le roi! Vive la reine!" After lunch, they were driven through the gates of McGill University and up to the Percival Molson Memorial Stadium, to be seen by 14,000 cheering Protestant students, each of whom had been given souvenir bronze medallions bearing the portraits of the king and queen.

Later in the afternoon the couple was driven to the top of

Mount Royal, where they were served afternoon tea by daughters of prominent families. Dinner at the Windsor Hotel followed in the evening, where a thousand guests including the expansive Mayor Camillien Houde (who apparently made the king and queen laugh loudly during a dinner conversation) and many members of the Mount Royal Club, dined on turtle soup and squab (young pigeon). Afterwards the king and queen appeared on a light-flooded balcony overlooking Dominion Square, acknowledging 100,000 people who cheered and sang "God Save the King."

Although the worst of the Depression was over, there were still tens of thousands dependent on relief in Montreal, and the need for work fuelled much of the support for the cause of war. The idealism that had characterized the beginning of the Great War had been replaced by a more pragmatic sentiment from which a sense of international responsibility emerged. Over the weeks of this particularly hot summer in the city, tensions increased in Europe, the latest news flashes interrupting radio programming and propaganda newsreels were played before audiences waiting to see *Confessions of a Nazi Spy* with Edward G. Robinson or *It's a Wonderful World* with Jimmy Stewart and Claudette Colbert. Open-air concerts became fundraisers for the Red Cross, who announced it was ready for war service and able to train nurses and ambulance drivers.

One Saturday afternoon that summer, Hartland took his 8-year-old nephew Hartland MacDougall up in a plane for a short flight that delighted the little boy. The MacDougall family lived in Cartierville, where the flying school operated at the time; Hartland flew the plane over their home and young Hartland could recognize his house, stables and the adjacent Montreal Polo Club from the air. The boy would remember this thrilling flight with his "fun uncle" for the rest of his life, but Hartland's sister Dorothy, the boy's mother, was reportedly furious.

News came on August 20 that German troops were massing on the Polish border, and two days later Canada learned that Hitler's

Germany and the Soviet Union had signed a non-aggression pact. In Montreal, infantry regiments were called into service to guard railway yards, bridges and power stations considered vulnerable to sabotage. On September 1, silent crowds gathered on St. James Street in front of news bulletin boards posted outside the *Montreal Star* offices to read that Germany had invaded Poland the day before. Britain declared war on Germany on September 2 and Canada did so one week later, after a vote in parliament. Hundreds of men had already started lining up to enlist at regimental armouries in Montreal. Hartland, having served his militia term at RMC as a gunner, remained on the reserve list down in the old Drill Hall in Montreal. Contrary to what some later claimed, Billy Bishop had not been the one to suggest to Hartland that he join the air force. Hartland went to Frank McGill, whom he knew at the Montreal flying club.

> *I thought … that my battery or regiment would start mobilizing and they would say, "We've got a job for you." But they didn't, and they had far too many officers on reserve and there was no prospect, they told me, of our unit being mobilized for six months or a year, but then … as I had flown as a private pilot quite a bit, I thought it would be more pleasant to go into the air force, and so I applied there and got into the auxiliary squadron in Montreal.*

A transfer from army to air force was duly arranged by a contact of Frank McGill's at Air Force headquarters. Thus Hartland joined the pilots in the auxiliary squadron known as No. 115 Fighter Squadron, formed in 1936 and now training aboard Fleet biplanes at the Montreal Light Aeroplane Club. He was told the squadron could be mobilized at any time. He didn't know how soon that day would come, but he knew there would be no time to wait to marry Magda.

Hartland and Magda were married on September 29, at his newly-renovated home on Redpath Street. His mother, brother, sisters and in-laws were there, and a few friends as witnesses. According to sister-in-law Celia, who wrote in her diary that evening, it wasn't a particularly happy occasion.

> *First and foremost, Hartland married his Magda. All the Molsons are awfully upset, but there is nothing they can do but make the best of it. Now the deed is done. I feel rather sorry for Magda, after all, it will be so lonely for her when Hartland is called overseas, especially as she is a foreigner and not particularly welcomed into the Molson clan. In fact, the more I think of it, the more I feel sorry for Magda. It seems such a pathetic snatching of happiness. There are an awful lot of war weddings. I do think it is foolish to rush into wedlock, and run the risk of being widowed in a year or so.*

The Molsons had trouble accepting Magda because their enclosed world did not easily admit a "foreigner." In time this may have been overlooked, but was impossible to forget, given her strong Hungarian accent, which she never lost. But Hartland had never been one to let the opinions of others change the course of what he wanted to do, particularly when opinions reflected narrow thinking. He'd been in love with Magda for a year before they married, noted Celia. Their affection for each other was evident to many. Not only was Magda gregarious, she was always cheerful and charming. When she began talking she spoke rapidly and barely stopped to draw a breath, a habit even more pronounced when she was ill at ease or nervous. When Celia invited her to lunch with some friends in early 1940, she noted in her diary: "Magda was very vivacious all the time. I had the feeling that she was putting it on a bit, possibly because she may have felt slightly at a disadvantage."

Betty Henderson Paul, who met Magda at a women's lunch, noted that she was a very good bridge player, better than Hartland. She recalled visiting her in the house on Redpath, where a maid

served tea on beautiful English china. Though she was very knowl-
edgeable about cuisine, Magda never did the cooking: at home and
elsewhere they hired local cooks. Hartland was rarely home that
autumn; days and evenings would find him either in meetings,
finalizing arrangements at the brewery with Tom and Bert or working with the squadron at the flying club.

Magda had bonded with Zoë immediately, and Zoë, who called
her "Gigi" (her grandmother, Bessie, was "Gaga"), remembers her
as a very good stepmother. Both kind and empathetic, Magda was
supportive and generous to her stepdaughter. Bessie too grew to
like her more and more, encouraged her and made her feel at
home, with little gifts and frequent invitations. After Hartland left
for flight training, Bessie invited Magda for dinner every day.

On November 15 Hartland's squadron was sent to Trenton,
Ontario, where they would train for a month on Fleet Finches and
Tiger Moths, camping at military facilities there. He returned to
Montreal for Christmas leave, then moved with the squadron to
Camp Borden, Ontario, where he stayed until spring, undergoing
service flying training in heavier more powerful aircraft such as
Wapitis, Harvards and Fairey Battles. He was home again on May
24, the Victoria Day weekend, meant to mark the beginning of a
scheduled ten-day leave. Instead, Hartland recalled, the telephone
rang. It was McGill's contact, calling from Ottawa, at Air Force
headquarters. "He said we want you and your friends from Borden
to go down to Halifax tonight and join No. 1 Squadron. I said, 'I
can't, my uniforms are all at the cleaners. I can go Tuesday, after
the holiday weekend.' He asked me to call my friends to go too, so
I called Dal Russel, Deane Nesbitt, Arthur Yuile, Paul Pitcher, Eric
Beardmore … we were six altogether."

Members of the No. 1 Squadron RCAF had been in Nova Scotia
since war was declared, flying Hurricanes and waiting for orders to
go overseas. But they needed more trained pilots, and headquarters
had their eye on Montreal's No. 115 auxiliary squadron. According

to 115 pilot Beverly "Bev" Christmas, their training was cut short and the pilots were given their wings early so they could fly to Halifax and join the No. 1 Squadron. The members of Hartland's unit had yet had no training in fighter tactics or formation flying, nor had any of their pilots flown Hurricanes. They would all leave for England within two weeks of the auxiliary pilots' flight to Halifax.

On June 8, the amalgamated unit now known as No. 1 Fighter Squadron was paraded in full marching order through the streets of Halifax, and at 4 p.m. began to board the steamship *Duchess of Atholl,* moored at the pier. They would depart at 10 a.m. on June 11, with an escort convoy of three destroyers and one battleship. On board, the squadron had two mascots: a hen named Unity and a fighting cock named Goebbels.

Bev Christmas recalled, "The squadron was really keen to get at the enemy. When we sailed for overseas in June 1940, there were at least 2 or 3 members of the squadron who were not listed to go, but they were smuggled on board, and fed under the bunks. No one knew they were there except everyone on the ship."

CHAPTER SEVEN

T HE RCAF No. 1 Squadron arrived in England singing. It was June 20, 1940. During the days since they'd boarded the *Duchess of Atholl* in Halifax the young men – some friends, some virtual strangers – had come to know one another and formed bonds that would grow firmer through the weeks that lay ahead. Most had thought they were scheduled to join the fighting in France. But the situation had grown much worse: the British withdrawal from Dunkirk had taken place, and the Germans were making plans to invade England. Three days before Hartland's squadron docked, word had reached them on board ship that France had fallen to the Germans. "The battle of France is over," stated Winston Churchill solemnly in the House of Commons, "and the battle of Britain has begun."

The men's voices rang out across the Liverpool pier.

From the shores of Canada we have come
To put old Hitler on his bum

We'll take the thug, and flatten his mug,
We're Canada's Fighter squadron!

To the crowds of British civilians on the wharf, the sight of the
hundreds of Canadian airmen – officers, pilots and crew – all in full
dress uniform, was more than a welcome sight. The *Manchester
Guardian* published photographs of the ship, her decks and ramp
crowded with disembarking troops. A reporter said the Canadians
were "boisterously cheerful" as they marched through the streets of
Liverpool, "the first to be seen on parade there."

Few of the twenty-two pilots in the squadron had been to
England before. However, even to those for whom it was their first
time, the "mother country" somehow felt like home. It was an
unseasonably warm June. The sun beat down on Hampshire as the
convoy of trucks made its way to the airfield in Middle Wallop,
where the pilots were to begin their training to become flying officers. Hugh Dowding, the Air Chief Marshal, was introduced to
each pilot. He inspected their small fleet of Hurricane aircraft.
Many years later, Hartland could still recall the exchange between
"Stuffy" Dowding and the Squadron Leader.

> *Stuffy said, "We are glad to have you. I understand you are oper-*
> *ational and you have your own aeroplanes." Ernie McNabb said,*
> *"We only have Mark I Hurricanes, which have no armour plates*
> *or self-sealing tanks, and all have fixed-pitch wooden propellers."*
> *"Good God," said Stuffy, "I didn't know that," and Ernie said,*
> *"I'm sorry to tell you further, Sir, that we are not operational, that*
> *half our squadron have never yet flown the Hurricanes." "Good*
> *Lord!" said Stuffy, "Nobody told me that!" Of course our news-*
> *papers and our government here had been saying they were send-*
> *ing over fully operational fighter squadrons to save Europe …*
> *which was absolute nonsense.*

Dowding ordered the squadron's fleet replaced with new aircraft, "diverting them immediately off the assembly lines." To the pilots' amazement, the new Hurricanes arrived the following day. The Air Marshal also arranged for the men to undertake several weeks of training that would begin the moment the planes arrived. Lectures and ground instruction were combined with in-flight training: there was much to learn. Besides the details of formation flying and how to manoeuvre turns while climbing and diving, the pilots had to master unfamiliar radio operations and learn complex navigation and armament procedures. They practised fighter tactics and staged mock dogfights. Each flying officer was taught to stick to his leader at all times.

The pilots developed great respect for the new Hurricanes. "They were wonderful to fly," squadron member Dal Russel remarked. "In our final period of training … we became so used to our Hurricanes that they were very nearly a part of us. We flew by instinct – without consciously handling the controls." Another pilot, Eric Beardmore, would later say, "There's nothing holds together like those Hurricanes. So long as your engine is turning over you can land."

"I was scared to death on that first take-off," Hartland remembered. "There was no such thing as a two-seat trainer, so you just got in and tried to remember everything you had been told to do … But, as it turned out, there was no problem and I vividly remember both my relief and then delight. It flew like a charm. My initial disappointment at not getting Spitfires was diminished as this airplane began to capture my heart."

The friendships the men were forging with each other were as vital as their flight training. They had more in common than animosity toward Hitler. Though some were in their 20s, most were in their early and mid-30s, which was quite unusual for fighter pilots. Hartland joked that they could call themselves "the tired businessmen's squadron." The men shared privileged backgrounds and many had attended the same private schools. At least two, Gordon McGregor and Deane Nesbitt, had earned trophies for aerial skill before the war. Their high spirits were buoyed and fuelled by this camaraderie – they depended upon one another, trusted one another.

In the barracks at Middle Wallop (described by some as "rustic" for they were still under construction), Hartland and the other pilots listened to the nightly news broadcasts on the wireless. The Luftwaffe had been launching daylight attacks on the southeast coast, and carrying out smaller, widely scattered attacks further inland at night. The Canadians could see occasional puffs of anti-aircraft fire in the distance. On June 27, the first air raid siren wailed in the town nearby, and bombs fell close enough to the air-field that the pilots could hear the whistle of the bombs dropping and feel the rumbling impact of the explosions. The scent of smoke was carried to them on the breeze.

On July 4, the squadron was moved to Croydon, an old civil air-field southwest of London, for the next stage: six weeks of inten-sive combat instruction. The men lived in boarding houses near the airfield and used the old airport hotel as their mess. In addition to attending lectures and submitting to written and oral tests, pilots in training now averaged three hours of flying per day.

The Luftwaffe was increasing its attacks inland by mid-July. "Big black bombers," said Dal Russel, "were coming on about nine or ten abreast, stepped up in succeeding rows like a big stairway." The heaviest formations yet, some made up of hundreds of bombers and escort fighters, relentlessly made their way across the Channel. Southern British aerodromes were systematically targeted; squadrons of RAF were sent out to intercept them. The German Air Force greatly outnumbered that of the Allies. The Canadian pilots' confidence and their impatience to see some action reached a peak; during the last weeks of their training they became more daring and more adventurous.

On July 23, one of the Canadian pilots – some insist it was
Hartland – flew his Hurricane under London Bridge. Staff Officer
Roy H. Foss wrote a stern memo the next day which read, in part:
"I impressed on the Officer Commanding No. 1 Squadron the
necessity for carrying out, at all times, safe flying by the pilots and
warned him that any breach of air regulations would be severely
dealt with. I also impressed on Squadron Leader McNabb the
necessity for dealing severely with Orderly Room or more serious
cases pointing out that the most effective method was to deal with
these cases severely in the first instances." No names were mentioned in the memo. When the orderly room at Croydon was
bombed in mid-August, it was Hartland who would later joke
about it: "They hit our own buildings … luckily they hit our orderly
room and got rid of all our criminal records – no more charges were
laid from past performances." Nevertheless a legend grew, as legends
do, and rippled through the military and familial ranks for years,
and even generations. Decades later, a young cousin asked
Hartland specifically whether he had flown under London Bridge.
His reply was ambiguous. "Well," he chuckled, "one had to do that
sort of thing in those days for the sake of morale, you know."

Soon after this incident, the Hurricanes were given their cam-
ouflage paint and their squadron markings. One afternoon in early
August the unit had a holiday from training when Canadian High
Commissioner Vincent Massey visited the pilots. Such occasions,
whether visits from high-ranking military personnel or members of
the royal family, were usually very formal. Buttons and boots were
polished, uniforms inspected, boisterousness reigned in, manners
buffed. The pilots, medical and senior officers formed a receiving
line where Massey greeted each man in turn, and spoke with them
briefly. Inevitably the effect of these visits was to emphasize the
importance of the job the men were doing, to build upon their
respect and loyalty and to raise their standards and confidence.

On August 15, the squadron pilots were completing their last few hours of flight instruction before their unit would become fully operational. They were preparing to return to Croydon, taxiing in their aircraft before take-off, when they were all suddenly ordered to stop where they were and stop their engines. As Hartland recalled,

> Croydon, our base, was being bombed in the first raid into London ... They held us on the ground until they got the all-clear from Croydon. Ernie came back and they told us that we could start up and we'd take off, and we were all simply livid. Ernie McNabb was arguing – he said "God damn it, if our own base is being hit, why don't you let us go, we've finished our training." They said, "We don't dare do it, if we did that and you had a casualty ... the Canadian government would say we'd acted without their authority ... you have no idea the stink that would be raised." So we might have caught those 110s that came in, or we might have caught one or two of them if we'd been let go just when we were on our way. We always flew across armed, we always had ammunition ... We'd finished our training – what a wonderful introduction it would have been to the battle if we'd had a crack at something that first day.

The following day the squadron prepared to move to Northolt aerodrome on the western fringe of London, to be their main base during the battle. They moved on August 17 and the next day became fully operational. Hartland described their new posting:

> The aerodrome we were on was not very large although very adequate and had several squadrons on it, including the first Polish Fighter Squadron. It was rather oval in shape with houses at one end and five hangars, messes and other station buildings on one of the long sides and with open country on the other two sides. The other long side was bounded by a well-traveled road. As in all

war, operations planes were widely dispersed in order to avoid the danger of losing a large number of them in a bomb attack. Our planes were around one end of this oval field and about as far away from the mess as you could get. The living quarters and messes were extremely comfortable and really seemed very much like you find them under peace conditions ... The hut was very comfortable, it had beds and blankets, chairs, reading material, cards, darts and a radio so that we kept ourselves occupied in some way or another, but waiting always seemed rather endless.

The squadron flew every day on operations and routine patrols. For the first week they didn't see any action. On August 24, the Germans changed the strategy of their offensive and began bombing London. The squadron was ordered to put up three or four patrols a day, in the morning, noon, afternoon and evening. With night raids over the airfields as well, the pilots and crew got little sleep.

Hartland's first sight of German planes, he said, "was quite awe-inspiring. They came in a breathtaking mass, thick as black midges." He hadn't felt frightened – just a queer dryness in his throat, an electric prickle under his tongue and a kind of disembodied detachment. At times of such high tension, he noted, "nature provided an internal anesthesia, and ... extraordinary emergency distorted the sense of time."

On August 26, everything the pilots had learned was put to the test. Back at the mess, Hartland wrote to Magda:

Nothing happened until about 3:15. We were rushed away then up above solid cloud into brilliant sunshine at 20,000 feet and about 20 minutes later told to look for some Huns. We looked and saw a big mob of what turned out to be about 24 Dorniers (bombers) and above and beyond a cloud of escorting fighters. We closed in ... we came in fast on the bombers who were in 3's stepped up from the front to the rear and looking pretty big and

*solid ... We knocked down two confirmed, think there were two
more probables and a couple damaged. One of our lads – Bob
Edwards ... went down and is missing. He might have bailed out
... I didn't notice what results I got. Deane, being right behind me
said ... [one] was at least badly damaged. As I broke away I saw
five little figures around the sky swinging in parachutes. They
looked quaint in the sunlight floating gently towards the great carpet of cotton wool formed by the cloud layer. Ernie, Desloges, Dal
Russel and I had bullets through our machines ... The speed with
which the whole affair happens is unbelievable and one has nothing but sensations and instincts while the scrap is on. It doesn't feel
real somehow, and one certainly doesn't have time to be frightened.*

Ernie McNab, who had shot down one Dornier, crash-landed his
Hurricane but was not hurt. Gordon McGregor (later president of
Trans-Canada Air Lines) had destroyed another; Deane Nesbitt
and Hartland each damaged one German bomber. Bob Edwards
shot the tail off a Dornier, but before it crashed, its gunners hit
him; he spun down out of control and was killed.

The first casualty in the squadron shook up the pilots, and
injected a new, intense emotion into their working life. Hartland
said, "When one of the boys gets it, there is a sullen undercurrent
– almost bordering on overanxiousness to get into the air to avenge
him. At such moments flying becomes a grim business, and all you
ask is to get on a Nazi's tail."

The awareness of danger was palpable, the tension always present. Even when they were sleeping, they might be roused unexpectedly to be at readiness. "If we were supposed to be at readiness
at 9 o'clock," recalled Hartland, "we would go to bed in our rooms,
as we did every night, thinking that we would have a very comfortable night's sleep ... [at] about dawn or perhaps a few minutes
before, an orderly would come in and shake you into consciousness

and say, 'No. 1 Canadian Squadron is called to readiness.' We would jump out of bed, pull on some clothing, probably over pyjamas, pull on flying boots and rush downstairs." They would board a bus to take them quickly to their dispersal point near their planes. "There was usually a light mist in the morning at this station," he added, "and as we drove along the tarmac around the field we would see the rosy glow of the exhaust pipes as the mechanics ran up the engines."

Flying officer Paul Pitcher recalled that every time the telephone rang in the dispersal hut, their stomachs rolled over. The first call was usually a warning that they would soon be summoned to action. "On your toes, boys!" the voice would say, and the pilots would pull on their vivid yellow "Mae West" life preservers over their uniforms and wait for the next call. Many pilots might "stroll around and look nonchalant," but this waiting period was the most stressful period of all. When the second telephone call came, the shrill sound signalled the start of the action: the pilots would be expected to be in the air in five minutes. The words "Scramble Red Section – Angels 15" would send twelve pilots dashing for their aircraft, ready to climb to 15,000 feet. Their flying equipment – parachutes, helmets, goggles and oxygen masks – would already be in the planes. Hartland explained, "As we reached our machines the engines would roar into life and our ground crew would help us into our parachutes and harness ... and on our way." By then there was no time to worry, just to act.

For Hartland, waiting for the last man to come back after an air battle was more uncomfortable than waiting for the scramble phone call. No talk was permitted about casualties.

That was the toughest part about life at an operational base, waiting after a patrol for tardy members especially when there had been any kind of a show up there. You'd walk into the lounge, and without being too obvious would count the number of men. Then you'd make a casual query and find three of your pals had yet to be accounted for. There wouldn't be much talking going on. Everybody would be busy with papers or magazines, and each time the door opened all would look up. Then comes a phone call – one of the boys had bailed out and was en route to the operational base in a truck. Another while elapses before somebody comes in with a report that one of our planes is just landing. You wonder which of the missing two it is. If one of them happens to be carrying a particular close friend you wait tensely. The door finally opens after an eternity and in comes a late arrival. He says, "Good show," and you reply, "Not bad at all."

More minutes pass and perhaps they blend into hours. Nobody speaks the thought that is uppermost in everybody's mind. Then the phone rings again – the last man is reported in a casualty clearing station suffering from only minor injuries. There is an immediate relaxation evident in the lounge. Ordinary jokes get a big hand. Some chaps whistle. The card game gets going and the regular, easy-going routine is underway once more.

On the wall of the dispersal hut next to the telephone were pinned travel posters, girlie pin-ups and Air Ministry publications. One of the latter depicted a mound with a cross standing in wild grass blown by the wind. The caption read, "What did he die of?" and there followed a blunt list:

He forgot to set his altimeter before take-off.
He thought everything would be all right.
He said that the chances of needing his parachute were one in a million.
He thought the bombers were unescorted.
He enjoyed low flying.
He thought he had set his compass correctly.
He couldn't see the point in learning how to use his dinghy.

Whether in readiness or "standing down" at ease, the No. 1 pilots spent nearly all their daylight hours at dispersal points around the airfield, where their planes were parked and kept ready for quick getaways. On sunny days they sat outside, talking, playing cards or pitching horseshoes. Inside the wooden dispersal hut they read books and newspapers, wrote letters or played darts.

Pilot's duty days were rotated; they were allowed every fourth day off from noon until noon. But casualties cut into leave time. The constant atmosphere of noise and stimulation at the base made resting there impossible: they would usually take their leaves in nearby country estates, when invited by landowners or families. Once in a while one or two airmen would go into London, where they would dine at the Dorchester or the Savoy; some would go to the theatre, where *Gone With the Wind*, *The Grapes of Wrath* or *The Wizard of Oz* were playing. Hartland and Jim Blaiklock hired a "sartorially impeccable" chauffeur named Sebastien who drove a 1911 Rolls-Royce, and travelled from Northolt to London on at least one occasion. Recalled one ground-crew member,

> *On the Northolt field was a taxi driver called Sebastien. He drove an ancient but most impressive-looking Rolls-Royce, so impressive-looking in fact, that the R.A.F. guards ... seldom bothered to stop it as it wheeled through the gates. So, into this car would crawl the pilots who felt they deserved a night in London, whether or not their superiors agreed. Sebastien would whisk them unchallenged, through the gate, wait until the small hours of the morning for them, and then have them back on the field in time to muster for the dawn patrol ... a whiff or so of pure oxygen would help them get off the ground on those mornings.*

In spite of the Luftwaffe's larger airforce and the strength of their offensive, the RAF and their allies flying Spitfires and Hurricanes had the advantages of radar and home territory. Allied strategy at first was to launch squadrons of twelve planes into four 3-plane "vic" formations. The most unpopular position were those of "tail-end Charlies," detailed to weave from side to side at the rear, protecting from stern attack. Pilots joked valiantly that they were either promoted from this duty or buried while performing it. Later the squadrons were reorganized into three sections of four aircraft each, which could split into twos when the battle began. Matching strategy with strategy, the defending formations were consistently destroying at least twice as many German aircraft to their own losses. Churchill's famous words in the House of Commons on August 20 were inspiring: "Never in the field of human conflict has so much been owed by so many, to so few."

The action became more intense at the end of August when the Germans began attacking Fighter Command bases. On the last day of the month, the Canadians were in action twice. In the morning, while the pilots were patrolling the English coast near Dover, a formation of Messerschmitt 109s came out of the sun and shot three of them down. All three pilots bailed out and survived, but two, Vaughan Corbett and George Hyde, were badly burned. Later that day, the eleven Hurricanes still fit to fly intercepted a formation of fifty bombers over Gravesend. Five enemy aircraft were damaged or destroyed, to the loss of one Hurricane, whose pilot, Jean-Paul Desloges (the only French Canadian in the unit), was severely burned before he managed to bail out.

On the following day, the squadron assisted in breaking up one of the afternoon raids, a formation of 160 aircraft that crossed the coast near Dover and headed inland towards Kenley and Biggin Hill. The Canadian squadron, one of eleven sent to meet the attack, flew directly into a group of twenty bombers to break up the formation. They succeeded in destroying two and damaging three "bandits" before the enemy retreated. This day marked the end of a week in which the No. 1 Squadron had fought four air battles. Their score was encouraging: they had destroyed eight enemy aircraft, and "probably" destroyed or damaged ten. Their own losses included one pilot killed, four injured, and seven Hurricanes written off.

In the early days of September there was no let up in pressure. Every day the pilots were scrambling after raids. It was "an impossibly delicate balancing act" to maintain morale and uphold skills while this intensive fighting went on, for the more practical experience the pilots gained, the more likely they were to be killed, wounded or mentally worn out. The squadron began to have problems with reinforcements: RAF pilots were posted as replacements, but there were never enough to fill the places of the casualties.

On September 7, the Luftwaffe switched their attack from radar stations and airfields to London itself. But in the morning, before Britain was aware of the change of German strategy, the No. 1 Squadron had been ordered to protect Northolt. Two other squadrons were based there, one RAF and one Polish squadron. Hartland and the other pilots watched helplessly as they saw a raid of more than 200 aircraft heading to London, where they carried out very heavy bombing. The squadron leaders pleaded to be allowed to launch sections to intercept them and engage, but "Control insisted on maintaining station defence."

Germans began sending Messerschmitts as "close escorts" for bombers on their way to London, that is, fighters instructed not to engage in fighting unless attacked, but to stick close to the bombers – some alongside, others above – to protect them. As Hartland later described it, "They sent the bombers over naked at first, huge waves of Dorniers, Heinkels and Junkers without any fighter escorts and depending on weight of numbers to break through. Our boys knocked them down at a terrific rate. So then they began sending over more and more fighters and fewer and fewer bombers until there were as many as 75 or 100 Messerschmitts swarming around, perhaps 10 Heinkels. Then our job grew more difficult."

On September 9, the squadron had its first experience with close escorts. Working in coordination with twenty-five other RAF squadrons, the Canadians tried to manoeuvre their planes into position above and behind the enemy, a formation of over 300 aircraft. The pilots succeeded in destroying one German fighter and damaging two others, but one flying as tail-end Charlie, was shot down and wounded.

On a battle on September 11, Hartland destroyed one Heinkel bomber. It was his second victory, as he had been credited with damaging a bomber the week before. This time, he was on an afternoon patrol near Gatwick when the squadron sighted about twenty Heinkels, escorted by fighters 3,000 feet below the bombers.

We dove in formation, broke the bombers into scattered groups and turned to pick our quarries. I chose one that was scooting away and took whacks at it from five different directions until suddenly, it nosed over with a funnel of smoke trailing from its cockpit and a soft rose-glow that turned gradually into a furnace. I followed it down a little way, expecting to see the crew bail out, but they didn't. I guess my bursts must have washed out the entire lot, for I saw the ship hit in the middle of a field and spread a great sheet of flame through the hedge and a fiery smear half way across the next pasture.

Altogether that day the squadron destroyed two and damaged two, while two Canadian pilots, Pete Lochnan and Tommy Little, were shot down. Lochnan crash-landed his Hurricane without injury, and Little, who took to his parachute, suffered leg wounds.

On September 15, later considered to be the climax of the battle, the No. 1 Squadron was dispatched to fly over London. The Germans had sent 120 bombers to the city, escorted by 650 fighters. Twenty-four squadrons were scrambled to counter this raid, including No 1. They left Northolt at 11:40, ordered to patrol at

15,000 feet, and were almost immediately attacked from above, out of the blinding sun, by Messerschmitt 109s. Two Canadians, Deane Nesbitt and Ross Smither, were shot down; Nesbitt bailed out with head injuries; Smither was killed. On a second scramble later that day, the Canadians shot down two Heinkels and damaged several others. The Allies totalled the losses of aircraft at the end of the day: the enemy had lost 61, and Fighter Command, 31.

On September 16, there was another "nerve-wracking, terrific battle." The Hurricanes climbed through a cover of cumulus clouds until they broke out to clear sky and could suddenly see 100 bombers escorted by 100 fighters. They continued climbing and saw a second wave, the same strength as the first. Just before going in to attack, they saw a third wave coming over the Channel, with RAF squadrons climbing to intercept. With nearly a thousand air-craft in the small area just south of London, tactics were reduced to "a quick shot and away, for someone was bound to be on your own tail."

On September 23 Hartland participated in two uneventful wing patrols in the morning. At 2:30 in the afternoon, Otto Peterson and Dal Russel spotted a single plane flying towards the English coast near the Isle of Wight. They took turns leading attacks from astern, expending all their ammunition. The plane dove into the sea; both pilots were credited with destroying the bomber.

Later that afternoon, Billy Bishop showed up at the aerodrome, wearing his Air Marshal stripes. Bishop was in Britain on a public relations tour as part of his job as chief of recruiting for the RCAF. Movie cameras and crew followed him, and the British press recorded the event. To the Canadian journalists, Bishop said "It is great seeing the boys so fit and keen for the job." The Air Marshal, who insisted on an informal visit, shared a drink with the pilots, and toasted them: "To your continued success and glory."

That night Bishop invited Hartland to London to dine with him at Claridge's. After dinner, the two climbed the stairs to the roof, where Bishop had a table and chairs and some brandy waiting. From the rooftop, they looked out over the darkened city; they could make out the domes and belfries of the tallest cathedrals silhouetted against the flickering, orange glow of fires burning. They could hear the throbbing drone of German aircraft and the whistling sound of the bombs as they fell, followed by the explosions. The friends peered through binoculars for a better view of the action. Later they learned that while they had been having dinner, the aerodrome at Northolt had been bombed. They were relieved to hear there had been no casualties there.

The Canadian squadron was now down to fourteen pilots and six serviceable aircraft. September 27, though in retrospect considered the Allies' most successful day, brought another loss to the Canadians. Russel, Peterson and McNab were attacked by Messerschmitt 109s in the skies over Gatwick. Russel shot down one, then teamed up with McNab to close in on another, setting it on fire before it crashed. Others had victories as well. But Peterson never made it back to base – he had been killed.

The pilots were exhausted from the intensity of the constant rigorous demands made on them. The tension due to the ever-present danger of combat exacerbated the fatigue brought on by so many hours of flying and the need to stay alert while waiting in readiness. The shortage of pilots in the unit was noticeable. At one point only nine pilots were available, then three wounded pilots returned, raising their number to twelve. Five others remained sick or were in hospital recovering from injuries. A cold or influenza virus swept through the quarters, affecting the morale of those still able to fight. Donald Rankin, the second medical officer for the squadron, had developed pneumonia.

Only four weeks earlier, first medical officer John Nodwell (who would also develop pneumonia) had said the Canadians were "the healthiest body of flying men" he had ever examined, and that "every man was superbly confident." But on September 30, he wrote:

There is a definite air of constant tension and they are unable to relax as they are practically on constant call. The pilots work with forced enthusiasm and appear to be suffering from strain and general tiredness … The constant strain and overwork is showing its effects on most of the pilots, and in some it is marked. They tire very easily, and recovery is slower. Acute reactions in the air are thereby affected. There is now a general tendency to eat irregularly or to have a sandwich in place of a hot meal. The pilots are becoming run-down and infections which would otherwise be minimal are becoming more severe. There is a general state of becoming stale. Needless casualties are bound to occur as a result of these conditions if continued.

On October 4, King George visited the airfield and presented Distinguished Flying Cross awards to Ernie McNab, Gordon McGregor and Dal Russel. The pilots, each of whom had destroyed at least four enemy aircraft and damaged more, were the first in the RCAF to be awarded battle decorations. The occasion lifted the spirits of the squadron at a time when they needed it the most. The pilots were released from duty that afternoon an hour earlier than usual, and everyone – from ground crew to senior officers – participated in the celebrations.

The following day, October 5, was a damp and cloudy Saturday; a continuous drizzle fell throughout the morning. An early attack by Messerschmitt 109s near Dover was successfully diverted by RAF squadrons, but more formations of fighters and bombers kept coming over the Channel. Soon hundreds of enemy aircraft were fanning across southeastern England and spreading through Kent.

The first call summoning the Canadian squadron to readiness came at 10:45, and the second call to action twenty minutes later. Hartland and the other eleven pilots in the unit sprinted to their aircraft, where the ground crew had the engines running for them. Gordon McGregor was their squadron leader; at his signal they began taxiing to take-off and "with scarcely a pause" took to the air in formation. It was exactly eight minutes after 11 a.m.

McGregor took over radio commands as he led the tight formation, four sections of three planes, one section behind the other. They began the climb, circling to gain height. At 5,000 feet they turned on their oxygen, so they wouldn't forget later. At 10,000 feet, the rear section of the formation began to move above the squadron and to fly in a series of S's to protect it from surprise attack from the rear. Nearing their destination, McGregor put up his hand with his fingers spread to indicate that he wanted his pilots to spread out into spans, the tight formation broken up so the pilots could spend their time looking for the enemy without danger of colliding with the others. Each pilot was getting ready for immediate action. Hartland took the safety devices from his machine guns, set his sights and checked his oxygen.

McGregor spotted the quarry first and led the sections toward seven Messerschmitt 109s flying in a line south of Maidstone. Farther to the southeast, he had seen another formation of "bandits" – he steered his pilots between the seven fighter-bombers and the coast to attack. The other German formation turned to join in, and immediately the squadron became separated. Individual dog-fights erupted, spread out across Maidstone and the coast, between 16,000 and 20,000 feet. Bandits were everywhere, and the sky was laced with the white contrails of the duels and the black trails of falling, burning aircraft. Hartland later described the sight of the swirling planes as being "like whirlpools of paper and rubbish on a windy street corner."

Each Hurricane had only 45 seconds of ammunition in its machine guns, so it was crucial to get into a good position and aim true. McGregor was the first to shoot down a Messerschmitt. Soon Paul Pitcher shot down a second one and damaged another. Bev Christmas fired a long burst and destroyed another bandit, while Eric Beardmore and Pete Lochnan damaged one each. To the south, Hartland saw "a large, milling mass of aircraft, like bees around a jam pot" and "the usual flock of vultures hovering above, hanging around in the sun." He saw two Hurricanes trying to attack them, and went up to join in. "I got short bursts at two Huns and missed them." Then he spotted a pair of 109s below him working together; he chose the closer one, and dove down to engage it. "I chased them around for a few minutes getting in short bursts whenever the sights were on." Shells passed by his windscreen, looking like red-hot bricks. He pressed down on his trigger but didn't see whether or not he had hit the Messerschmitt, for it "rolled off and disappeared toward earth."

Hartland would later describe a feeling of detachment as he took action in a dogfight, "as though you were sitting on your own shoulder watching someone you know very well, criticizing him and encouraging him, trying to help him along." But at this point, he would later say ruefully:

> I forgot all that I had learned. I slowed up and straightened up too without looking around. Not looking around is by far the most elementary way of getting mowed down in a dogfight in existence. And one must never fly straight in a fight. Keep twisting and turning, otherwise you're cold meat. There was a gentleman behind just hoping I'd do something stupid and he knocked my machine out of control with his little cannon in about two seconds.

Hartland may have forgotten about the first fighter, "but he had remembered me. Just as I was about to let the last blast, my own controls were shot away by an explosive cannon that wiped out my 'plumbing,' exploded in the cockpit and got me in the leg and side. My instrument panel and canopy started disintegrating, glycol engine coolant and smoke began streaming into the cockpit and the aircraft ceased to obey any of my commands."

Hartland realized that he would have to bail out. The stick moved around "like a spoon in weak coffee." Even as his Hurricane was plummeting nose-downward and slightly on its back, as it was falling faster and faster, Hartland was able to note that the one control that still functioned was the throttle – he closed it before he began struggling to slide the hood back. Air pressure kept forcing it back again. He tried not to panic. He feared that if he forced his body through the opening and wriggled out of the aircraft, he might scrape off his parachute. The plane had already dropped 2,000 feet. He made one last Herculean effort to push the hood out of the way, released his harness and suddenly he "shot out with great gusto," and found himself hurtling through the air at 450 miles per hour. Tossed around, twisted about, sprawled without control of his limbs, "I was," he said, "like a rag doll without any joints." Soon, Hartland's falling body slowed to a terminal velocity of about 125 miles per hour.

> *Funny thing! I found now that I could adjust my body to any position in the air, somewhat like rolling over in bed. There was no sensation of falling, no paralyzing rush of air, dizziness, or nausea. It was more like floating in a swimming pool. So I twisted around on my stomach and waited for the first sight of the ground, then as I broke through the ceiling [of cloud] I pulled the rip, felt the tug of the chute straps under my crotch and armpits & began to float gently down. I knew I was wounded, but not how badly. I didn't feel any noticeable pain. No great discomfort was felt and the descent from there on seemed slow, in fact, too slow. One feels as though the earth will never arrive.*

The real danger of a parachute jump, Hartland would explain later, was not the landing, nor the fact that the chute might not open.

At high altitudes one dares not open it for fear of being riddled by the guns of an unsporting Hun. Near the ground there are additional hazards found. The enthusiastic farmers and farmerettes who may take a pot at you with the old family muzzle loader, or assist you to a three-point landing on the prongs of a pitch fork. Naturally, it is difficult for them to identify friend from foe from their worm's eye view as you float down.

After he pulled the rip cord and engaged the parachute, Hartland noticed that his right flying boot was missing and his leg was bleeding. He explained a few days later in a letter to Magda:

The descent now seemed so slow, that I amused myself by trying to make a tourniquet round [my] knee, out of the rip cord. As it is made of finest metal cable I couldn't get it to stay for an instant and threw the thing away in disgust, then looked down in horror to see if I was going to kill anyone below by letting it fall on them. All I saw was sheep. Then I floated through a cloud – like walking in dense fog – and came out about 255 feet above the ground. This is the part which is interesting because one wants to avoid obstacles and to be as near habitation as possible. I saw a nice town [Ashford, Kent] in the distance, a railway underneath, and a wood coming up with a good road beyond. I missed the tracks but not the woods. Fortunately, the tree I chose was a nice soft one and broke my fall quite a bit. I must have pulled up my sore leg because I landed with a plunk on my popsi on some nice damp ground. I hobbled about 30 yards to a wide path and sat down, then started to call every minute or so.

In about ten minutes Hartland's calls were answered. Six Cockney soldiers appeared; they had seen him come down. They put field dressings on his wounds. When Hartland began to tremble with the effects of shock, they all took off their tunics and cov-

ered him with them to keep him warm. They offered him a cigarette and lit it for him. One of them went off to get their truck and
returned with a medical officer. They handled Hartland "like a
baby," made him comfortable in the truck and took him to their
billets, where the medical officer checked the dressings and
arranged for him to go to a casualty clearing station. Only then was
Hartland able to send a message to the Squadron, "and then one to
… the Padre who very kindly volunteered to call anyone else."

CHAPTER EIGHT

B ACK AT NORTHOLT, the eleventh pilot from the Canadian squadron had returned to the base by 12:30, less than an hour and a half since they had all set out. The air battle had lasted about thirty minutes.

A telegram from the airbase was sent to headquarters:

PRELIMINARY COMBAT REPORT NEAR MAID-STONE AT 1140 HOURS 5/10/40 12 HURRICANES NO 1 CANADIAN SQUADRON LEFT NORTHOLT 1108 HRS. 11 HURRICANES LANDED NORTHOLT 1229 HRS. OUR CASUALTIES 1 PILOT NOT YET RETURNED (F/O MOLSON) ENEMY CASUALTIES 3 ME 109 DESTROYED 2 ME 109 DAMAGED 1 ME 110 DAMAGED

Members of the squadron were hoping Hartland was just late returning; some feared the worst. About thirty minutes later, a second telegram confirmed that he was missing, which was the news passed on to Magda in Montreal.

When no one seemed able to tell her anything more, Magda became hysterical with anxiety. Late in the afternoon a Canadian Pacific telegram (addressed not to Mrs. Hartland Molson nor even Mrs. Herbert Molson, but to "Mrs. M. Molson"), referring to Hartland as "your son," was telephoned then delivered to her home on Redpath Street. This did little to calm her. Could the sender have been mistaken also about the nature of his injuries?

FROM ROYCANAIRF LONDON
REGRET TO INFORM THAT YOUR SON FLYING OFFI-
CER H DE M MOLSON SUSTAINED MULTIPLE
WOUNDS OF LOWER LEFT LEG RESULT ENEMY
ACTION OCTOBER FIFTH FULL STOP WOUNDS
NOT CONSIDERED SERIOUS FULL STOP LETTER
FOLLOWS

It was not until the next day, Sunday, that Billy Bishop heard about Hartland's misfortune. Bishop, in Ottawa, telephoned Magda immediately. His words, as Bishop's son Arthur remembers, were, "He's in the hospital and he's safe. He's fine, he's going to be alright. There's nothing to worry about."

The Cockney soldiers who had seen Hartland come down and found him were from the 1st Kensington Regiment, stationed nearby. When he landed, Hartland was "a clammy mess of glycerine," his uniform soaked through from the combination of glycol and radiator fluid. (It seemed not to occur to anyone that offering Hartland a cigarette may not have been a wise choice. He accepted it as gratefully as he did all their ministrations.) The soldiers took him to their billets, then to the battalion clearing station before taking him to a special casualty clearing station at Ashford, which Hartland remembered as "a very charming little hospital."

Oddly enough, the medical officer didn't go right to work on my wounds, didn't even strip off my blood- and oil-soaked clothes. He just put me under a big electric cooker with layers of blankets and let me lie for several hours. I learned later that this was to reduce the nervous shock. And it worked. I began to feel warm and relaxed and presently felt quite snug. Then about 5 in the afternoon they came and rolled me to the operating room and sewed me up.

Staff at the little hospital kept four blankets and the heater on Hartland from 2:30 to 5:15. Then he was x-rayed and given an anesthetic, his wounds were cleaned and a doctor removed the shrapnel and bandaged his leg. Hartland would stay there for thirty-six hours. Orderlies burned his uniform and gave him a blue flanelette hospital garment. Medical officer Donald Rankin came down with an ambulance the next night and drove him to the Canadian Hospital at Taplow.

The Duchess of Connaught Memorial Hospital, with 480 beds and a research centre, had opened in July of that year. It was built and run by the Canadian Red Cross at the invitation of Lord and Lady Astor, on the grounds at the eastern edge of their estate.

According to Joyce Grenfell, Nancy Astor's niece, the nursing sisters at the hospital wore "bright-blue poplin uniforms with gold buttons, stiff white collars and cuffs, and floating organdie veils." (The bright blue uniforms gained nurses the nickname "Bluebirds.")

Donald Rankin, who had developed pneumonia, joined Hartland as a patient at Taplow a week later. Rankin was able to bring him news of the war and of their regiment: attacks had begun to peter out after Hartland's last flight, and as the autumn weather came it looked as though the Germans had given up invading Britain altogether. The No. 1 Squadron had been posted to Scotland for a rest.

The hospital was just a short walk across the grounds from Cliveden, the Astors' stately home. Though she was often away in Plymouth, where she was an MP and her husband the Lord Mayor, Lady Astor visited the patients almost every day. An indefatigable politician and society hostess, she maintained an involvement in the day-to-day operations of the hospital and developed special bonds with both the staff and the Canadian servicemen who were patients there.

Described by former Canadian Prime Minister Sir Robert Borden as someone of "immense earnestness, brilliantly clever and witty, and amazingly vivacious," Nancy Astor was an unusual woman of her generation. She was known for her verbal exchanges with Winston Churchill, and was at the centre of controversy during the years leading up to the war. Her personal and political opinions were extreme and intractable. As Lieutenant-Colonel Athol Gordon recalled, "a non-smoker and a teetotaler with a predisposition to Christian Science, her forthright comments were very amusing to the troops, and the impingement of such a personality upon western Canadian doctors can better be imagined than described."

Hartland admitted they had some differences. "She … didn't understand how 'a nice person like me could possibly be in a filthy business like the beer business.' I got on very well with her because … one thing she couldn't stand was a 'yes' man, and when she said something rather rough like that to you, as long as you responded in kind, she thought you were alright."

Nancy Astor used to come down and take a look around every day, and when she was visiting me one day, she said, "Where are you going when you get out of here?" I was beginning to get up and walk around a bit and I said, "I don't know yet," and she said, "Why don't you come up to us at Cliveden?" And I said I thought that would be very nice.

Lady Astor also invited Medical Officer Donald Rankin, who was recovering from his pneumonia, so he and Hartland were moved up to the house together. They would stay at Cliveden in adjoining rooms (two of the forty-three bedrooms) for nearly a month. The Astors' home was a lively centre of social and political affairs, which filled with invited guests – famous and influential people – every weekend. Politicians, journalists, royalty, celebrities and industrialists mingled with intellectuals, social workers, artists and senior military officers. The Astors' deliberate assemblage of weekend guests who represented different points of view was widely acknowledged. Hartland enjoyed both the "hotbed of political debate" and the Astors' glamorous lifestyle.

In Taplow Hartland met many people with whom he would maintain lifelong connections. He became reacquainted with Lester Pearson, who as first secretary to the Canadian High Commission was a frequent visitor to Cliveden. He became particularly close to members of the Astor family, including Lord Waldorf Astor, and the couple's five children, most of whom joined their parents on the weekends. Bill, Nancy's eldest son with Waldorf, was Hartland's age.

> [Lady Astor] was quite a gal, she took up riding ... one of those motor assisted bicycles. It had a large wheel on the back with a little engine somewhere, and she'd come weaving down the gravel driveway and some of her family might perhaps be there, one of the boys or something on the weekend, and they'd just close their eyes, and say "We can't look!"

Lady Astor and Hartland had much in common, which they may have sensed rather than spoken about. The difference in their ages didn't mean much to either of them. Most of Hartland's friends were older than he was, and Nancy had friends of all ages. Both Hartland and Nancy had experienced unhappy first marriages from which each had one child. Both came from families who had long histories of prosperity and public service. They may have discovered that they'd each known Henry Ford. The Astors had invited the Ford family to stay for a fortnight, and when Henry left, he gave each of her children a Ford motor car.

Some days, but for the blackout curtains on every window, it was easy to forget there was a war on. There were dances for the Nursing Sisters and Officers in the grand hall. Guests continued to come and go on weekends. Hartland and Donald Rankin spent many pleasant hours boating and canoeing on the Thames, sharing access to the Cliveden boathouse that was also open to the Nursing Sisters. Bobby Shaw, Nancy Astor's son by her first marriage, sometimes joined them. Shaw, an air raid warden in London, had been hit and injured in an incident there and was convalescing at Taplow as well.

Hartland recalled that:

Lady Astor had very strict rules about drinking in the house, which we had to find out how to circumvent, which we did, with the capable assistance of their butler of about 40 years called Mr. [Edwin] Lee. He used to make sure that we got our ration of booze every day. They passed wine and barley water [around] at dinner, they had to I suppose … When Lord and Lady Astor went to clean up before dinner, Lee would then expect a buzz on the buzzer. He would come in with a tray of whisky and ice and soda and it would mysteriously disappear just before Lord and Lady Astor came back in for dinner.

"Waldorf was influenced into being a teetotaler by Nancy," Hartland explained. "He was a most gentle man, very nice, but Nancy certainly ruled the roost."

On Sunday, November 17, Major-General AGL ("Andy")

McNaughton was one of the guests at Cliveden invited for dinner. McNaughton, a Canadian "soldier-scientist" had been the chief of general staff in the early '30s, and the force behind the work-camp program in which jobless civilians were employed to construct airport landing fields. Between 1935 and 1939, he had been president of the National Research Council in Ottawa. Hartland had first met General McNaughton through his father Herbert, who was a close friend of his and considered the General "an artillery genius." Hartland and McNaughton had connected again in 1936, when the NRC was collecting data on soy production, and again two years later, when the institute tested Grettir Algarsson's variable-pitch propeller. McNaughton was, in 1940, the Canadian senior-most army officer overseas, subordinate only to the War Office in London.

"Brilliant, charismatic, and outspoken," McNaughton "differed from his own government about keeping Canada's overseas army as united as possible." His was an awkward and demanding role, for though he was responsible for maintaining control of Canada's armed forces, the British considered Canadian formations overseas to be an integral part of the British forces, and therefore subject to the direction and control of London. The Canadian government fought to maintain their separate identity. It was a delicate balance that demanded the utmost in strategy and diplomacy for people like McNaughton and Lester Pearson to navigate.

Hartland and McNaughton had different opinions on this issue, a subject that came up when they met at Cliveden, and which Hartland didn't hesitate to defend. This exchange was characteristic of the sorts of conversations that went on frequently under the Astors' roof.

> One weekend General McNaughton and his wife came down and I just knew him and said, "How do you do?" and chatted with him and, on the one evening before dinner, they all went up to wash their hands or something and General McNaughton and I were

left in front of the fire in the big hall and he said: "How are your chaps getting on in the Squadron?" And I said, "We are getting on all right, but they are very bloody-minded." And he said, "What do you mean?" And I said, "Well, we all feel that being called the retired-business-men Squadron may be amusing, but we feel it's a hell of a way to run a railroad." And he said, "What do you mean?" I said, "We mean that we think that Canada should certainly have equal service and sacrifice for everybody. We don't think that this business of pulling a few volunteers here and there and throwing them in is a very good system. We think that everybody should have to do their share." "Oh," he said, "That's not the role of Canada at all." And I said, "Well, what do you mean?" He said, "Canada's role is to provide food and munitions, both of which we are very good at, and only a token force, because that is not what is needed and it is not what we are capable of doing. As far as I am concerned Canada's Expeditionary Forces should be as small as will let us hold our place." I don't know if he used the word "token" but he inferred small and minimal and I said, "Well I am terribly sorry to hear you say that Sir because I can just assure you that a hell of a lot of people like myself think that's a rotten way to organize."

Hartland's words, "the business of pulling a few volunteers here and there," referred to American pilots who had volunteered to join the RCAF and RAF, and were readily accepted by these squadrons who needed reinforcements. By September 1940, the RCAF had accepted 197 American pilots. These pilots were considered volunteers not because they were unpaid but because at the time the U.S. government was still officially neutral over the war.

When it was time for Hartland to leave the Astors, he was sorry to go. His departure was timed so that he accompanied the couple on one of their frequent trips to Plymouth. "I went down with Nancy and Waldorf to Plymouth, when he was being installed as the Lord Mayor for the second term … there was a hell of a raid that night in Plymouth … she had been a member there for years … we went down by train, and she read her bible all the way down in the train, the special [Christian Scientist] bible that they have, by Mary Baker Eddy."

Immediately after they parted Lady Astor sent a telegram to Hartland, wishing him a safe journey and telling him she was in tears following their parting. Later she dictated a letter, which her secretary typed on a large black Remington, to Hartland and Donald Rankin (to whom she would always refer as "the Committee") to Hartland's home address. Lady Astor would write to many Canadian friends, including servicemen who had passed through the hospital at Cliveden during the First War, but none of these hundreds of now published letters match the affection she expressed to Hartland and Donald.

> No one knows how much I miss you. I think your loved ones at home would be alarmed, and you would be surprised, for it feels as if I had lost two really true and loving friends. I find the Lord Mayor not at all comforting and even the boys do not seem so lov- ing as the dear Committee. Jean [Lloyd] and I sigh for you, and old Meanie Winn [niece of Lady Astor's] moans occasionally. However, my maternal affections are stronger than all the others, and I rejoice that you are safely back in Canada.

Back in Canada, Rankin went home to Halifax and Hartland to Montreal. Hartland found himself on the same train with fellow squadron member Eric Beardmore, who had also been injured. Their wives met them at Bonaventure Station, where a photogra- pher and reporter were waiting to introduce themselves the moment the airmen debarked from the train. A photo of Hartland, Beardmore and their wives clad in fur coats dominated the front page of the *Montreal Star* the following day.

During his six weeks leave in Montreal, Hartland was kept very busy. He was interviewed by the *Evening Standard,* then was asked to make a speech at the Erskine United Church for December 8. Invited to be guest of honour after the church social hour, it was the first time he was called upon to speak to an audience. Hartland replied that he didn't know what to say, so the organizer of the event helpfully wrote an outline for him. The outline was a series of topics, beginning with "Training in England," to "Life on the Ground During Combat Duty," to "Principles of Fighter Technique" and ended with a "Tribute to Civilian Morale." Hartland would use this outline for all subsequent speeches in the months to follow.

Other interviews followed, and articles appeared in Canadian and American newspapers and periodicals. There were more invitations to give speeches. The RCAF set up a speaking tour for him and arranged his itinerary to work around his duties with the air force in Ottawa. The Boston *Evening American* ran an interview in January, and Hartland delivered a speech to the Ottawa branch of the Canadian Legion in early February. On February 14 he was a guest of honour at a Military Ball in Holyoke, near Springfield, Illinois, sponsored by the British War Relief Society. Three days later he spoke to the Toronto Canadian Club. Each time he spoke his confidence was bolstered, and his ease with an audience grew to the point that he could include humour in his remarks. In March, he made a speech in New York, and another in Maine, to the Explorer's Club. He was not, he confessed, ever very comfortable speaking. "It really isn't my 'cup o' tea' but someone seems to think it worthwhile so I go with my usual unreasoning obedience!"

They sent me off on a speaking tour to the Air Force Establishments to describe the Battle of Britain as I saw it. That wasn't any particular amusement for me ... in Maine, at the Explorer's Club, I was met by a Canadian expatriat, who had

*come down from Toronto … He said, "Lindbergh's a member of
the Explorer's Club, and as you know he is very anti-British, he's
very pro-German and so he has been asked to stay away from this
meeting, but you may find some of his friends there, they may ask
you some questions." I thanked him for the warning … I had
some combat film and stuff to show and Lindbergh's friends
weren't too much trouble; they asked a couple of stupid questions
to which I was able to give a couple of stupid answers, but it was
interesting in a way.*

One of the highlights of Hartland's speaking tour was meeting
Sir Hubert Wilkins in Maine. The 52-year-old Australian aviator
and his wife picked Hartland up and took him to dinner before his
presentation at the Explorer's Club. Sir Hubert, a former war corre-
spondent, explorer, naturalist, balloonist and war hero, fascinated
Hartland, who doubtless enjoyed his many stories spanning his
extraordinary career.

Hartland's speeches would always end with an appeal to help the
British air raid victims. To aid Lord Astor's efforts with his "Lord
Mayor's Fund," Hartland established a Canadian Fund for the same
purpose, to be donated to the British account. Although he didn't
want to carry on a campaign – because "a campaign must end" – in
April 1941 he gave $10,000 to the fund, a gesture he publicized in
order to inspire others. The response was immediate and generous.
In May, Hartland wrote to Lady Astor, "I'm hoping that some of
the now $420,000 given to the Queen's Canadian Fund (for the
Lord Mayor's Fund) may have given some little help to your grand
people there … we are getting about £1000 (equivalent) a day …
I expect the contributions to continue steadily and indefinitely …"

Promoted to Lieutenant Flight Commander just before he came
home, Hartland's pay had increased from his flying officer's wage of
$4.25 per day to $6.50. Two weeks after Christmas, he was posted
to Air Force headquarters in Ottawa. There he took over com-

mand of No. 118 Fighter Squadron based in Rockcliffe, a new squadron that they were forming for the defence of Canada, which was to become part of Eastern Air Command.

Hartland lived in Ottawa for six months, leaving on short trips to give presentations to flight clubs, Legions and private clubs. In the early part of the year, Magda and Zoë joined Hartland in Billy Bishop's house in the upscale Sandy Hill suburb, not far from Parliament Hill. Bishop was away at the time in northern Ontario, taking part in a Hollywood film called *Captains of the Clouds* starring James Cagney and others. There, Bishop was amused to tell Hartland, some of the old Dominion Skyways aircraft had been leased for use in the picture.

The Astors, meanwhile, were "waiting breathlessly for the invasion." Lady Astor wrote, "Whether it will come or not, I don't know, but anyhow, they tell us we are well prepared, and if Hitler arrives, he will have to take England over the bodies of every man, woman and child in it, if he is going to win. It sounds brave, but it is just common sense." The Germans had been carrying out raids on Plymouth. "I cannot tell you what it has been like. It is beyond all belief – terrible," she wrote.

Hartland had read in the papers how Lady Astor had been working tirelessly to keep up the morale of the people who had lost their families and possessions. "It is a great relief to know that you are safe," he replied, "but it must have been a real ordeal and of course you worked like a beaver as usual. Since then we hear that the raids on London have been tremendously heavy, and I hope, with the people of those bombed areas, that we blow the daylights out of every town in Germany."

Hartland was beginning to doubt that he would be sent back overseas, but he continued to hope. "Whether they will send back any of those in their thirties," he wrote Lady Astor, "is quite a question. I am led to believe that the rulers of fighter command in England have pretty definite ideas on such subjects."

For the first three months in Ottawa the new squadron flew with an ill-assortment of aircraft, including two Lysanders, a Yale, two Harvards, and a pair of Fleet Finches. This evidence that their squadron was a low priority affected the morale of the men. The squadron diarist reported in March that "Unit personnel are a bit fed up." When the news came that Grumann Goblins were to be delivered for their use as replacement aircraft, they were dismayed. The planes were clearly inappropriate, even obsolete: an RCAF report submitted four years earlier had concluded the Goblins were "not in keeping with the performance required by modern aircraft, and the design is several years old."

The grievances against the Goblins were many. A heavy and solid aircraft, the pilots called it "the pregnant frog" in reference to the contours of the fuselage. The Goblin was considered useless as an operational aircraft and unsuited as an advanced trainer. Its ground visibility was poor, it lacked blind flying instruments and had no provision for winter flying. Yet as they were the only planes available at the time, the unit was forced to accept them.

The bitterness at having been given inadequate aircraft still rankled many decades later. In 1979 Hartland referred to the Goblins as "very tired old discarded airplanes ... which I think the Turks or the Mexican Air forces had turned down." "Second rate old beat-up aeroplanes," he called them on another occasion, adding, "They were just ridiculous: two machine guns, a top speed of 200-220 – we couldn't catch the standard bomber." In 2003, Dal Russel agreed: "They weren't worth a damn."

The Goblins had no speed or manoeuvrability. "They were two-seaters. They would only fly reasonably if we put a slug of weight in the rear gunner's seat and they thrashed along," explained Hartland. Soon after service flying began, it was found that wing fabric on many had badly deteriorated, the canopies were defective and the mechanism of the controllable pitch propellers was corroded. (Later in Dartmouth, Nova Scotia, when aircraft were taken out of their hangars into the winter air, the cockpit hoods shattered.) Some wings, propellers, ten engines and all the defective canopies were removed and sent to contractors to be put into shape, but the repairs would take many weeks.

Meanwhile, the unit made do with Harvards for instrument training, Finches for formation practice and the few operational Goblins they had for familiarization. They could not begin their gunnery and interception training until the end of June 1941 when most of the Goblins were back. On July 15 the squadron was finally ready to move to its war station on the east coast. The No. 118 Squadron pilots – the first air defence unit in Eastern Air Command – flew their fifteen Goblins and one Harvard to Dartmouth over two days.

Hartland was frustrated in his new post from the beginning. "We started out with this role of defending Canada," he explained, "and we knew we couldn't do it." He and other members of the squadron participated in formation flying, air-to-air and air-to-ground firing practice. "We had very poor facilities. When we flew cross country we had no range radios we could use ... we had not got the equipment. We just did it by the old seat of the pants." An average of eight to ten of the Goblins were unserviceable every day that summer. Moreover, accidents were frequent: one Goblin crashed on July 23 at Lawrencetown Lake, killing the pilot. Another accident occurred on July 29, and a third on August 5. Hartland narrowly missed being a casualty himself. "I had a rough engine and landed at Moncton and I had sweat about four pounds off over those New Brunswick woods, but I couldn't get in touch with anybody about it."

Magda travelled by train and joined Hartland in Halifax, Nova Scotia. Soon after arriving they set about looking for a house, but at first had doubts that they could be comfortable there. "The place is pretty scruffy," he wrote Lady Astor, "and the housing problem acute. We have been trying to find a house so that my fat daughter (6 yrs.), dog and servants can come down, but so far have found nothing. Of course we are making it pretty tough by asking for two bathrooms in one house! At present Miss Zoë is enjoying the sea air on the Gulf of St. Lawrence with my mother. It's probably better for her there as there is, apparently, no summer down here."

Hartland, Dal Russel, Arthur Yuile and Ernie McNab missed their days being in the No. 1 Squadron, where they flew their beloved Hurricanes and all the modern equipment they needed was delivered promptly. Most of the other original members of the No. 1 Squadron had been dispersed, transferred or reassigned; their old squadron, meanwhile, had been renumbered 401. McNabb was transferred from the No. 118 Squadron in August, and Hartland became Squadron Commander.

Morale continued to be a problem. The Maritime squadron required a variety of aircrew, for flying so many different aircraft operationally required not only pilots familiar with the aircraft but also mechanic crew and engineers. Their squadron had been initially set up to defend against the possibility of a bomber attack, which everyone considered highly unlikely. Their unit was given low priority in equipment and inadequate accommodation, added to which the lack of public recognition (compared to their time in the Battle of Britain), caused pilots' camaraderie and inter-service relationships to suffer. Hartland felt the squadron could have been more useful. "If [the RCAF] had really thought it through, they could have done a great deal more with what we had at the time, but they did not."

The tedium of patrolling was lessened when the CAM-ships arrived. Catapult Armed Merchant ships, a new concept invented by Winston Churchill to intercept German raiders, were freighters with concrete-reinforced bridges, fitted with catapults on their bows. For take-offs at sea, Hawker Hurricanes from the Royal Navy were placed on the catapults, pilots would strap themselves in and open their engines absolutely full, and the catapults would be fired when the boats were "on the rise." As Hartland explained, they usually got off quite successfully, and the problem was that the pilots never had anywhere to land, so they parachuted out and used their little dinghies.

The CAM-ships and their aircraft cargo arrived in Halifax in a convoy from Europe. After being at sea for three weeks, the Hurricanes were coated in salt, which would seize their engines and propellers. The aircraft were loaded by crane onto barges, towed over to Dartmouth Harbour, their wheels lowered, and then pulled by tractor to the hangar where the mechanics and engineers from the squadron would proceed to revitalize them. Hartland explained, "We could not see the Hurricane for salt. It was just completely coated … our fellows proceeded to clean that up … right through the guts … their guns were all out and the whole [air-craft] completely washed out. The guns were recalibrated and the [aircraft] test flown." The Hurricanes would then be towed back to the harbour, loaded back on the barges and towed across to the CAM-ship, ready for take-off. "It was a frightening sight," Hartland recalled, "that blast hitting the bridge … [the plane] would go shooting down … a hundred and fifty feet or so – not very long for a take-off."

In September the unit learned they were to be the first RCAF squadron to receive Kittyhawks, new aircraft from the United States. Pilots and crew were sent to Rockcliffe in October to famil-iarize themselves with the aircraft, and in early November flew them to Dartmouth. They liked the Kittyhawks. To their relief, the last of the Goblins were taken out of service on December 12. The 118 Squadron finally had the aircraft it needed to provide a "suc-cessful strike force."

Hartland had not been confiding his frustrations to the Astors, but he had continued his correspondence with them, and, begin-ning in June, had arranged for weekly parcels to be sent from Canada to the family at Cliveden. The parcels contained cheese, tea, coffee, marmalade and other goods that he knew were hard to come by in England. Lady Astor, meanwhile, had found, at Hartland's request, a suitable British painting for him to hang in his dining room in his Montreal home. But the subject of money, considered vulgar, had never been discussed with the Astors.

> *It was really marvelous of you to find time amongst your other worries to first of all get a picture for me and secondly to cable. My wife and I are extremely grateful … I am writing to the Bank of Montreal's manager [in London] … asking him to complete the financial arrangements. If you could have your people advise him what to do I hope he will do it. One never knows – I s'pose it depends on whether I owe him enough to be interesting or not.*

To Hartland's embarrassment, yet to the amusement of his brother and sister-in-law, the painting came to "several thousands of pounds" more than he had intended to spend. Nevertheless, he was thankful to and gracious with Lady Astor, who had the painting shipped to Canada. Hartland closed his letter with the words: "It is very sad to see pictures of the damage done to places like the Abbey and the House. People must feel very savage at the destruction of so many treasures of old England. Perhaps it's symbolic – if we are to build a new world perhaps it will be easier and more thorough if we have fewer reminders of and ties with the past. That's cold comfort if any comfort at all."

CHAPTER NINE

THE WEEK BEFORE Christmas in 1941, Hartland was having dinner with Frank McGill, then a Group Captain, in a hotel dining room in Halifax when he met a young recruit who considered him a hero. Arthur McMahon, who sat a few tables away from them with his cousin, Andy O'Brien, was thrilled when the latter pointed out the flying officers about whom the young sergeant from Renfrew, Ontario, had heard so much. O'Brien, who'd met McGill before, offered to make the introductions. "Despite his protests that 'one doesn't barge in on superior officers,' I took him over to the table and introduced him," remembered O'Brien. "Both the Group Captain and Squadron Leader jumped to their feet and shook the youngster's hand warmly – dropping a few remarks in the Air Force line. McMahon was a plenty tickled lad."

Hartland's unit was one of eight squadrons that the RCAF assigned to Coastal Command. With a total of nearly 3,000 personnel, each squadron had a different role to play. Some flew aircraft with loaded submarine depth-chargers aboard and set out to locate and sink submarines, others were commissioned to patrol for enemy aircraft. All grappled with similar problems – Hartland's wasn't the only unit equipped with "obsolete and inappropriate" aircraft, whose operations were allocated "less than overwhelming" importance. However the government's attitude to Canadian Coastal Command postings took on new significance and a higher priority after the Japanese attacked Pearl Harbor in December 1941. Suddenly the war was no longer confined to Europe. The United States joined the Allies, which generated a sanguine feeling that now, the tide would turn against Germany.

Former members of the original No. 1 Squadron – "all our key people" as Hartland referred to them – began to return from overseas and were sent to Hartland's unit. The most experienced of the Canadian pilots would become commanders and take over new squadrons as they were formed, including one in Sydney, Nova Scotia, and one in Torbay, Newfoundland. Hartland and Arthur "Jeep" Yuile were the first Commanding Officers for the Home War Establishment.

Early in the new year, the role of Hartland's squadron was considered that of an unofficial (or, as Hartland put it, "low-grade") Operational Training Unit (OTU). A large turnover of pilots and personnel went through the unit at Halifax; they would come from the training scheme, stay with them for a while and get posted to other squadrons to go overseas. Over the winter, the officers and crew had to deal with new problems caused by weather, battling freezing conditions, cross-winds, icy runways, snowstorms and thaws.

One day in mid-April Gordon Sinclair visited the unit and interviewed Hartland. He had been intrigued to meet the "streamlined and clean cut" pilot who since his return to Canada had been the focus of "publicity which made it appear as though he were a combination of Superman, Buck Rogers and the Rover Boys." The resulting article, called "Aerial Galahads," appeared in the *Toronto Daily Star* later that month.

> *The speedy fighter aircraft look delicate; the pilots who fly them are almost baby-faced, and their chief, Squadron Leader Hartland Molson, wears an innocent air of blandness and unconcern. Then you stick around the swank new hangar for a day or so and you learn that beneath the surface the men and planes of this squadron are anything but fragile or unconcerned. The words you reach for now have to do with alertness or intentness or something like that. The men and the planes are ready and they are not fooling.*
>
> *Typical of his men is Molson, son of one of Canada's famed clans ... Squadron leader Hartland Molson is the product of the present war, a hard-boiled gentleman. None of the group would dare say such a thing, because it would sound like bragging, but it's dollars to doughnuts they'd sooner fight than eat.*

Hartland would spend the first year of his Maritime posting in Dartmouth running the OTU, which (in July 1942) was training forty-seven pilots in tactics and armaments, on a strength of six Harvard aircraft and twenty-three Hurricanes. Glycol leaks and poor oil radiators kept serviceability low. One pilot was killed flying into the water. On July 10, Hartland wrote former squadron mate Carl Briese in Calgary,

> *I have been more or less looking after fighters down here on a rather extraordinary and unsatisfactory basis. Theoretically I have a squadron to which is attached the Sea Hurricane Flight, but in practice I get told to interfere with other squadrons from time to time, making it awkward for everybody concerned. I have flogged away trying to get the best fighter picture possible – without walking on toes – as it did appear in the best general interest, but it has its difficult moments.*

We are using Sea Hurricanes out of the crates as fast as we can assemble and now have about 23, as well as 6 Harvards, but our serviceability is lousy because the engines are just plain tired.

The role of RCAF squadrons on the east coast was a defensive one, involving more than training. Officials at headquarters were pushing for fighter protection, displaying what some would call near paranoia about the possibility of the enemy landing on the east coast, rumours having reached their ears of a German aircraft carrier being sighted in the region. Hartland's squadron, standing guard at Dartmouth, did over-water patrols, carrying underwing depth charges lest a U-boat was sighted.

On the last day of July 1942 came Eastern Air Command's first kill, when a pilot flying a Harvard sank a German submarine southeast of Cape Sable. Although, Hartland noted, the Canadians had had little coordination with the Eastern Sea Frontier (the U.S. Army Air Force), the "flying boat people" and the "anti-submarine patrol fellows" worked well together. The Squadrons in Coastal Command would sink nine submarines in total, although after the summer of 1943, the U-boats introduced the snorkel-tube, thus reducing the ability of aircraft to locate and destroy them.

In October 1942 Hartland was posted to Halifax and promoted to the position of Wing Commander. As Fighter Air Staff Officer of Eastern Command, he helped build up a fighter organization comprising several squadrons, which served as an operational training unit for qualified pilots. That assignment, which would last for a year, involved the coordination of all the squadrons with Eastern Air Command with the war room in Halifax, which was primarily dealing with shipping and the navy. He rented a house on Lucknow Street, and Magda joined him there.

A letter came to Hartland in May 1943, from RCAF headquarters in Ottawa, indicating that he had been tentatively selected to be the Air Liaison Officer to Moscow. His appointment would not be confirmed, said the letter, until the foreign affairs minister established himself in Russia and advised the government upon the advantages of adding an air attaché to his mission. For a few months Hartland was optimistic, until he learned he would not be going after all.

> *Earlier I had heard I was posted to Moscow as Air Liaison Officer and if I was not going to get overseas I was really delighted, I even started to think about trying to learn a little Russian and then the grapevine from my friends in Air Force Headquarters [told me] you are not going to get this. It turned out that our Minister in Moscow had been evacuated to Kuibishev and he wrote and said: "Don't send me any more of these Armed Forces Liaison Officers. They don't learn anything anyway and the Russians won't talk to them and anyway it's very uncomfortable here." And so my posting was scrubbed. I was very angry.*

Instead Hartland was posted back to flight training and given command of No. 8 Service Flying Training School in Moncton, New Brunswick, one of many schools in the British Commonwealth Air Training Plan. Still smarting about not getting to go to Moscow, Hartland "reluctantly" moved to Moncton in October. Billy Bishop, who wrote to congratulate him on his move, sympathized, adding, "I only wish it had been in a better part of the country." Bishop and another friend dropped by to see Hartland there later in the month, stayed overnight at the station and borrowed a twin-engine Anson aircraft the next morning to do a bit of sightseeing.

Magda moved to Moncton to join her husband at the end of October, bringing 8-year-old Zoë with her. There the little girl was enrolled in a local primary school, but before the end of the year her father was transferred again, this time commissioned to move Moncton's entire training staff out to Weyburn, Saskatchewan. This flight school, built in 1941 by the Royal Air Force, had been used by them until the end of 1943 when they were ready to hand it over to the RCAF.

Hartland recalled that on New Year's Day in January 1944, they packed up 1,200 people in three trains in Moncton and arrived in Weyburn the following morning. It was dark, and the air was damp and cold. At first light, Tommy Lawrence, the AOC in Winnipeg, arrived to introduce himself, and after settling in Hartland had a look around. He was dismayed by what he saw. The following day he telephoned Lawrence and told him he couldn't take over the station.

> [Lawrence] said, "What in hell are you talking about?" and I said, "Do you think you could come out here?" And he said, "Sure I'll try." So he came out to see and that station was such a mess ... physically unbelievable, unbelievable ... the hospital had 10 or 12 beds but . . . [was] overrun with cockroaches, he agreed with me that the station had a little less than reasonable housekeeping. But a more serious thing was that of the hundred, [or] hundred and five aeroplanes ... we had less than 20 that were serviceable.

Tommy Lawrence told the previous station commander, an RAF officer from New Zealand, that Hartland would not take over the station until he was completely satisfied, and that "he had to stay there with his rear party until they got the place cleaned up." Such was the attitude of the CO, Hartland added, "that he really didn't give a damn. But of course they were scratching for people to do these jobs, so they couldn't all be good."

The flight commanders and engineering officers discovered that the aircraft were in bad shape. Hartland test flew one of the Harvards and at first it seemed to be in reasonable condition. Then "I went up a little bit and it did a roll over and a whole cloud of dust and sanding stuff fell all over the aircraft, all over me, including one pencil that went by. I mean, the things had not been cleaned in a while."

We could not go on with our night flying training, we could not go on with our cross country flying, and we could not keep our schedules, so I had to slip our whole course back … two weeks or four weeks … We stopped all flying training. We took the aeroplanes at one end and we started there and we rushed them through our three hangars like Henry Ford, doing the electrical and the hydraulics and the various things on the way through.

Hartland remarked that flying over the Prairies was very much easier than flying over the Maritime provinces, because the weather was so much more predictable and the terrain was conducive to training purposes. Once the premises, aircraft and equipment were cleaned up, the Weyburn school began running three classes at a time, each class handling between fifty and sixty pilots in training. Cadets were from all over the world, some from as far away as Australia, France and India. Other personnel, including instructors, support staff, hospital, catering, mechanics, service police and transportation crew, helped manage the station.

Weyburn flight training school was a self-sufficient community. Besides the hangars and runway, armament building, rifle range and guard house, the airmen had food supply stores, a small hospital and dental building, a legion hall and their own YMCA. Dances were held at the drill hall. The "camp bus" – an old truck with an extended frame fitted with planks for seating – was provided for rides to town and back. Every time it snowed, tractors and big steel rollers packed the snow for the flying to get started. By March, the station was "one big mudhole," and wooden boards were placed for walkways to connect the buildings.

Hartland's posting at Weyburn lasted only three months. At the end of March 1944 he was promoted to Acting Group Captain and, to his astonishment, ordered back to Moncton. There, the former air training school had been converted to a construction and maintenance squadron for aircraft known as "heavy transports" and "ferry fighters." The crew in Moncton was composed mainly of tradesmen, who were taking supplies from Goose Bay up to Newfoundland. "I had been sort of settled back there rather glumly," Hartland explained, "and then I was pushed to St. Hubert [Quebec]."

Posted to St. Hubert in April 1944, Hartland described his new construction and maintenance unit as a "mixed bag." It was a much smaller operation than in Weyburn, with between 200 and 250 stone masons, plumbers and electricians of all ages, sent to build or repair air force facilities. As the station commander, Hartland rarely saw any of the pilots, who flew Mosquitoes or heavy aircraft on long-distance trips. Although very competent at their trades, the personnel presented quite a problem to military administrators like Hartland, for they were "not used to living in barracks and making them very tidy in the way in which we, who had grown up in a more military sense, believed was necessary."

> *We had a lot of trouble in that station, because of the nature of the characters making it up: the real sort of fly boys, the ferry squadron pilots who didn't ever have to spend much time in a unit for discipline ... and the construction and maintenance chaps, who weren't really interested in anything other than a pipe or a plank and a hammer ... they were in constant mischief ... it was a very unattractive air force station, but it was a necessary one I suppose.*

Shortly after arriving in St. Hubert, Hartland participated in a radio broadcast live from the parade ground to promote the official opening of the sixth Victory Loan Campaign. At the request of the school he travelled to Lennoxville to present prizes to the graduating class at Bishop's College School in early June.

During his tenure in St. Hubert, the issue of conscription was introduced, prompting rioting in Montreal. Referring to the bad relations between the police force and the military, Hartland recalled the police were singling out his service men.

> I remember I had to go down to bail out three of my chaps who
> had been watching a police raid on some place and the police just
> thought they were nice candidates, so they threw them in the
> paddy wagon too and they split the head of one of my chaps. And
> I had to go down and bail them out of the tank with all the drunks
> in the Montreal police station.
>
> I was very upset by it, I got in touch with the city authorities in
> Montreal and complained very bitterly and I went down to get
> these three fellows. They were in with all the drunks and the pros-
> titutes and that sort of thing … it was very revolting … and about
> a three hundred pound policeman, when I claimed them, said,
> "Ten dollars bail," and I said, "There has never been bail for ser-
> vicemen and there was no such thing, that we worked between the
> police and our own Provost Corps," and so on. He said, "The
> bail is ten dollars." So I gave him thirty dollars for the three men
> and then I said I'd like a receipt. He said, "THE BODY IS THE
> RECEIPT!" And that was the end of my conversation.

The serviceman who'd been struck on the head developed an
infection in his scalp and was ill for three or four weeks. With
Hartland's support he took the unprecedented step of filing a civil
suit against the Montreal police authority, and won.

Just after D-Day on June 6, Hartland was promoted to Group
Captain and abruptly transferred again, this time to Ottawa, where
he would stay for a year, working in the "great and glorious Jackson
building." Hartland's brother-in-law Tommy MacDougall had also
been posted to the RCAF headquarters there. With other "tour-
expired" officers, Hartland worked as a director of personnel, under
the command of Air Vice Marshal Jack Sully, from London,
Ontario, and Air Marshal Robert Leckie, from Glasgow, Scotland.

After about a few days I heard rumours that my appointment had been competitive. I had word that the Chief of the Air Staff wanted to see me and I went over to see Leckie. He told me about the fact that he wanted tour expired people in all the directorates and then he said, "I have to tell you another thing." He said, "You know Sully didn't want you." And he said, "I am telling you quite frankly, you had probably suspected it. You may have a difficult time. I'll tell you another thing; if you have really serious trouble, I want you to come and tell me about it."

I had to watch my flanks because Sully, in peacetime, had been in business and I think had probably had to play favourites a little bit. He always struck me as a very small PR type. He was quite a nice fellow, but he did have a collection of his friends around him. This is normal I guess, but it was of not much interest to me. I was trying to do what I was supposed to do. In fact I never had to go to Leckie and tell him that I was having this sort of a problem, real trouble with Sully … it would have been awfully embarrassing. Finally Sully got moved or retired or something and they brought Hugh Campbell back from 6 Group overseas and then everything was just dandy.

The source of the animosity Sully felt for Hartland remains unclear, but it may be simply attributable to professional jealousy, for at some point earlier in the year Hartland had been asked to be honorary aide-de-camp for the governor general, the Earl of Athlone. Geoffrey Eastwood, the principal ADC at Rideau Hall, had written to Sully to advise him of this in March, which meant that a summons from Athlone had priority over air force duties. Hartland may have been singled out for this honour for any number of reasons – Herbert had been an honorary ADC for Athlone's predecessor, Lord Tweedsmuir in Montreal, and Hartland's name may have been suggested by a member of the staff. It is also possible that Hartland may have been introduced by Lady Astor to Athlone and his wife, Princess Alice, at Cliveden in November 1940.

At any rate, Hartland was glad to have Leckie on his side, and it is not difficult to understand why Hartland respected him. The Air Marshal, who had transferred from the RAF to the RCAF in 1942, was highly regarded, known as "one of the outstanding men in British Commonwealth aviation." Described by the *Toronto Daily Star* as a "short, rugged man with a ruddy, pleasant face," Leckie had "the uncommon faculty of sitting completely motionless yet giving an impression of vibrant liveliness. You feel he wastes no motion or words – at the same time, he is … a man of great vigour."

As a stern taskmaster, Hartland tolerated no laxity in either behaviour or dress. He insisted that the personnel hold the same standards as all air force men, with "their buttons shined and buttoned up and wearing their hats and saluting officers and just marching reasonably down the street … not leaning against a lamp post picking their teeth … with their hat tucked into their belt and so on. I felt there had to be some sort of pride maintained in the corps." A newspaper article written by Blair Fraser took Hartland to task, calling him a "martinet" who wished to be saluted everywhere he went. Hartland wasn't put off by the journalist's accusations, but merely found the article amusing.

Hartland would later describe his time in Ottawa as uninspiring.

It was mostly frustrating … and dull, dull, dull, but [the work] did have to be done. And in my directorate there in personnel, I had all sorts of odd things. Canteens, bands, discipline, discharges, relationships of families of serving people, and chaplains also … all sorts of odd things like this were clustered under the Directorate of Personnel … discipline in all its phases, that included people returned from overseas or LMF [Lacking Moral Fibre*] cases and plenty of problems with that enormous number of enlisted people. So it was interesting to that extent but it never felt that you were fighting a war.

* Today this syndrome is referred to as post-traumatic stress disorder.

By 1944 most of the pilots who'd gone overseas with No. 1 Squadron had been killed. Those who were left kept in regular contact with each other. Hartland and Nancy Astor also kept up their correspondence, most of hers which began, "Dear Air Marshal (you must be that by now)," or "(I hope you are that by now)." The hospital at Cliveden had closed in the summer of 1943 and had been replaced by a new state-run administration, she told Hartland. Lord and Lady Astor had been very busy in Plymouth, helping the people in the aftermath of devastating air raids. "We are ... coming out to visit you after the war is over. Jean (Lady Lloyd) will have to bring her husband and I know you would like mine, but I am not at all certain we'd have more fun without them! Jean, being young and in love, doesn't understand that! ... Alice (Meanie) [Lady Astor's niece] sends her love and says she is coming to see you too."

Hartland continued to send parcels of food to the Astors. In April 1944, Lady Astor wrote, "I can never get over your unending gifts which really mean more to me than I can ever express ... I have to hide the Canadian cheese from the family!"

During Hartland's year in Ottawa he was invited to many receptions, ceremonies, concerts and dinners, both in his capacity as director of personnel at RCAF headquarters, and as honorary ADC for Governor General Lord Athlone. In December 1944 he attended a reception for Athlone and Princess Alice. In February, at Athlone's request, he joined the Governor General in Montreal to take him on a personal tour of Molson's Brewery. In March Hartland attended the opening of parliament as Athlone's ADC, and shortly thereafter was invited to become a "privileged member" of Ottawa's Rideau Club.

Apart from taking Lord Athlone on a tour of the premises, during the course of the war Hartland had little contact with the brewery in Montreal. However while on his Atlantic postings he had occasionally facilitated shipments of beer to various officers' mess stations, dealing with authorities when shipments were held up and ensuring that "carloads" of ale from Molson's were earmarked for them, in spite of frequent shortages. At the same time, the Canadian brewery was supplying beer to navy, army and air force units in England, through the British Ministry of War Transport.

During his time in St. Hubert, Hartland had learned from Tom that in October 1942 the *Curlew* had been formally handed over to the American Navy for war use, and that their beloved yacht had been refitted as a warship and entrusted to a new crew. (Following this sale, Tom, who had enlisted in the Royal Canadian Artillery but never got overseas, had been sent on a secret mission to the U.S. to purchase another privately owned yacht. For purposes of the purchase he acted as a civilian, but in fact he was commissioned by the Canadian government to procure it for the war effort. The U.S. was still neutral at that point, though Roosevelt knew about the "secret" arrangement.)

Following Germany's formal surrender in May, Hartland had begun winding down his duties in Ottawa. He would have no time off between his air force work and the family business in Montreal. On May 29, 1945, three months before his official retirement from the RCAF, he was called back to the brewery by his cousin Bert, who had succeeded Herbert as president in 1938.

> I do not wish to put too much pressure on you but you will realize that with the war in Europe ending we are taking stock of our position in regard to post-war planning and we realize we must get busy. During the war years we let a lot slide. As a matter of fact we did very little in improvements so as not to impede the war effort. Therefore, at the earliest possible moment we must start on these improvements. For this reason it is desirable that you return here at the earliest possible date. I would like to hear from you when you think we could expect to see you back in harness again.

Hartland replied to Bert and returned to the brewery as assistant secretary in September. There he joined the others back from service, including his brother Tom and their cousins Stuart and John Molson. Since 1939, eighty-eight employees had joined the armed services, including the four Molson directors; the staff, Hartland noted when he returned, was "pretty skinny." With Bert the only Molson left at the helm, the brewery had been, in Hartland's words, "coasting quietly through till the end of the war."

In spite of production cuts (necessary to comply with shortages and rationing), for the last four years the brewery had been understaffed and the staff overworked. The stress was evidenced by three near-strikes, the first of which had been successfully mediated by Bert; the second settled by direct conciliations to the workers; and the third, which resulted in eleven employees – who'd refused an order to return to work while their grievances were being considered – being fired. In 1944 the employees rejected an invitation to join an international union and instead formed their own, calling it the Molson Brewery Employees Association. Their contract would be renegotiated annually, incorporating fair handling of complaint procedures, improved working conditions, safety education, a shorter working week, rest periods and overtime pay.

By 1945 over a third of the 700 employees had been with Molson's for more than fifteen years, and seventy-four of these had worked there for twenty-five years. For the latter, Bert Molson instigated and established the "Quarter Century Club," whose members were given gold watches and their own lounge in which to relax. Similarly, for workers on various production lines the "Curlew Club" was set up "for recreation and rest so that all employees in their rest hours have the benefit of comfort and relief from monotony." At the same time, various organizations were established for Molson employees, including camera and rifle clubs, an athletics club that had its own bowling facilities and a lending library.

Until February 1945, six months before Hartland rejoined the firm, Molson's had been privately owned by family members. At that time, Bert anticipated that the company would see an enormous rise in sales once the war ended and would need money for expansion. As long as Molson's remained a closed, private and limited-liability company, growth would be inadequate to meet the need, and valuable market share points might be lost to other breweries if they couldn't respond to demand on time. In early 1945 the brewery's total assets were $11 million, and shareholders' equity was $9 million, with an annual net profit of $1 million. Bert initiated the procedures to change the legal character of the company and created a public company by splitting the existing shares twenty-five for one, creating 750,000 shares, of which 150,000 were offered for sale at $20 each on the stock exchange.

It was also with future expansion in mind that in 1944 Bert had purchased a block of land to the west of the brewery. The purchase reflected Bert's long-term vision of a series of expansions that would bring the capacity of the brewery as high as two million barrels a year. As Hartland later pointed out, this series of prescient decisions enabled Molson's to expand from a comparatively small operation to become the largest single brewery in Canada.

Settling back into life in Montreal was bittersweet for Hartland. He had to change the focus of his energy and become accustomed to more predictable routines at home and at work. He would be acknowledged throughout his life for his contribution to the war effort, particularly as a pilot in the Battle of Britain, for which he was awarded the Order of the British Empire (OBE) honour. But the high conflict in the skies was over; his days of military administration and its attendant privileges and frustrations were past.

Hartland would never fly a plane again, even for pleasure. As he explained to a *Globe and Mail* reporter, flying "is something you should either do a lot of – or none at all." It was all too easy, he added, "for fliers who get rusty to get themselves killed." His exposure to sports was now limited to attending hockey games at the

Forum, where he had maintained the family's box seats, and playing rackets with friends at the Montreal Racket Club. Business occupied most of his time, and family life revolved around Zoë, Magda and his mother.

Tom and Celia decided to live separately after the war. Like for many others life had changed significantly; they'd grown apart and become disenchanted with each other. During their separation and subsequent divorce, their relationship continued to be amicable; their four children (Deirdre, Cynthia, Eric and Stephen), ranging in age from 11 to 6, spent time with each of their parents. Hartland's brothers-in-law Larry Mather and Tommy MacDougall also returned in good health to their families and appeared to settle back into their previous vocations easily. Dorothy, the elder sister who was the closest of the siblings to Hartland, took to scolding her brother for being so strict with Zoë. Hartland continued to nourish his relationship with his MacDougall nephews and nieces, who with the rest of their family had left their house in Cartierville and moved in with Bessie on Ontario Avenue for the duration of the war. Young Hartland MacDougall, who had also gone to boarding school, spent some of his holidays with his uncle in Ottawa during his tenure at RCAF headquarters. Hartland Molson had become "like a second father" to his nephew, and the two would continue to spend time together whenever they were able.

The societal framework in upper- and middle-class Montreal had changed irrevocably. Former domestic servants had found better-paid work in factories, in many of which they were mass-producing appliances for consumers who needed them because they no longer had maids and cooks. Sustaining the growth of industrialization and a new social attitude, both married and unmarried women were joining the work force in record numbers; they were also heartily taking up untraditional habits such as wearing trousers and smoking cigarettes in public.

Some traditions were irrepressible, however. The St. Andrew's

Ball, which had been suspended during the war, was revived at the Windsor Hotel in the fall of 1945, with "more splendour than ever"; this year the event was hailed as the Victory Ball. Hartland and a delighted Magda joined over 2,000 others all sporting their most formal attire, the women in bejewelled ball gowns, the gentlemen in white ties and tails, kilts or military uniforms. The Earl of Athlone and Princess Alice presided as guests of honour in a ballroom ablaze with flags.

In October 1945, Lady Astor wrote to Hartland that she had decided to postpone coming to Canada until after the New Year, as her children wanted to have a "Peace Christmas" and she felt she ought to be with them. She wrote again in December, outlining her plans to be in Virginia in January and then to travel on to Florida. "After that I don't know but if I come to Canada I will let you know. I do want to." But by the end of February she was in California for a month, still "hoping I can stop a long time and go to Canada." But instead she would return home from New York in early April on the *Queen Mary*; she never made it to Montreal.

CHAPTER TEN

I N 1945, HARTLAND's first few months back in the brewery were spent interpreting and negotiating the changing reality of operations while becoming reoriented to civilian business life. He had become more serious-minded and more sure of himself, more determined than ever to live up to his responsibilities and to fill every day with as much useful activity as he could. To the advantages of family, education and position, Hartland would now be adding experience and ambition. His training and work overseas – first as a pilot and then in various levels of leadership and administration – had forged and fine-tuned his earlier convictions and abilities. It was as though the intervening years had served as a crucible which took his many burgeoning talents, hastened them to maturity and coalesced the best of them.

Though the idealistic 33-year-old who had left Montreal to follow the call of military defence in 1940 was very different from the man he was upon his return five years later, Hartland's appearance stayed much the same. Always immaculately groomed, an elegant and careful dresser, he arrived at his office in fashionable suits complete with Ascots, spats and shined shoes, his sense of personal style giving him an air of dignity and easy authority. Sometimes his conservative brother and cousins would radiate amused disapproval of his dandyism, shaking their heads and rolling their eyes. But if Hartland was aware of this he made no indication, and in any event their attitude didn't compromise the respect he earned in the hierarchy, which was firmly built on his aptitude.

As an executive secretary, the particular talent Hartland brought to the management team of his brother and his cousins was as much a reflection of his background in accounting practice as it was of his most recent series of experiences and his confident imagination. Moreover, among his key personal characteristics were impeccable manners, natural charm and an unfailing sense of courtesy. He worked well with the other directors, discussions almost always leading to unanimous agreements.

Minutes of bi-monthly management committee meetings record Hartland's contributions and that his opinions were noted, his suggestions acted upon. Tasks assigned him were promptly carried out and reported upon. He was able to synthesize information provided to him in sales figures broken down by geography, brand and sizes, and juxtapose these with industry analysis figures. Keeping a close eye on the competition, Hartland recommended modifications; he projected profit estimates and share earnings. In 1946 he proposed that the board consider employing a firm to carry out a study of the job and wage rates of Molson employees, and recommended undertaking research on employee profit sharing plans. He was appointed to lead a committee to arrange an appropriate reception for veterans who'd returned to work after service in the Armed Forces, and settled upon a beer and oyster party in the reception hall.

When the brewery purchased a sales and distribution agency in

Toronto in 1946, which became Molson's Ontario Limited (MOL), Hartland was made its president. On behalf of the company he purchased a property on Avenue Road to be used as their head office. To the board in Montreal he presented information on the standing of negotiations between MOL and the Ontario Brewers' Association and reports on visits he had made to other breweries in Ontario. He hired superintendent staff in Ontario and Quebec.

Hartland would play a critical role in an incident that arose in the summer of 1946. A manager for an agency in Drummondville who worked for one of Molson's competitors, National Breweries, was getting drunk frequently and quarrelling publicly, and the Quebec Liquor Commission refused to renew the agency licence there. As a result Maurice Duplessis telephoned Molson's and offered them exclusive rights in Drummondville. Molson's general manager informed the premier that "such an arrangement would be wrong, and could not be entered into ... because of agreements in the Quebec Brewers' Association." But the situation was prolonged and Molson's was in an uncomfortable position. Norman Dawes of National Breweries, incensed about what he called "political interference about his staff appointments," went to meet Duplessis to see if they could work out a compromise. Meanwhile, Hartland was authorized to impress upon Dawes and his partners that they considered the situation urgent, could not support their quarrel much longer, and that if the premier repeated his offer to Molson's the company would have difficulty refusing it.

Hartland's return had been economically timely, and now he made the most of unprecedented opportunities. While he had been away in uniform, the family business had worked its way through a host of difficulties under Bert's leadership, dealing with the short supply of vital materials such as barley malt and having to overcome equipment breakdowns without the aid of qualified machinists. Moreover, machine parts had been scarce or unobtainable, and the economy had been in a suspended state while resources of people, supplies and capital were funnelled into the war effort. Through 1946 and into 1947, drafts of the brewery's long-awaited plans for a new building program were revised and fine-tuned. Meetings to discuss the future were constantly interposed between the duties and daily reality of running the company. A dynamic expansion was about to be launched, the largest in their history, and one which would take the longest time to complete.

Hartland worked on the extended calculations of new production capacity and net profits, while Tom drafted and edited organization charts, display flow charts to model the plant operations and procedural manuals for all departments. The series of carefully-ordered expansions, which would take six years, would, over that time, triple the plant's production capacity while also tripling the company's gross profit, from $3 million to $9 million. The changes would be visible externally and internally. Capital investments in buildings and equipment would rise from $4.6 million to $15.5 million. These included an addition to the eight-storey brewhouse, new fermenting rooms, new cellars and a new bottling plant, while the old one was converted into space for storing inventory. New kettles were installed in the brewhouse and 100 brown and gold-painted trucks were purchased for local deliveries, replacing the small fleet of black flatbeds. At the annual meeting in December 1948, Bert announced, "For the first time in our long history Molson's does not own a single horse. An era has passed."

New records were set as production capacity gradually caught up with demand. Greater efficiency at lower cost was an integral part of the plan, necessary to cope with the price increases in raw materials and new taxes. The growing general prosperity was shared: employees saw payroll increases, extended vacations and equality of pay for women. Annual addresses to shareholders and fiscal reports read like panegyrics.

In September 1949, a celebration was held to mark the first year of production of a million barrels of beer. Bert spoke in front of an audience of agents and employees, praising "the quality of our product and the extent of our output" and singling out father and son brewmasters John and William Hyde, who between them had "established a unique record of 70 years in this responsible office." He further commented, "I said earlier that we have never been as conscious of history as perhaps we should be. The fact is we do not believe in living in the past; our history has been made by men whose minds and hearts were pointed to the future. In that spirit we must now consider our Millionth Barrel record as part of Molson history and say to ourselves, 'What next?'"

Less than four years after he had returned to Molson's, Hartland was promoted to the position of co-vice-president of the company with his brother Tom. At the time Bert Molson remained president, his brothers Stuart and John Henry were assistant secretary and general manager, respectively, and the latter's son David was apprenticing as an assistant to Tom and Hartland. To eliminate the confusion as to which Molson they were addressing, brewery employees referred to each of the family members by their first names, as in "Mr. Bert" and "Mr. Tom," a practice that has continued to this day.

Every day now the company filled and shipped a million and a half bottles of ale. In December 1949 Bert summarized another superlative-laden address at the annual meeting. "There has never been a time in Molson history when the future of Canada appeared brighter, and we look with confidence on our 164th year."

Hartland took a few days off for Magda's birthday and Christmas in 1945, taking her and Zoë up to the family home in Ivry, north of Montreal. It was enjoyable to be back at the country property which his grandfather, father and uncles had bought in 1909, and where Hartland had been staying regularly through the seasons of his life. The land, 1,200 acres encompassing three small lakes, was ideal for hiking, swimming, fishing or skiing, depending on the season. At the time, two large log homes accommodated extended family members, who would take turns visiting the property. Hartland determined that he would have another house constructed there the following summer, on a side of Lac Violon away from the others, where he could entertain his own guests and have more privacy.

The interval was short but restorative. Their return to Montreal after the New Year was followed by a trip to Ottawa, where the couple had been invited to attend a ball at Rideau Hall. Geoffrey Eastwood, the governor general's aide de camp, had first telegraphed, then written, to urge the Molsons to stay overnight following the ball and join the Athlones for luncheon the next day. Special permission had been granted, wrote Eastwood, for ex-officers to wear their uniforms, in case they had outgrown their tail-coats and had not had time to order new ones. For Magda, who loved an opportunity to dress in the highest fashion and wear her best jewellery, the event was the highlight of the winter.

Two months later Hartland took his first post-war extended holi-day in Jamaica, where he had promised to take his wife once travel restrictions were lifted. A popular holiday destination for many Canadians, Jamaica offered beauty, warmth, tranquillity and a con-genial social life. For Hartland, who had bought shares in the Jamaica Public Service Company in the 1930s and was now a director, the trip coincided with the company's annual general meeting. They flew KLM airlines from Miami to Jamaica; Hartland was "very much impressed with the difference the war had made" to flight service to the island.

The couple might not have expected that their 1946 arrival in Jamaica would be featured in the social column of the local news-paper. But Hartland's name appeared in the "Plane Arrivals" list with other notable Canadians, and next to the column, a photo-graph of Hartland and Magda flagged an article with the headline: "Hero of Battle of Britain Visitor." Hartland's friend and business associate, Russell Bell, president of the Jamaica Public Service Company, had alerted Governor Sir John Huggins, who sent a formal invitation to the Molsons at their hotel to join the vice-regal couple for dinner at King's House. Magda enjoyed their three-week stay on the island so much that before they left they made enquiries about booking a similar trip the following winter.

Hartland's first trips to Jamaica had involved flights from Miami to Kingston on KLM airlines. He wrote to Gordon McGregor, one of his former squadron mates and now head of the ten-year-old Trans-Canada Airlines. Hartland asked him if TCA was going to offer a service to the West Indies, but McGregor replied that it was extremely doubtful that they would be operating to Jamaica that winter or even spring. He would, he promised, put the Molsons' names "at the very top of our first West Indies waiting list, and if the service does materialize, I would hope that you people would be on the inaugural flight."

When Hartland and Magda returned for another month in Jamaica in February 1947 they flew from Miami to Kingston again, but the following year they traded flying for sailing. Although never vocal about it, Hartland had been much disappointed at the loss of his father's yacht, which Tom had sold to the U.S. Navy in 1942. In 1948 Hartland quietly bought another yacht, one that had been converted from a naval sub-chaser, christened it *Curlew* in the family tradition, and rehired Captain Thibeau from the old *Curlew*. Thibeau hired a "first-class" crew of six French-Canadians, including an engineer, deckhand and sailors. Hartland would keep the new *Curlew* for three years, before concluding that it wasn't a financially prudent choice, considering that his crew had to be employed year-round but that Hartland was only able to use the yacht for three weeks a year.

Upon his return from one of his Jamaica trips, Hartland found a letter waiting for him in Montreal from Waldorf Astor. He and Lady Astor were winding up their rest-holiday in the U.S. and were to be returning separately to England in early May. Waldorf, who was chairman of the Institute for International Affairs in London, was planning to come to Montreal to have dinner with two of the institute's local executive members on April 18 at the Ritz Carleton, and hoped Hartland would join them.

Hartland's re-integration into civilian business and upper crust social life was aided by the support of colleagues he had known before the war, those with whom he had forged strong friendships, who now heartily welcomed him back to the establishment. Through entitlement and past achievements, it was a natural fit. Because many of his friends were older, they tended to look upon Hartland's youth and war experience with a bit of envy.

War had made Hartland a hero, though he carried this knowledge with modesty and conscientious reserve. That others were drawn to him and actively sought his company was evidence that he was held in high regard. The name he had already made for himself attracted those who wielded power and prestige; trust, which began as a function of kinship ties, flourished with familiarity.

Those who knew and valued Hartland appreciated his high personal standards, natural intellect and his teasing, challenging directness. His wit, sophistication and style were all his own. Not only was he always immaculately turned out, but he was also physically fit. His demeanour was elegant and, in the right company, even courtly. Inwardly, Hartland was completely comfortable in the atmosphere of money and social standing; in conversation he was an amused participant in the subtleties of expression and body language that said little but revealed much.

The post-war rise of industrial capitalism and a new social consciousness whetted Hartland's appetite for new challenges, whether business-related or humanitarian.

He was learning that he didn't have to seek such stimuli – they would come to him. He was not tempted to become complacent, coast or slow down. At his office in the brewery he accepted

responsibilities as they were offered and executed them competently. He built up a strong reputation of versatility and reliability.
In and outside his profession, he found himself learning how to
negotiate the complex terrain of commercial operations, how to
deal with personalities and shifting power plays and how to weigh
his actions' political and social implications.

Magda's influence in Hartland's life had led him to become more
politically and ethnically conscious in a wider world perspective
and at home. As he formulated a sense of his own part in the social
picture and his base of knowledge and resources grew, he became
aware of his own potential power to enable events and effect
changes. His network of associates would be mutually helpful in
garnering support for causes large and small, from arts and sports to
social justice and political reform.

One of his earliest efforts was among the most rewarding:
Hartland and his brother-in-law Tommy MacDougall financed
Barbara Ann Scott's trip to Switzerland in February 1948 to compete in the Olympic winter games, where she captured the gold
medal in figure skating. Later that year Hartland was asked to join
the Canadian Council of Christians and Jews and lent his support
to the B'nai B'rith Youth Services and the Boy Scouts Association.
He took on the War Memorial Campaign fundraising project for
Bishop's College School, his alma mater in Lennoxville. In
Montreal he helped raise funds for rebuilding McGill University's
student dormitories.

In recognition of his public-mindedness, Hartland began to be
awarded memberships in countless sports and education-related
associations. Meetings filled up all his lunch hours, late afternoons
and evenings. He had taken on so many commitments that he had
to start turning down new requests, but worthy causes kept being
presented to him and he continued to make extraordinary efforts.
In early 1951, he accepted an invitation to be a sponsor of the
International Rescue Committee, dedicated to help bring refugees

from behind the Iron Curtain to Canada. He was elected to two boards representing the Montreal bastions McGill University and the Bank of Montreal, on both of which his father, grandfather and other ancestors had served before him.

When Hartland became chairman of a joint Montreal Hospital Fund Drive, with committee member E.P. Taylor and others, the organization reached their objective of raising $18.5 million within three months. The money went directly to the Montreal Children's Hospital, the Royal Edward Laurentian Hospital and the Montreal General Hospital, the latter of which had become structurally unsound. Tom Molson, chairman of the Montreal General's building committee, saw to it that nothing, from tiling to the arrangements of pipes and valves, escaped his detailed inspections.

Endorsements from Hartland were consistently thoughtful and discriminating. As a reflection of his efforts he was invited to many awards ceremonies, banquets and receptions, through which his name became more known and, inevitably, requests became more numerous. Some people were manipulative enough to try to use his influence to further their own personal gain. One such "operator" was Paul Parent, who approached Hartland with a request that he stand on an advisory committee for *The Social and Historical Register*, essentially to help screen applicants for membership in the publication, for which Parent was soliciting subscriptions. Hartland initially agreed, but soon realized he had been misled by a hoax perpetuated to line the pockets of the unscrupulous social climber. He sent a furious letter to Parent demanding that he withdraw his name completely from any association with his *Social Register*. "Such a situation is entirely distasteful to me," he added, and refused to answer Parent's obsequious reply. (When, four years later, Hartland's name appeared in the well established *Who's Who of Canada (1951/52)*, one wonders if he felt at all ambivalent about that.)

Magda was an ideal spouse for someone who recognized his duties more than his desires. She accepted that her husband's work at the brewery, outside directorship agendas and extra-curricular meetings kept him away from home much of the time. But when they were able to step out together, she enjoyed the occasions to the utmost, appearing in designer dresses and hats. According to one acquaintance, she was pleased and proud to be seen with her husband and thrived on being in the public eye. At home Magda was able to busy herself keeping the staff in tune to her perfectionist standards in household routines and played hostess to Hartland's business associates as well as their mutual friends. She did not, unlike some "Grande Dames" of Montreal, volunteer her time to charities, but lent her name to worthy causes so that others would be inspired to give. A reliable anchor who could also display a wide range of emotions at home and in private company, Magda provided both domestic security and a refreshing, colourful balance to her husband's demanding business career.

Zoë had left for boarding school in the fall of 1947, to come home only on extended school holidays – Easter, Christmas and summer. Hartland had chosen Netherwood, the girls' boarding school in Rothesay, New Brunswick, which had promised a "very strict, thorough education under competent instructors, amid healthful surroundings and wholesome influences." Both the headmistress and vice-principal were women from Montreal and graduates of McGill. At age 12 Zoë joined seventy-seven boarders and fourteen day girls, finding herself in the company of several friends from home including Ann Yuile, the daughter of a pilot from Hartland's old squadron.

Netherwood was one of the strictest Canadian boarding schools, where, remembered another pupil, Zoë's second cousin Verity Molson, "they lined us up in 'crocodile' formations to walk to church every morning." When Zoë's aunt Celia took the train down to visit, the headmistress refused to allow her to give the girls a gift basket of biscuits and chocolate, considering only hampers of fruit to be appropriate.

Nancy Astor and Hartland Molson had kept up a prodigious correspondence over the nearly ten years since they had seen each other. Waldorf Astor had seen Hartland more recently in Montreal, where he had noticed that Lord Astor's health had begun to deteriorate. Two of the couple's sons had written to Hartland as well. John Jacob "Jakie" Astor, the youngest and "most witty and amusing" of the boys, now in his mid-30s, had an unusual request.

> You may remember we met at my father's house, Cliveden, when you were recuperating early in the war … I am trying to get some Wild Rice and Wild Celery seed to put in a lake I have, to attract wild duck. It is impossible to get this in England, and the present Lord Tweedsmuir has told me Canada is the only place one can get it.
>
> I wondered if you could possibly get someone to send me a few pounds of each. It would have to be a gift! As you know, we cannot use dollars, and you are one of my few contacts in Canada. I hope you don't mind me asking you this.

Hartland replied that he remembered Jakie quite distinctly. "It might be added that I shall never forget the kindness and hospitality of your parents to me in 1940." Once Hartland received the letter, he made some inquiries about wild rice and explained to Jakie that it was hard to get, and the results reputedly poor. He offered to make more inquiries, however, and wrote again a month later. Jakie thanked him "for the trouble you have taken over my blasted duck problems," read through Hartland's "extremely thorough and clear notes," reconsidered his project and decided to abandon the idea of growing rice. (Some time later Jakie ran for parliament in Plymouth and won his mother's old seat there.)

Jakie's brother David later wrote to Hartland explaining that a close friend of their family's, a psychiatrist named Alistair MacLeod, was moving to Montreal. "My mother, being a Christian Scientist, has maintained a sparring relationship with him as, you will know, her religion makes her think that doctors are somehow connected with sin." Hartland assured him that he would look up Dr. MacLeod "and see how things go with him." He added, "I am not particularly alarmed about your mother's view on the worthy Doctor's profession, because after all she has never been overly interested in brewing either, and yet she has been a wonderful friend to me, and both Magda and I are very deeply attached to her."

In early April 1949 Hartland and Magda set out for New York, to sail from there for England. After staying a few days at the Ritz-Carlton, they boarded the Cunard White Star Line Steamship *Queen Elizabeth* the evening of April 12 and sailed the next morning. They had paid $1,090 for one of the best staterooms on the ship, an outside room with two beds and a private bath. Arriving in London on April 18, Hartland hired a chauffeur-driven car, with which he would make all his social and business calls.

High on Hartland's list of people to see in England was Nancy Astor. Hartland had sent a letter to her and one to Jakie, suggesting that if the latter was going to be "knocking around London" he would be welcome to join him for a cocktail. Lady Astor wrote from her London home in Berkeley Square, to Montreal: "I am delighted that you are coming over and can hardly wait to see you, and hope that you will come to Cliveden as soon as you arrive. This is to say that I shall be there, and awaiting you with open arms." When Hartland drove out to Cliveden and brought Magda to meet Lady Astor, he found her much changed; she was no longer MP in Plymouth, no longer made public speeches, entertained far less, now devoting much of her energy to directing her siblings and her grown children. Waldorf, whose health was quite frail, was staying with his stepson Bobbie Shaw in Kent.

One business-related appointment was on Chiswell Street, to

meet the president of Whitbread's brewery and be taken on a tour of the premises. In March, Bert had written to Whitbread's and other British brewers that Hartland "would like to get some view of contemporary British practice, and may call upon you." Hartland was also commissioned to buy hops while he was in England and have them shipped to the brewery in Montreal. After three weeks in London and a week in Paris, Hartland and Magda returned to Canada on the *Empress of Britain* sailing from Liverpool with their niece Lorna MacDougall on May 24.

A month after their return, a letter from Nancy Astor arrived, in which she waxed as enthusiastic as ever.

> *Having met your Magda, coupled with my affection for you, you may expect me for a long visit [this winter], but I have so many friends in Canada whom I want to see that you may have to take me on a tour! Just in a small car – I wish you would. It would be such fun stopping at all the little towns where my friends are. If you are anything like Waldorf you won't consider it fun, so I won't ask you to do it, but I do ask you to keep a lot of time for me!*

Once again, Lady Astor's plans to visit Hartland in Montreal did not materialize. She wrote Hartland in April 1951 from New York to say that she could only get to Toronto for one night and asked if he could go there to have dinner with her. He couldn't. Then she asked him if he could get to New York. "If you flew down it would be fun and I would have a family dinner on the 19th ... Please think about it." But Hartland was unable to consider it, being inundated with commitments including work, meetings and preparing to bring Zoë home from school.

A summer trip to Europe was being planned for Zoë and four of her friends, including Margaret Ogilvie, daughter of Hartland's old travelling companion Bart Ogilvie. The girls would be spending five weeks in Europe, escorted by Catherine, Duchess of

Leuchtenberg. The Duchess was a member of the Russian Imperial family, whom the Molsons had met in St. Saveur, near Ivry, where she and her husband Dimitri, Duke of Leuchtenberg, ran an inn for paying guests. The Duchess took Zoë and her friends to Europe, where they toured Spain, Germany, Italy, Belgium, France, Portugal, Switzerland and Austria by automobile. Lady Astor, having heard about Zoë's trip, wrote to Hartland, "Please tell me where your daughter is & if I can catch up with her I would love her to come to Cliveden – anytime from now until the middle of August when I hope to go down to our cottage by the sea."

In July Lady Astor wrote, "I cannot tell you how glad I am you are having Princess Elizabeth, who is nearly as remarkable as her mother, the second only to the great Elizabeth. A real wonder." She was referring to the Canadian visit of newlyweds Princess Elizabeth and Philip, the Duke of Edinburgh, scheduled to take place in October. Montreal Mayor Camillien Houde had persuaded Hartland to be joint-president (with businessman Wilfrid Gagnon) of a coordinating committee for the city's hosting days of the royal tour, to deal with the agenda of events there. Regular committee meetings were held through the summer and early fall, in which budgets were set and a program was organized. Molson and Gagnon drew up route plans for processions, booked venues for receptions and hired entertainment for luncheons and dinners. A fireworks display was added to the agenda, and a presentation to veterans. The co-presidents of the committee allocated various duties to other committee members and scheduled press-briefing conferences, which were held at regular intervals.

In honour of the royal couple, a banquet was to be held at the Windsor Hotel, and it fell to Hartland to organize the event. He was given a budget of $17,000, which would include the meals, musicians and decorations. The invitation list included a cross-section of Montreal notables, such as Montagu Allan, John Bassett, Philip de Gaspé Beaubien and his wife "Babs," Billy Bishop and his wife

Margaret, three members of the Bronfman family (Allan, Harry and Samuel) and their wives, Tom Molson's former brother-in-law George Cantlie, John Henry Molson and his wife Hazel, Bert Molson and Robert Reford and his wife Elsie. Seating plans were confirmed and a booklet of regulations and procedures for ushers and guests was drawn up. When the last details of all events were in place, federal authorities gave the requisite approval to the plans.

The royal couple's three-day Montreal visit marked the end of the Canadian tour; when it was over, on the last day of October, Mike Pearson and his wife Maryon accompanied the party on their RCAF flight from Montreal to Washington. Hartland's work wasn't finished, for he had to undertake follow-up duties for all the events and send official letters of thanks and appreciation to all those who had been involved. He wrote Nancy Astor on November 15, saying that although the work he did turned out to be a lot more complicated than he had anticipated, he thought the visit had been "a tremendous success." It seemed rather a miracle, he added, that they got through the program without "something rather appalling going wrong. Unfortunately I did not get any opportunity to talk to the Princess or the Duke quietly, which I would have enjoyed."

All across Canada their reception could not have been more enthusiastic, & in this 2nd largest French city in the world, it did our hearts good to see the way all races and creeds came out on the streets in the greatest numbers in our history. With a population of a million and a half, it was estimated that over two million people were on the route, or in other words, people went around to several points to have another look and give another cheer.

Hartland also wrote the Earl of Athlone about the event, who replied from Kensington, in London, on December 22, 1951.

I am most grateful to you for your excellent account of the visit to Montreal of two very charming people and full of intelligence. Your account of the entertainment arrangements of course amused me intensely ... I know all about [Houde] from among others no less a person than Queen Elizabeth. You will remember on that occasion Houde took her, I think to unveil some stone he had put up as a trysting place much to the annoyance of many ... I congratulate you on the way you coped with the meals and surplus numbers. Montreal most certainly produced the largest crowd and Princess E. was impressed with them and the reception they had from clapping and voices which are very shrill. They enjoyed their drive and all they saw. To my mind, Montreal beats the lot of the cities. In Ottawa the people are very silent on such occasions and do not show much enthusiasm except perhaps [when they] notice the driver of a car! Anyhow you can feel your arrangements had met with approval, and enjoyment by those for whom you slaved is worth the work and worry.

Bert recognized by 1949 that the profits being made at Molson's Brewery had risen to a point where the taxation level was unsustainably high and thought it might be advisable to change the capital structure of the company. To approach this in the wisest manner he contacted Walter Gordon, a chartered accountant and management consultant who was prominent in civic affairs, for whom he had high regard. Gordon (who would later be appointed minister of finance in the Pearson government) helped the company set up a new structure of shares and recommended that they be divided into A and B groups, separating non-voting from voting shares, thus gaining capital while enabling the family members and other key shareholders to maintain control.

In 1950 Molson's Brewery purchased land on the north side of

Notre Dame Street opposite the original premises for the erection of an administration building. They had been for years accommodating office needs in inadequate facilities, as Hartland described later, "bursting at the seams with makeshift space all over the brewery." In spite of production and construction problems, which they met with ingenuity and improvisation, expansions in the plant had led to unprecedented production and sales figures. Inspired to express his feelings metaphorically Bert declared, "Ever since 1945, the lights down the Canadian boulevard have been a constant green as far as one could see."

At the mid-point of the century most of Molson's beer was sold in Quebec, with an additional "satisfactory volume" in Ontario, a small amount to the Maritimes and a trickle to Newfoundland. Confederation of the latter province saw an increase in shipments there; at the same time arrangements were being made for exports of beer to Manitoba and Saskatchewan. The company also re-entered the American market, sending beer to New York State for the first time in ten years. For twenty-four years the wholesale selling prices had been unchanged; however, with the introduction of new taxes that fluctuated from province to province, the retail price was inconsistent. Bert noted that in 1950 taxes paid to or collected for governments by Molson's was $19 million, and in 1951, that figure had risen to $28 million, not including Liquor Commission profits made in provinces where all beer sales were made through government stores. Noting that the latter figure represented 55 percent of their total sales, they acknowledged there was no choice but to increase the price of beer, which they did reluctantly. As Bert pointed out at the annual general meeting, "There is a vague and ill-defined point above which prices cannot rise without mass consumer reaction. When that point is reached, the Law of Diminishing Returns inexorably functions; sales and tax collections drop, bootlegging begins, revenue collecting and police costs mount, jails are filled and a new and sorry chapter opens."

Bert admitted to board members and shareholders that he had more worries than the extent of taxation's effect on the brewing business. Despite what he saw as the fundamental wealth and vitality of the country, the general level of business in Canada gave him some concern. Hartland, who shared his perspective of national and international events from an investor's point of view, agreed. He and Bert discussed what the latter referred to as "too much economic tinkering going on in our world," including exchange and monetary controls, international customs and raw material deals, gifts of goods and arms to other countries, and "one active state of hot war and a never-ending cold war." It created a confused picture. Though Canada's resources were being well developed and the country had a high level of immigration with virtually no unemployment, both he and Hartland sensed some trouble ahead. The truth, as Bert worded it, was not without touches of irony and humour: "We have an extraordinary mixture of both stimulation and discouragement out of which ample justification could be found for gloom or happiness."

CHAPTER ELEVEN

ALTHOUGH HARTLAND hadn't seen Mike Pearson since 1940 at Cliveden, events marking his career had been regularly reported in the press. Pearson had left London in 1942 to become Canadian ambassador in Washington, in 1945 he attended the founding conference of the United Nations in San Francisco and by 1946 he had been called back to Ottawa by Prime Minister Mackenzie King to be deputy minister for External Affairs. Pearson's appointment marked the time that Canadian foreign policy started to define itself, with peace-keeping placed at the forefront of diplomats' and administrators' agendas. Co-operative global opportunities began to flourish. The North Atlantic Treaty Organization (NATO), which Canada joined in 1949, initiated the first appearance of Canadian forces in Europe during peacetime. To Hartland, it was fascinating to follow these burgeoning national and international developments and to discuss them among some of the people who contributed to their shaping.

In October 1948, Pearson had entered and won his first election, thus securing his place as minister of External Affairs with a seat in the House of Commons. Hartland sent him a congratulatory telegram, to which Pearson replied by letter on October 27.

> As you can imagine, I am very relieved and not a little pleased at having passed my first electoral test successfully. I realize, of course, that I may have a more difficult one in the future; but, on the other hand, I think I have learned something about election-eering in the past few weeks and possibly I shall be a better candidate next time. I should love to tell you about it some time as it was, to me, an immensely interesting experience which had its amusing sidelights. I am off to Paris on Friday and will look forward to seeing you when I return.

When Pearson was in Montreal Hartland invited him to early-season hockey games at the Forum, where they sat in the box seats that had belonged to the Molson family since the arena's inception. At one of these games Pearson told Hartland he was considering hiring the latter's cousin Percival Talbot (called "P.T." by some and "Pete" by others) Molson, to be his personal assistant. Pearson had met Pete recently, as their paths had crossed at External Affairs, and he had heard glowing reports from others about the young man.

A graduate of McGill and a Rhodes Scholar in 1941, Pete Molson had never made it to Oxford, joining the Canadian Navy instead. He spent the duration of the war at sea, ending up as a Lieutenant Commander in charge of a frigate in a food-supply convoy. Following the war, Pete's dreams of Oxford were forfeited again when he was given a chance to write the External Affairs exam – a notoriously difficult exam, in which he excelled – and immediately became a foreign service officer. For two years he worked in London, England, as private secretary to Canadian High

Commissioner Vincent Massey. When Massey returned to Canada (to become chancellor of the University of Toronto), Pete stayed on at the High Commission in London until he was posted to Berlin in 1948. There was talk that he might be called to Ottawa on the recommendation of those who thought he was a candidate for a brilliant diplomatic career. When Pearson met him, Pete was only 27 years old.

Two years later Pearson hadn't forgotten his first impression of Pete Molson. When a position of executive assistant fell open, Pearson called the young man back from Berlin and installed him at External Affairs in Ottawa. The challenge suited Pete's talents perfectly – he was able to apply his experience abroad and his sensitivity to international issues to many facets of work in the department. Pete's contribution was, by all accounts, complementary to Pearson's vision and abilities; it seemed his destiny to continue on this particular career path and that nothing would stand in his way to being promoted through the ranks.

In 1951 Molson's Brewery in Montreal was nearly at the end of its post-war expansion program. The new administration building had been completed and the new steam plant construction was underway, and despite the heavy tax burden, operating profits were still setting records. Future expansions on the original site were no longer realistic, given that all the available adjoining land had been purchased and put to use already. Recognizing a growing market for their beer outside Quebec, the board discussed for the first time the possibility of expanding into Ontario and building a new plant there.

Although the Toronto-based Canadian Breweries Limited (which owned O'Keefe, Brading and Carling breweries) had been eager to enter the Quebec market, they had so far been unsuccessful. President E.P. "Eddy" Taylor had made two attempts to take over National Breweries – first an offer to Norman Dawes, then another public offer to the shareholders – but both had turned him down. Finally Taylor increased his bidding price for the preferred shares and over a year managed to acquire half the company's votes, giving him effective control. Taylor dismissed most of the company's former management and appointed a new team of directors to replace the old, these actions inviting much resentment from the Montreal business community. Taylor didn't stop there, however. Attempting to circumvent anti-monopoly laws, he made National Breweries a subsidiary of Canadian Breweries, then changed its name to Dow Breweries, and introduced lighter lager brands to the market. Another Ontario brewer, John Labatt Limited, entered Quebec at the same time and launched a major advertising campaign. All at once Molson's, Dow and Labatt's were engaged in a battle for the Quebec market. Promotions took different forms as the contenders aimed at all strata of beer drinkers – Labatt's stressing the family's French roots and Canadian Breweries giving away millions of dollars' worth of free beer. The potential of television as a new advertising medium was seized upon in 1952; managing directors re-wrote adverting budgets, and the competitive brewers sustained deep cuts in their profits that year.

Like the other breweries, Molson's was dealing with new strategic competition and adapting to modern marketing methods, while at the same time developing plans to expand from Quebec into Ontario. Meanwhile Bert, who had been president for fifteen years and had long been considering retirement, decided it was time to do so. His departure necessitated at least two decisions: first, that a successor be chosen, and second, that a new family member be invited to join the management team. He had pondered the first question throughout the last year of his tenure and came to a decision that he kept to himself for a while.

The second question was relatively uncomplicated. As Bert was single and childless, and Tom's boys were still at boarding school, the choice fell between John Henry's eldest son Billy, then working as a stockbroker, and Pete Molson, engaged under Pearson at

External Affairs. Bert, Hartland and Tom all agreed that Pete's personal qualifications for a position at Molson's, in spite of his lack of business experience, eclipsed Billy's.

In December 1952, Hartland asked Pete if he would consider leaving his position at External Affairs to join the family brewery. He offered Pete a starting annual salary of $7,500.00, matching what he was earning as Pearson's assistant, and proposed that he spend the first year getting to know the business. After that he would be appointed as an assistant to the president or vice-president and would be trained for an executive position. Pete's wife Lucille, knowing her husband's talent and love for the diplomatic service, advised him against it. Instead Pete agreed to consider the proposal, and went to speak to his father Walter about it. Walter, who was ill in hospital at the time, had never taken his "turn" in the family business and welcomed the idea. His health worsening daily, in the weeks before his death Walter strongly urged his son to accept Hartland's offer.

Pete eventually acquiesced. In January Hartland brought up the subject with Pearson, who by that time was president of the UN General Assembly and chairman of the NATO Council. A date was fixed upon; Hartland told Pearson he thought May would be a good time for Pete to join the brewery. At the end of March 1953 Pearson wrote Hartland:

> *I am planning to go to the meeting of the North Atlantic Council which starts in Paris on April 23, and it would be very helpful if I could take Pete with me as I have done on similar trips during the last two years. I expect to be back in Ottawa about May 1st and to leave a couple of weeks later to fulfill certain speaking engagements in the U.S. It would be useful to have Pete around in Ottawa for those two weeks to hand over to his successor and to clean up the various matters that inevitably arise at the end of a parliamentary session. My suggestion is, therefore, that Pete*

might finish his work with the department on May 15. I know you well enough to be sure that you will be frank with me, but I hope that my suggestion will be agreeable to you and to your colleagues at the brewery.

A postscript to Pearson's letter read, "I look forward to Pete's departure with acute displeasure!" Hartland's April reply was characteristically courteous and straightforward in equal measure.

Thanks for your letter of March 27th about Pete. As we said when the matter was first discussed, we do not want to do anything to inconvenience you in any way; consequently the date suggested by you, about May 15, for Pete to leave your Department, is quite satisfactory.

When I look at your program, I can easily imagine that changes in staff do not go very far towards making life simpler, and I am sorry that we should be the cause of any discomfort to you. However, I think because of its particular nature our business can be excused for making demands on some members of the family, and in this case we felt that the opening we foresaw should be placed before Pete in preference to going outside for some stranger. It is probably unnecessary on my part to mention this as Pete told me that you understood the situation and were sympathetic.

It is difficult to imagine the enormity and extent of adjustments Pete had to make in exchanging his working environment of international diplomacy for that of his family's brewing business. During the first year of the company's management meetings, which he attended regularly, he was silent as he listened to the others discuss subjects ranging from manpower reports and sales positions to tank inspections, safety boots and foil versus paper labels. He knew nothing about the science of brewing or specifications of engineering; he'd had no experience with market analysis or accounting.

Hartland and the others interpreted his silence as a focused effort to absorb and understand his new role and failed to realize how ill-fitting a role it was. They saw Pete as a man whose abilities knew no bounds; they attempted to mould and encourage him to be an able administrator of their wants and needs. But over the years that followed, the problems, including their expectations and his lack of fulfillment, were never addressed.

Plans to establish a Toronto brewery had been underway since 1952. Tom and Hartland knew they had to proceed cautiously given the competitive climate in which they now found themselves. They had set up a numbered company for anonymity, and Hartland made several trips to Toronto to scout around the city looking for suitably sized lots in key locations. He found the perfect site in early May 1953 on Fleet Street, a prime piece of reclaimed land on Toronto's lakeshore not far from the entrance to the Canadian National Exhibition Park. The ten-acre lot, one third larger than the ground area of Molson's Montreal brewery, had railway and highway access and plenty of room for future expansion. The only problem was that half of it was owned by Canadian Breweries' O'Keefe Brewing Company. Hartland was well aware that E.P. Taylor was vigilant about avoiding and quashing competition, even going so far as to dismantle plants that he closed so that no rival could use them for future breweries.

To close the deal Tom and Hartland took no chances, and to avoid even the possibility that they might be recognized together in Toronto they travelled separately, holding reservations at two different hotels under assumed names. A lawyer facilitating the "cloak and dagger operation" drew up the offer to purchase under the auspices of the numbered company and was vague with the vendors about the principals. In the absence of the O'Keefe Breweries president, who happened to be out of the country that day, Canadian Breweries Limited chairman, E.P. Taylor, signed the deed of sale himself. When he discovered who the purchasers were, he was livid. Hartland described the denouement:

> *In those days advertising was severely restricted, and O'Keefe's had developed the smart dodge of continually parking one of their trailer trucks on the property so that it was, in fact a unique billboard in full view of the heavy lakeshore traffic.*
>
> *The day following the purchase, George Craig of our Ontario Division phoned Mel Kelly, president of O'Keefe. The conversation went something like this: "How are you, Mel?" Fine! Yourself, George? "Actually I'm rather upset today Mel." Oh? What's wrong, what's bothering you? "Your damn truck on our property, that's what! Will you please remove it?" There was a long pause at the other end of the line – and then an almost unrecognizable voice said, "Oh no! Not you people?"*

Choosing a successor to Bert as president of Molson's was not simply a matter of seniority or of proportion of shares owned, but of suitability. The three board members who were the likeliest candidates were John Henry, Tom and Hartland. Bert's brother John Henry had a valid claim to the presidency based on competent service and seniority. On the other hand, Tom Molson, as the largest shareholder, was also a serious candidate to succeed Bert. In some ways Hartland seemed the least obvious choice in that he was younger and somewhat unproven as a business executive. However, Bert felt that John Henry, by virtue of his age and outlook may not have the drive and energy necessary to direct the company's national expansion, and that Tom, uncomfortable with public exposure, lacked the requisite skills and character attributes to be an effective leader.

As he revealed to Hartland some time later, Bert had been thinking seriously for a year about who should be his successor and had already decided in his own mind that Hartland was the best choice to take the brewery forward. His conclusion was that Hartland's character, temperament and business training represented the right balance to ensure Molson's continuing progress and prosperity, and that he would be the best one capable of executing Bert's plan of national expansion and industry consolidation.

Although confident in his selection, Bert feared that family tensions might develop if he pressed his choice against the others' tacit expectations. Believing that the best interests of the company and family harmony would be served by having his decision validated by an independent third party, Bert suggested that Molson's again retain Walter Gordon for professional advice, and the directors agreed. Gordon interviewed all the candidates and their senior management colleagues, and studied the implications of personnel shuffles of responsibility, then prepared a report that addressed the issue of succession. The report, which made recommendations to modernize Molson's board and management structure, concluded that Hartland was the best individual to lead the brewery.

To some of his closest colleagues, Hartland was very open about how his relationship both with his cousin John and brother Tom changed somewhat for the worse when he was appointed in preference to either of them. Even with the understanding of the role Walter Gordon had played as an outside advisor, Hartland felt that Tom Molson's family particularly long resented this decision.

Gordon's recommendations were promptly implemented. A special general meeting of the shareholders legalized the new appointments: Tom became the first family member to occupy the new position of chairman of the board, John Henry and Stuart became co-vice-presidents and the latter secretary as well, while former director of sales, Edgar Genest, and former assistant to the president, Campbell Smart, were elected to the board, increasing its members from five to seven. Pete took the position of executive secretary, and Hartland, the youngest of the directors at age 44, was the new president of Molson's Breweries Limited.

Molson's released an announcement to the press in June, detailing the new executive structure. At the same time, they made public their plans to build a large brewery in Toronto. They'd had no experience building a brewery from the ground up, the one in Montreal being a series of structures, each one having undergone countless modifications and renovations. Architects' blueprints and engineers' designs incorporated every want, need and efficiency into the new Toronto plant's design. The new plant, Molson's declared, would be "the world's most modern brewery." With the board's final approval, and a budget of $12 million, construction began in November. The name of the Ontario subsidiary was formalized as Molson's (Ontario) Limited, and David Chenoweth was appointed executive vice-president in charge of the Ontario operations.

The recession of 1953–54 didn't slow down Molson's construction plans, although it did force many small breweries to close their doors. Advertising costs (mostly channelled into the new medium of television) broke all previous records, and competition was fierce in an already saturated market. These conditions prompted Molson's to look at curbing expenses in the Montreal plant, where they were overstaffed. Accordingly, many of the older employees were offered early pensions, and 115 of the newest workers were laid off. Responding to consumer preference for lighter brews, after many months of detailed preparation and planning, the brewery introduced a new beer. This lager was made with rice malt and after some discussion the board agreed on a name – Crown and Anchor – and a new shape and style for the label. Encouraged by the positive market response, Molson's introduced a second lager beer in December 1954 and called it Golden Ale.

The Fleet Street brewery opened in April of 1955. Everyone marvelled that it was completed $1.5 million under budget and that only one year had passed between the assemblage of the first structural steel and the production of the first commercial brew. However, Bert's sudden death of a stroke on April 11 in Montreal prompted the Molsons to postpone the official opening of the new plant until the summer.

Tom and Hartland were sorry their cousin didn't live to see the project he'd initiated become a reality. Hartland reflected that under Bert's leadership the brewery had expanded from a comparatively small operation to become the largest single brewery in Canada. The company's financial performance during Bert's time had also been impressive: in 1945, when Molson's became a public company, it had total assets of $11 million, shareholders' equity of $9 million and an annual net profit of $1 million. On the date of Bert's retirement in 1953, these figures had reached levels of $27 million, $23 million and $4.5 million respectively. Over the next decades Hartland would frequently point out that it was Bert who had skillfully positioned the company to enable the growth and development it achieved later.

In August 1955 the *Toronto Telegram* devoted twelve pages of accolades and articles to Molson's Brewery, to commemorate the official opening of the new facilities. Accountants had predicted that the Toronto plant would lose money for a year before it began to make a profit, but once again the performance exceeded expectations. By the end of September the operation had broken even and would continue to expand steadily over the next several years. As Hartland's nephew Eric Molson recalled, "the construction crews stayed at that lakeshore site for twenty years."

In the spring of 1955 Hartland was in the full stride of his career. As president of the newly-expanded Molson's Brewery he directed successful promotional campaigns and was himself the subject of a new series of interviews and publicity. He continued to crowd much activity into his life, in business, philanthropy and family interests. He caught the attention of ordinary as well as powerful people as it became clearer that he was a unique and admirable person who had much to offer.

Hartland's personal image was one of unassailable style and substance. His past history as a pilot in a destiny-shaping battle and his experience in and support of amateur sport had not been forgotten by the public. He was already a life member of the Amateur Athletic Union of Canada and honorary patron of the Olympic Athletic Club. This year Hartland accepted two other prestigious positions, agreeing to become vice president of the Canadian Olympic Association and honorary president of the British Empire Games. Well-tuned to the needs of the community, he continued to give generously of his time to lower-profile charities and business organizations and rarely turned down any request. He endorsed fund-raising efforts at Bishop's College School, attended memorial services for his old RCAF squadron and agreed to be guest speaker at the annual conference of the Canadian Institute of Chartered Accountants in Toronto.

In July Hartland took a telephone call in his office in Montreal from the prime minister. The contact was so unexpected and Hartland so unassuming that at first he had presumed a brewery employee was on the other end, and to the statement "I'm Louis St. Laurent," he quipped, "Sure, and I'm the Prince of Wales." But the call was legitimate, to ask if he would accept a seat in the Senate. The prime minister offered Molson forty-eight hours to think it over. Hartland wrote Nancy Astor a week later:

> One of the larger surprises of my life occurred last week when Mr. St. Laurent, our P.M., asked me to go into the Senate. It was particularly surprising because this is the first time any non-political appointments have been made. I could not find any valid reason to refuse such a request, so altho' I never took your advice to go into politics, I find myself close to it. I wish I had some of your gift for speaking!

Lady Astor was encouraging. "I am delighted to hear that you are going into politics after all," she wrote. "You should have done it years ago."

Though he had never been affiliated with any political party nor spoken publicly in support of a politician, Hartland's point of view was generally understood to be liberal. However in accepting the appointment of a Senate seat (then, a lifetime commitment) he told the prime minister he needed to maintain his political independence and not be expected to echo the position of any person or party. St. Laurent accepted the condition, and thus, sitting on the crossbenches, one of the most important undertakings in Hartland's life began.

Hartland travelled to Ottawa and took his seat in the Senate chamber for the first time in January 1956, where he and the thirteen other newly appointed members took their oaths. Hartland would travel to the capital every week from Tuesdays to Thursdays, attend debates and committee meetings through the days and evenings, and sleep at the Chateau Laurier. For the first several months, though he applied himself to the committees to which he was appointed, he did not speak up during the debates. Senator Percival Burchill, who later became a close friend, was particularly kind to Hartland, welcoming him to the Senate and helping him become accustomed to the traditions of the chamber. One senator derisively mocked Molson's independent status, and called him a "mugwump."

It was not until November that he felt confident enough to speak out. The two subjects that motivated his maiden speech were Canada's participation in the emergency force for the Middle East and the recent insurrection in Hungary. He confessed that he felt hesitant to speak, "partly because of the very brief time I have been a member of this chamber, and partly because I realize my contribution will appear drab ... in comparison with the eloquence of my colleagues," but he spoke forcefully and with conviction nevertheless. He began by blaming American foreign policy for its role in Israel's decision to invade Egypt, sparking the incident that would later be referred to as the Suez Crisis. Canada, Molson pointed out, had to make "the most important decision of her young international life," between whether to follow Britain and France – their founding nations – or the UN charter, which denied war as an act of policy. Hartland praised Pearson (who would later be awarded the Nobel Peace Prize) for "his handling and presentation of our responsibility at the United Nations Assembly," which words were interrupted by a chorus of "Hear, hear!" from his fellow senators. He resumed, admitting that although he felt himself to be "the poorest authority on matters political," he believed that Canada's position in the outside world would be reflected by her actions at that time, and that it was the duty of the Senate to support External Affairs and deal with the situation as a matter of national urgency.

Hartland then turned his comments to address the vote on relief for the Hungarian people, who, after uprising against communism, had been invaded by Russian tanks and occupied by Russian forces. Hartland echoed the widely held Canadian sentiment that it would be wise to apply sanctions and break off diplomatic relations with Russia.

> It is difficult for anyone brought up as Canadians are, to speak rationally on this issue. Believing in God as we do, and accepting murder, rape, slavery, deportation, starvation, brain-washing and any form of torture to be weapons employed only by barbarians, how can we view the magnificent courage, the suffering of these Hungarian heroes without emotion? And conversely, how can we look on the actions of Russians without emotion? Perhaps the time has come to invite the Russians in our midst to go home … We can lend our full and unstinting support to the United Nations. We can open our doors and our hearts … we can open our purses to give a little mite of relief from suffering to those who survived within Hungary.

Arthur Roebuck, one of the senators present at the time, spoke next, calling Hartland's address "remarkable and excellent."

> *He is a comparatively new member of this house, and I under-stand this is his maiden speech. For his own gratification I would call to his attention the rapt attention with which he was heard, and the round of applause with which his address was closed. His very wide grasp of public affairs, the effective language in which his sentiments were expressed and the excellent viewpoints which he placed before us proves at once that he is indeed in his right place here among the elder statesmen of Canada. I wish him a long and happy sojourn among us. If he continues to give us the benefit of his wisdom and literary ability, I am sure he will occu-py an important place here and make a great contribution to the welfare of Canada.*

On November 29, Immigration minister Jack Pickersgill announced that the government would provide free transportation for Hungarian refugees who wished to immigrate to Canada. Hartland would follow up on his sentiments over the next several years by financially supporting many newly arrived Hungarian students at McGill University.

Hartland and Magda continued to attend their beloved hockey games at the Montreal Forum. Seated as usual in the Molson box just behind the players bench, they became more recognized now that the games were televised for the second season, and the cameras regularly caught them cheering for the Canadiens. Twenty-five years of radio coverage had been superseded by visual coverage and play-by-play announcers on French and English channels, the game periods interspersed with advertisements from the sponsor

Imperial Oil. Those days a vortex of controversy reigned over out-bursts of competitive fervour displayed by players and their fans. In the winter of 1955 Canadiens player Maurice "Rocket" Richard had been suspended, banned by President Clarence Campbell for striking a referee. The hockey idol was still off the ice by playoff time in March when Campbell was punched by an angry fan at the Forum, which triggered a riot. Never had collective passion over the country's favourite game seemed so out of control.

Hartland had many close ties to hockey, from the ranks of owner-ship and control through to the players themselves. The Canadian Arena Company (controlling the Forum and the Canadiens hockey team) was owned at the time by 75-year-old Senator (and director of National Breweries) Donat Raymond, whom Molson had known for three decades. The Raymonds' and the Molsons' box seats adjoined each other's – Raymond and Herbert Molson had been members of a small group who financed the construction of the Forum in 1925. Clarence Campbell, the president of the Hockey League, had played hockey with Hartland in Europe in the 1920s, as had Carl Voss, now referee-in-chief of the National Hockey League. Hartland's brother-in-law Tommy MacDougall was now a director of the Canadian Arena Company. And on the strength of a handshake, in 1953 Hartland hired Jean Beliveau, a rising young hockey star who had just signed a five-year contract with the Canadiens, to work for Molson's in public relations.

Donat Raymond's attachment to the Canadiens was a passion-ate one, and in spite of having received offers from several indi-viduals and syndicates, he didn't want to relinquish control of the club. Yet by the mid-1950s his health was failing and he feared that if he died, trustees might sell the club to the highest bidders who might not necessarily be best for the team. Tommy MacDougall, who knew Raymond was ready to consider selling the Canadiens, approached Hartland and suggested that he offer to buy the team. The idea appealed to both Molson and Raymond, the latter who had never forgotten that when depression arrived in Canada in 1930, Herbert Molson had been the only one of all the Montreal millionaires and bankers who had not cancelled their box seats at the Forum.

In spite of the fact that Raymond and Molson saw each other regularly both at the Forum in Montreal and in the Senate chambers in Ottawa, the communication was initiated indirectly. Raymond told Frank Selke, vice president of the Canadian Arena Company and the Canadiens general manager, to pass a personal message along to Hartland that he would welcome an offer, and Selke spoke to Zotique l'Esperance, Molson's director of public relations, who had a word with the president. Finally in 1957 a meeting was arranged between the senators on an August afternoon in St. Agathe, at Raymond's summer home. Raymond agreed to sell control of the franchise to Hartland and his brother Tom for $2 million.

As the negotiations had been so quietly handled, the transaction, finalized and made public at the end of September, came as a surprise to fans and sports reporters. Both parties refused to disclose the sum, which newspapers speculated was "one of the biggest ever made in the history of sport." Hartland's comments after the sale reassured the fans that they had no plans to change the management or its philosophies. "We don't own the Canadiens, really. The public of Montreal – in fact the entire province of Quebec – owns the Canadiens. The club is more than a professional sports organization. It is an institution – a way of life." The players must have felt the same way, for they went on to win the coveted Stanley Cup for the next three years.

Hartland and Magda drove up to their Ivry property almost every weekend, where Hartland would "survey his domain" in a golf cart. Family legend purports that he didn't know what name to give the house until one day he overheard Magda saying "fiddle-dee-dee" over something, and the name stuck. He referred to the property as "God's country" and took a great interest in its well being and in the family and people who worked and lived there. His eldest grandson Charles Hardinge would later describe Hartland's extraordinary attachment to Ivry as an exemplification of "home earth." Hartland's youngest grandson, Max Hardinge, would one day recall, "He was never afraid to get his hands dirty, and I have fond memories of helping him cutting down trees, and clearing paths down to the lake."

In those days at Ivry, depending on the season, Hartland went fishing for trout, golfing, or skiing, and entertained friends. He and Magda also valued the quieter times that they spent playing bridge or reading. Guests included the Astors' friend Dr. Alistair MacLeod, who'd recently moved to Montreal, and former pilot Paul Pitcher and his wife, who joined them frequently. A new guest in the summer of 1954 was Nicholas Hardinge, the son of the 4th Viscount Hardinge (then president of investment firm Greenshields & Company). Nicholas was a descendant of Viscount Henry Hardinge (1785–1856), British field-marshal and governor general of India, and Charles Hardinge (Lord Hardinge of Penshurst), Viceroy of India from 1910 to 1916. Nicholas, a junior executive for the Royal Bank in Montreal, had recently become engaged to Zoë. Shortly after their marriage, Hartland would help Zoë and Nick have a house of their own built on his property. The Hardinges called their house Simla, after the name of the summer residence of the Viceroy of India.

In the fall of 1954 the Princess Marina, Duchess of Kent, and her 17-year-old daughter Princess Alexandra made an official visit to Canada. Governor General Vincent Massey's aide-de-camp, Brigadier J. Aird Nesbitt, who was a good friend of Hartland's, suggested that the young princess might enjoy the company of girls her own age such as Zoë and her friend Eve Gordon, who was engaged to Hartland MacDougall. After attending a tea at the Ritz in Montreal followed by a dinner dance at the Forest and Stream Club, the young people "danced the night away" after dinner, the Canadians teaching Princess Alexandra how to jitterbug and do the Charleston.

Nesbitt had arranged with Hartland to have the royal visitors, their ladies-in-waiting and a team of Mounties there to protect them stay at his house in Ivry for the weekend. Accordingly, he, Magda and Zoë moved out of "Fiddle-de-dee" and had their own staff of five, including their butler, house maid and cook, re-organized for the royal guests and entourage. Zoë and Eve and other friends went riding at a lodge nearby, then played tennis with Princess Alexandra, while Hartland rowed around the lake with Princess Marina.

Hartland was to come into contact with members of the royal family very soon again. In May of 1955, Geoffrey Eastwood wrote to Hartland from London, England, to tell him that the Princess Royal (Mary of Great Britain) was planning to visit Canada that fall, including a stay in Montreal. Eastwood wrote that he hoped that Molson would be in town, particularly since the Princess Royal's itinerary included the official opening of the new Montreal General Hospital, which Hartland's fundraising efforts had helped to realize. The summer would turn out to be the busiest for Hartland in many years. The official opening of the Toronto brewery was scheduled in August, with publicity events spreading across five days. While Hartland was busy helping finalize plans for the royal visit, Magda was left to handle all the arrangements for Zoë's wedding, both events scheduled to take place within the first two weeks of October.

By now the Molsons were well-practised at organizing complex occasions, and both series of events were carried out smoothly. During the Princess Royal's stay, the reception at the hospital was particularly well received, and the hosts were grateful for her participation. The Molsons, who had helped to plan the local civic and private receptions, convocation luncheon at McGill University and official dinners at grand venues, enjoyed themselves at every event but were relieved when the four days were behind them.

Zoë's wedding on Friday October 14 at Christ Church Cathedral was a sumptuous affair where the bride, Magda and Viscountess Hardinge all wore Christian Dior dresses, and five bridesmaids shone in "frocks of golden yellow paper taffeta." For a wedding gift, Zoë's godfather Billy Bishop gave the couple an octagonal china bowl and Lady Astor sent six silver Georgian teaspoons. The ceremony was followed by a reception at Bessie's house on Ontario Avenue; the next day the couple left for a European honeymoon.

That autumn Hartland was also involved in introducing a new and unique labour agreement for the 1,100 employees at the brewery. When finalized, the contract – the first of its kind in North America – guaranteed weekly wages, lay-off payments and sick pay for up to a year. Punch-clocks were eliminated and the weekly wage ranges increased. In an interview with the *Montreal Gazette*, Hartland commented that the new contract reflected the good faith and understanding between management and the Employees Association of each other's roles. He would always take time to praise the employees, consistently holding them responsible for the success of the family business. "There is only one key which opens the door to success, and that is the quality of people. Integrity, location, machinery, solvency and background all have an important place in the portrait of a company, but it is only the people who compose the team operating the company who can use these tools intelligently and give life, character and success to a corporate entity."

A sudden explosion at the brewery in the early hours of May 18, 1956, left a large portion of a building badly damaged, with two employees injured and one dead. An ammonia tank had exploded, shattering all four walls on the eighth floor of the largest of Molson's fermenting and grain-storage buildings, and hurling bricks and debris for hundreds of feet in every direction. About twenty men had been on duty at the time, including 32-year-old chief night brewer Paul Cheese, whose body was found in a pile of rubble out on the street where it had been blown by the blast. A night foreman suffered a broken wrist and severe shock; another had multiple face wounds from flying glass. Although no smoke was visible, noted a reporter, "pungent ammonia gas billowed from a severed pipe, and a stream of partly-fermented beer and ale flowed from the building and bubbled back up through nearby sewers."

Distressed though they were to learn of the accident, over the next few days the Molsons realized that the damage could have been much more severe, and the loss of life much higher. An investigation was launched, following which demolition and rebuilding began. Engineering surveys and reports were studied and professional recommendations were applied to replace equipment, including twenty-five tanks.

Once the reconstruction of the damaged building was underway and stricter safety precautions in place, Molson's board members applied their attention once again to the acquisition of new plants – this time they had their sights set on the western provinces. Two years of speculation in the press was confirmed in October 1958 when Molson's announced a two-for-one split in their stock and the creation of 500,000 new shares to increase the company's capital. Hartland said the purpose of the change was to enable the company "if it sees fit, to acquire certain assets in connection with which we now are in negotiation." He would not elaborate, but did admit that discussions were taking place with Sick's Breweries "with respect to a possible association."

The discussions had been complex and difficult; however by the end of that year, Molson's had purchased the western chain of five breweries – one each in Vancouver, B.C., Regina and Prince Albert, in Saskatchewan, and Edmonton and Lethbridge, in Alberta – plus two in Washington State, U.S., for $4.3 million. It was Molson's first venture into the American market and would be managed separately. The Canadian breweries were all upgraded and converted to Molson's; with the addition of the potential 700,000 barrel output, the acquisition made Molson's Brewery's capacity the second largest in the country.

At the end of the decade, it seemed that everything Hartland touched was turning to gold. Arena ticket sales had been phenomenal, the arena selling out not only for hockey games but for boxing matches and concerts as well. The Canadiens had won the Stanley Cup three years in a row. Hartland invited family, old and new friends, business associates and some of the most distinguished plutocrats in the country, including Governor General Vincent Massey, who were all happy to join him in the owner's box at the games.

The publicity value accrued by Molson's Brewery through ownership of the team was also invaluable. The company already had exclusive national television rights to advertise during the Grey Cup football games, as well as the sponsorship of other broadcasts including French and English television sports panel shows. But the most lucrative advertising contract of all would soon be theirs, when they would take Imperial Oil's place as sponsor of the NHL games.

Hartland's Redpath Street house, which he purchased in 1939 and where he and his wife Magda lived until 1975. Photo: Courtesy Molson Collection.

Hartland Molson at the 56th anniversary of the Battle of Britain in 1996.
Photo: CP/ Montreal Gazette.

Hartland Molson was made an Officer of the Order of Canada at an award ceremony in Ottawa in 1995. Left to right: Hartland Molson, Governor General of Canada Romeo LeBlanc, Diana Fowler LeBlanc, and Margaret (Peggy) Meighen Molson.
Photo: Courtesy Zoë Murray.

Hartland seated beside his daughter Zoë Murray, and in front of his grandsons Charles, Max and Andrew Hardinge, at his 95th birthday party celebration held at the Forest and Stream Club in Dorval. Photo: Courtesy Max Hardinge.

Hartland's villa which he called Belmont, near Port Antonio, Jamaica.
Photo: Courtesy James B. Paterson.

Hartland Molson Charterhouse School photo. Godalming, Surrey, 1920.
Photo: Courtesy Zoë Murray.

Top: Flying Officers of the No. 401
Squadron relax between training
exercises in Hampshire, summer
1940. Seated left to Right, Deane
Nesbitt, Edwin Reyno, Hartland
Molson, Paul Pitcher, and (stand-
ing) Eric Beardmore. On the grass,
Otto Peterson and Dalzell Russel.
Photo: Courtesy Zoë Murray.

Right: Wing Commander Hartland
Molson, as a flight instructor in
the viewing tower at the Flight
Training School in Weyburn,
Saskatchewan, 1944.
Photo: Courtesy Department of
History, DND, Ottawa.

Hartland in RCAF uniform beside his Hawker Hurricane, in an airfield in Kent, summer 1940.
Photo: Courtesy Max Hardinge.

Flight Leader Gordon McGregor standing with flying Officers Jean-Paul Desloges, Paul Pitcher, and Hartland Molson, Croydon, 1940.
Photo: Courtesy Max Hardinge.

Hartland Molson, 1955.
Photo: Courtesy Zoë Murray.

Lester Pearson and Hartland Molson watch hockey game, 1965. Photo: CP/Montreal Gazette.

John W.H. Molson and Hartland at Molson Brewery in 1970.
Photo: Reprinted with permission from The Globe and Mail.

Eric, Hartland and Stephen Molson, 1996. Photo: Courtesy Molson Inc.

Listening to a speech at the official opening of Molson Industries' new brewhouse and reception area in 1986 are (left to right) Prime Minister Brian Mulroney, Premier Robert Bourassa and Mayor Jean Drapeau. To their left are Eric Molson, Jim Black and Hartland Molson. In the background CJG (Jack) Molson is flanked by two unidentified people. Photo: Courtesy Canadian Heritage of Quebec Archives.

Hartland, David, Tom, P.T., and Eric Molson, in the brewery's board room in 1966.
Photo: Courtesy Molson Collection.

Single-engine bush plane belonging to Dominion Skyways Limited, a partnership founded by Hartland Molson in 1935, with a shipment of Molsons Ale destined for a mining
settlement in northern Quebec. Photo: Courtesy Andrew Hardinge.

Hartland Molson standing outside the family business in 1978.
Photo: CP/ Montreal Gazette.

M.Y. Curlew, 189 tons and 117 feet long built for Herbert and Fred Molson in 1926.
Photo: Courtesy Canadian Heritage of Quebec Archives.

Hartland Molson and his
brother-in-law Larry
Mather, shucking oysters
at Ivry in 1955.
Photo: Courtesy
Elena Heard.

Back row: Hartland Molson, Bessie Molson. Front
row: Dorothy (Dosh), Herbert and Betty Molson,
Murren, Switzerland, December 1921.
Photo: Courtesy Zoë Murray.

Magda and Hartland Molson at Ivry in
the winter of 1957.
Photo: Courtesy McCord Museum.

Herbert and Bessie Molson's house and garden at Metis Beach.
Photo: Courtesy Zoë Murray.

Zoë Molson at her father's house on
Lucknow Street, in Halifax, 1942.
Photo: Courtesy Zoë Murray.

Hartland Molson at Ivry c.1924.
Photo: Courtesy Zoë Murray.

Hartland Molson, age 4, look-
ing at the St. Lawrence River
from the rocks at Metis Beach,
Quebec.
Photo: Courtesy Canadian
Heritage of Quebec Archives.

Betty, Tom, Hartland and Dorothy
(Dosh) Molson with nanny,
'Culloch,' in Metis, 1911.
Photo: Courtesy Elena Heard.

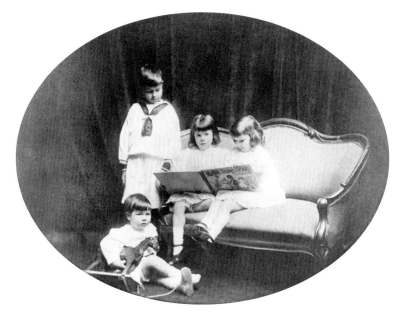

Tom, Dorothy (Dosh), Elizabeth (Betty) and Hartland Molson, 1910.
Photo: Courtesy Molson Collection.

Tom, Hartland and their father Herbert Molson, outside their house in Montreal, 1915.
Like other young sons of officers, eight-year-old Hartland was keen and proud to wear
his own Black Watch uniform. Photo: Courtesy Molson Collection.

Hartland Molson Charterhouse
School photo, Godalming,
Surrey, 1920.
Photo: Courtesy Zoë Murray.

H. DE. M. MOLSON
FORWARD

Hartland Molson, Royal
Military College football
team forward.
Photo: Courtesy Zoë Murray.

Herbert Molson
c.1905. Photo:
Courtesy Canadian
Heritage of Quebec
Archives.

Elizabeth Zoë (Bessie)
Molson c.1930.
Photo: Courtesy
Canadian Heritage of
Quebec Archives.

Chapter Twelve

ARTLAND'S MANNER HAD been wrought slowly by his privileged upbringing, but his politics were rapidly fused by his life experience. The combination created a dynamic that was difficult to resist, or at least impossible to ignore. Many treated him with deference tinged with awe. His effect on people, something he'd first noticed during his pilot years, seemed to simultaneously baffle and amuse him – yet he knew he'd have to eventually accept it and become accustomed to it. Though he'd never sought this kind of admiration or claimed to have earned it, he treated it respectfully. Hartland was certainly no egoist. Indeed if he felt any sense of entitlement it did not derive from birth or experience – rather, it sprang from his sense of duty. He negotiated a fine line between cognizance and reserve, maintaining a directness that was an attempt to span the invisible gulf that lay between him and so many others. Sometimes this backfired; some felt intimidated by and even fearful of him.

In the late 1950s and early '60s it was evident that Hartland began to separate his public persona from his private self. His outward manner became somewhat more polished; his unwavering opinions were conservative, his calm was genuine. In areas where he felt less confident he wouldn't hesitate to say so. He had grown far more comfortable with public speaking since the years just a decade ago when he had dreaded it. In fact he found he had a gift, that he spoke easily and well, many times without notes, and soon grew so at ease that he developed a characteristic humorous touch – a teasing, sometimes sardonic manner that often poked fun at himself but was never at anyone else's expense.

Since Hartland had become a senator, both the temperament and pace of politics had heated up. Under St. Laurent, who had been a leader of moderate nature and "gentle, upright bearing," the Liberal party had a strong majority and politics were stable and predictable. In 1957 when Diefenbaker became prime minister and Pearson the leader of the opposition, business in the House of Commons became more turbulent; many easy, unwritten rules were challenged, and the dynamics took on overtones which some saw as invigorating and others, as tiring and destructive. Serious issues – some with unprecedented implications, such as nuclear weapons testing – became more complex.

An ideological shift had taken place in the social and political climate. The government, as it had always operated, was now under close scrutiny. A whole generation of concerned and idealistic youth began to question their elders' values and formed groups that became active in non-violent anti-war protests, joined the struggle in the civil rights movement and spoke out against multi-national corporate interests. In sharp contrast, the French separatist group – Le Front de libération du Québec – whose original purpose had been to politically separate Quebec from the rest of Canada – began to organize in individual and independent cells, some of whose members planted bombs and threatened to shoot the Queen.

It was a challenge for Molson to keep up with the changing face and rules of politics and not become unduly anxious or agitated. Keenly aware of his inexperience and seeming lack of qualifications (admitting he was "extremely conscious" that he was one of the few senators who had not been trained as a lawyer), nevertheless he tackled problems head-on, familiarized himself with subjects by thorough research, and gave his opinions without reserve.

Although Hartland tried to keep as low a personal profile as he could when in Ottawa, he committed himself assiduously to his work as a senator. Whether the business of the day was mundane or stimulating – from making motions for readings of private bills or participating in debates – Hartland's contribution was significant. Very early on he took up positions on committees and subcommittees where he presented reports and frequently raised questions whenever he perceived weaknesses in works of legislation or their amendments. He participated in proceedings of the Transportation Committee, was appointed chairman of the Standing Committee on Rules of the Senate and became a member of the Committee on Banking and Commerce, the latter making relevant his professional experience.

Hartland believed he was "representing not any group or class, but a certain small section of the public," the English minority in Quebec. Asked once by a journalist if his privileged background was a help or a hindrance to his career, he insisted it was both; that the possibility of one's not striving to do one's best was more tempting because it was a viable option. The question was put differently during a CBC television broadcast in 1958 called *Men at the Top*. Again Hartland summed up his philosophy while answering a question about ambition: "What's the driving force that pushes a man forward in business?"

I think it varies with the character of the individual. After all, people are so very, very different. In some cases the sense of power would be the driving force, in others the acquisition of wealth. For very many people, I think, it's the idea of being able to achieve something in one's lifetime. When one's forebears have made some contribution in the business world, or in the community, one should try to do at least as much in the present generation.

In the Senate chamber Molson spoke often about issues that particularly invigorated him, one being the encouragement of young people's participation in sport. He believed "youngsters" needed to be given more support; that parents and society needed to take more interest in their development, not only by providing better coaching and facilities but ultimately also by making the child feel he was making some contribution to society. Moreover, he maintained, the rules and discipline in sport developed qualities of leadership, while teaching the "spirit of teamwork," demanding "quick reflexes and rapid decisions" and making "bloodstreams work to improve the tissues of the brain as well as the muscles of the body."

The problem of physical fitness needs to be recognized as an item of very real importance and made the subject of discussion between the various levels of government. It is an item of extreme importance to the future of this country. It would seem to me that … some method could be found whereby every boy and girl in this country, during his or her school years, would be exposed to some physical training. Then we would stop producing soft youngsters who puff after going up a flight of stairs, or who sit and gaze at television or who stand whistling on street corners. In connection with standing on street corners, we must remember that very few athletes ever become delinquents.

Hartland was vehement about his points of view, from insurance companies' stock performances to financing and guaranteeing bills for Canadian National Railways. He offered suggestions for how the government might support secondary industries and thus move towards solving the problem of unemployment. He worked tirelessly on redrafting archaic and unclear Senate rules, and urged that the Diefenbaker government initiate a "searching reappraisal" of the tax structure.

The senator didn't hesitate to challenge his dissenting colleagues, and often contradicted them with alacrity, consistently putting forward the merits of his logic and beliefs. In politics at least, it seemed the more difficult the dilemma, the more invigorating its effect on him. He applied his wide breadth of vision to every subject and he invariably offered points of view that were unapologetically rooted in the conservatism of his father's generation.

A Latin quotation from Cicero, which at the time hung on the wall of the Senate chamber, translated, read: "It is the duty of the nobles to oppose the fickleness of the multitudes." The patronizing overtones of this quotation did not strike Hartland or the other senators of the day as offensive. Hartland's attitude was characteristically stable in these times of hard decisions, and he maintained his points of view with great energy and rare ability. However, these strengths were not best used given the tide of social change in the '60s. Instead of attaching any relevance to the growing body of experimental and alternative social perceptions, or allowing any of the emerging philosophies to shape his contribution, Hartland resisted giving credence to new thought and operated instead through a retrenchment of his old positions.

During a debate on the amendment of the Food and Drugs Act in 1967, Hartland singled out Harvard professor of psychology Dr. Timothy Leary, self-styled high priest of LSD, who had published a major theoretical work addressing the evolution of consciousness. Calling him "vicious" and "wicked" and declaring that "he should be locked up, or worse," Hartland added, "anything that could be done to [him] would not be enough." Though this only echoed the sentiment of his peers, the thoughtless violence of such words proved to those attracted to Leary's philosophy of peace, love and expansion of the mind that the generation gap was inevitably widening.

As a young man, Hartland had been precociously accepted into an older age group, and he adopted philosophies that had been in keeping with those of his entourage, not necessarily with those of his contemporaries. Now that his elders were passing on and he was becoming the elder, the traditional values that worked to his credit in the past were now beginning to work against him. By 1972, when the Senate dealt with a motion to abolish corporal punishment, Hartland, like many aging politicians in the new era of erupting social change, could give the impression of being unenlightened and out of step with the times. In his day, boys at private schools were beaten regularly, and that form of discipline – applied "within reason" – was not only an accepted fact, but also thought to be beneficial. Though in the 1970s the public attitude was changing, Hartland stalwartly clung to the old adages, which to some served to show his rigidity and unwillingness to grasp new concepts. When speaking about this motion, his sharp speech was widely quoted in the French and English press.

I wonder how many members of this chamber were thrashed when they were young … I do not mean just a slapping of the hand; I mean a good whomping on the backside. I should think probably quite a high proportion of the members of this house have had that experience. I know I have, and remember it very well. I certainly remember it far better than the times I was kept in, had privileges reduced, forced to write a thousand lines, and suffered other punishments of that type. I would like to ask those members of the house who remember being beaten: can you look back and say it has embittered you, or made you feel hostile to society? If so, it is not apparent to me, but perhaps I cannot judge. I really do not

*think it ever hurt anybody unduly to suffer some physical punish-
ment ... I feel that the only lesson the bully understands, and the
one which frightens him, is a good old-fashioned beating ... They
will remember their beating, as I remember mine.*

In private company, Hartland was always able to be more animatedly "himself," especially when he was spending time with his
family. When his first grandchild, Charles, was born in 1956, and
his second, Andrew, in 1960 his joy and pride were unsurpassed.
Because the Hardinges lived in a house on Roslyn Avenue, not far
from Hartland and Magda, he could see them often. He arranged for
his own and Zoë's former nanny, Culloch, though now in her 80s,
to move in with the new mother to help out. When Zoë found a
Dutch nanny and was trying to make arrangements to bring her to
Canada, she asked her father if he could help expedite the process.

A dinner on Ontario Avenue to celebrate the engagement of
Hartland's niece Cynthia Molson to Clive Baxter brought twenty-
seven family members together in early January 1959. Hartland's
Aunt Mabel wrote to her niece, Winnifred, that it had been "a
very jolly happy party." Hartland sat at the head of the table opposite his mother, and stood up to deliver a speech about the young
couple, with jokes and interruptions from the others. Winnifred's
brother Meredith Molson, the aeronautical engineer who had
worked for Hartland at Dominion Skyways and whom he had sent
to flying school in California, was at the dinner as well. Meredith
was now a member of a team designing, building and testing com-
ponents of the Canadian twin-engine sensation called the Avro
Arrow, the world's largest jet interceptor. Test flights the year
before had been extraordinarily successful; five prototypes had
been built; the aircraft flew at twice the speed of sound. But to the
shock and dismay of the Molsons and the entire Canadian aircraft
industry, one month later the $250 million project would be can-
celled by Diefenbaker and all the aircraft destroyed.

A reference from Nancy Astor's son David (editor of the London *Observer*) brought Hartland an invitation from Prince Bernhard of the Netherlands to attend the April 1961 Bilderberg meeting, held for the first time in Canada. This gathering of "men of outstanding qualities and influence" – including eminent statesmen, financiers, representatives of international organizations and academics – referred to by one as a "brotherhood of friendship and trust," represented the western world's highest echelon of financial and political elite.

Named after the hotel in eastern Holland where their first meeting had taken place, the Bilderberg Group (of fifty to eighty people selected by Prince Bernhard) had been meeting annually since 1954; it was now reputed to be the most powerful organization in the world. Each meeting was held in a different country, where an entire hotel would be taken over and closely guarded; participants attended sessions on site; all lived, ate and drank together for three days. The purpose of the private meetings was not to formulate policy or make conclusions but "to reach a better understanding of prevailing differences between the western countries." Meetings were closed and off the record, giving the participants the opportunity to be frank, to say what they really thought without fear of international, political or financial repercussions. No votes were ever taken, nor were statements issued after the meetings. Unfortunately the exclusion of the public and press also invited suspicion of the group's objectives, to the extent that they were seen as a "secret society" and fuelled conspiracy theories of global control.

Hartland's participation in his first Bilderberg meeting, held at Le Manoir St-Castin, Lac Beauport, near Quebec was a unique experience. Thirteen other Canadians, including Mike Pearson and Walter Gordon, made up the delegation of seventy-two representatives from Europe and North America. Each participant pledged not to repeat publicly what was said in the discussions; even the speeches, printed and bound for distribution among the members, omitted the names of those speaking. At this time, the group discussed such contemporary issues as the role of NATO in the world policy of member countries, the control of atomic weapons and the implications for Western unity in light of changes in the economic strength of the United States and Western Europe. With the memory of the last war still fresh in the minds of many of the attendees, Western protectionist policies were the norm. Hartland, being a product of his class and time, didn't nec-essarily have the ability or inclination to embrace a more equitable global political analysis.

Hartland's impressions at the Bilderberg conference were undoubtedly carried with him in his role and contributions in Senate sessions and committee meetings. After the election in 1963 brought in a minority Liberal government and Pearson became prime minister, Hartland would have more opportunities to rub shoulders at international delegations, to influence and be influenced by world representatives. A long-coveted trip to Russia materialized in early August 1964, when he joined Pearson at the latter's insistence and accompanied the Parliamentary Group who travelled to this country and Czechoslovakia. Pearson again invit-ed Molson to accompany him at the twentieth session of the General Assembly of the United Nations in August 1965, to be one of the parliamentary observers.

A Canada–U.S. Interparliamentary Conference spanned four days in Montreal and Ottawa in May of 1965. Hartland joined seven other senators including Grattan O'Leary and Sydney Smith, and eighteen MPs including Jean-Luc Pepin and Stanley Knowles, where discussion groups and plenary sessions dominated the agenda. The participants heard speeches by the U.S. and Canadian delegation leaders, and between meetings attended receptions (at the U.S. Ambassador's residence and at Montebello), and in Montreal toured the World's Fair Expo '67 future site, and enjoyed dinner at the St. James Club and a luncheon at the Ritz Carleton Hotel with mayor Jean Drapeau. Unlike at the Bilderberg meeting, press conferences were scheduled, and wives were welcome to accompany their husbands to the social events.

Municipal honours and obligations continued to be presented to Hartland, many out of Montreal. As early as 1960 he had received his first Honorary Doctorate, in Commercial Science from the University of Montreal. He was invited to the Grande Salle of La Place des Arts for their opening concert in the spring of 1963. In October 1966, Montreal's subway system was opened, boasting "tiled stations, op art, spacious comfortable cars, and a swift, quiet ride," all for twenty cents. Molson obliged the city and the press with a photo opportunity by depositing the first ticket stub at the Metro station under the Forum; he and a city councillor rode the train on its six-minute run from Atwater to Berri Street. Though not a fan of op art, Molson was quoted in the *Gazette* as saying the stations were "tasteful and practical," and that he was very impressed with the ride, which was the quietest and smoothest he'd ever experienced.

In spite of his seemingly infinite stores of energy, Hartland recognized an increasing need to get away from public life for longer periods of time. When he took time off, he enjoyed extended vacations, seeking either rest or a different kind of stimulation. Early summer would find him fishing on the Godbout or the Bonaventure River. Winter and some summer weekends were reserved for Ivry. Hartland and Magda travelled to New York from time to time to visit her mother, to Europe to tour France and Italy for six weeks one spring and continued to spend many weeks in Jamaica every winter.

As their particular interest in Jamaica continued, their concern for the welfare of the country grew, and Molson was invited to become a director of the Jamaica Public Service Company. While on a tour of power installations of the island on behalf of the company, Hartland visited the Port Antonio area and was invited to a mansion called the "White House" on Alligator Head Peninsula. Next door to this property was an undeveloped lot known as "the mule pasture," then for sale, and Hartland decided on the spot to buy it. He would wait some years, however, before building a home on the property.

One winter Hartland chartered a 77-foot yacht named *Windjammer II* for a month, for $6,400.00, for which the owner provided four officers and men including a captain, steward and two deckhands. In it they cruised through the islands of the West Indies, where at one point the couple encountered Montreal mogul Izaac Walton Killam. Killam (who owned the investment empire Royal Securities and was said to be the richest Canadian of his day) invited Hartland and Magda aboard his yacht and to his house in the Bahamas. There Hartland was slightly embarrassed by Killam's daunting displays of wealth and extravagance; at dinner, he remembered, there was a footman behind every chair. Hartland was impressed by a story Killam related about how he gained control of Price Brothers Limited by first feigning disinterest and then outbidding a competitor who'd told him the amount he was bidding.

Upon his death Killam willed a generous amount of money to charitable foundations. One of his bequests enabled the formation of the Canada Council in 1957. One year later, Hartland established the Molson Foundation, a philanthropic body separate from the brewery whose mandate was to support "innovative projects in the fields of health and welfare, education and social development, and the humanities." Hartland and his brother Tom directed the foundation's first year's distribution of over $1 million to 300 organizations. In 1959 the foundation's gifts included $150,000.00 for construction of male students' residences at McGill and hundreds of thousands of dollars to a number of research foundations. The brothers earmarked nearly $1 million to endow annual Molson Prizes through the Canada Council, for achievements in arts, humanities and social sciences. The first two of these prizes, awarded in 1964, went to nationalist historian Donald Creighton and Quebec poet Alain Grandbois.

Philanthropy was always an important part of Hartland's life; the establishment of the Molson Foundation continued to be, over the years and decades that followed, one of the accomplishments of which he was most proud. His own contributions to the foundation were larger than those of other family members, however, and his often-expressed wish that others give more generously became an ongoing source of acrimony between Hartland and Tom, and later, Tom's sons Eric and Stephen.

Hartland's circle of friends and family began to diminish when death took its toll on the oldest of them. Billy Bishop passed away in Montreal in September of 1956; his funeral, at which Hartland was asked to be a pallbearer, attracted thousands who knew or admired Bishop. Senator Donat Raymond died in 1963, and in 1964, Lady Astor succumbed to a short illness. Hartland's mother Bessie died peacefully at age 94 in the summer of 1969. She had, said Hartland, "been pretty well immobilized for some years, and in recent months age had caught up with her to the extent that she really did not recognize us, nor did she get any pleasure out of life."

Other friends who began to spend time in Hartland's social orbit of the 1960s included businessmen, senators, politicians, accountants and lawyers. Senator Louis de Gaspé Beaubien became a good friend, as did Anatole Savard, Jock Findlayson, Ken McMurray and Harold Stikeman. Brother-in-law Tommy MacDougall and his sons Hartland and Bart, as well as former pilots Paul Pitcher and Deane Nesbitt, and the latter's brother Aird Nesbitt were frequent companions.

Hartland was unfailingly loyal to his friends, and with them he shared the pleasures of holidays and hockey games, luncheons at the Mount Royal Club in Montreal, the Forest and Stream Club in Dorval or the Rideau Club in Ottawa, and games of rackets at the Montreal Racket Club. The Pearsons often accompanied the Molsons to hockey games, where Magda and Maryon (a Toronto Maple Leafs fan) would vociferate their friendly rivalry. After a controversial call during one game between the Canadiens and the Leafs, Magda was observed shouting in protest and flinging her program at the referee. As Hartland tugged at her from behind to sit down, coach "Toe" Blake said, "Any more noise from the bench and you'll get a bench penalty!" The press was amused; Hartland, visibly chagrined.

Somehow Molson managed to effectively apportion work and time to his two major responsibilities, the Senate and the family brewery. The Senate was in session in Ottawa through the fall, winter and spring months, three days and evenings per week, which left Mondays and Fridays for Hartland to be at the brewery in Montreal. Much of the contact with both offices was limited to long-distance communications: at the brewery he depended on his faithful secretary Marie Desmerais (whom Hartland used to affectionately call "Miss IBM"), while on Parliament Hill, another efficient secretary, Claire Bourdon, took care of correspondence when he was away.

Hartland never considered giving up the presidency of Molson's Brewery in favour of his work as a senator, or vice versa. Before he assumed his Senate seat he had made it clear that he could only accept this appointment as an independent "because beer is sold through provincial governments of all parties," and he "couldn't get mixed up in the political fight and remain in [the brewing] business." Hartland was always scrupulous about avoiding conflict of interest positions. Yet it was inevitable that from time to time he would be questioned about the ethics of being the brewer of a product that was subject to being abused. "I'm all in favour of real temperance," he once countered, "and I'm completely opposed to prohibition. Beer is a drink that has been popular for a very, very long time. In England, during the war, when most things were in short supply, it was never suggested that beer should be rationed. It's a drink that helps, rather than hinders, moderation." "Of course, I drink it," he added another time, "but I don't spend my life doing that."

Though Molson's was the largest brewing company in the country when Hartland became president, the industry itself was highly fragmented and his brewery's market share was less than 10 percent. He realized that Molson's needed to adopt an aggressive expansion strategy and to participate very actively in the inevitable consolidation that the Canadian brewing industry would experience in the next fifteen to twenty years. In addition to executing Bert's plan to expand into the Ontario market, Hartland was also instrumental in overseeing his predecessor's more ambitious acquisition strategy that would result in the company becoming a truly national brewer.

Under Hartland's direction, the momentum of the brewery's growth through the 1960s was impressive. More land was purchased adjacent to the Toronto property for future expansions. Molson's had expanded out west by buying the chain of Sick's Breweries, including plants in Regina, Prince Albert, Edmonton, Lethbridge and Vancouver. The Fort Garry Brewery in Winnipeg was acquired in 1960, filling in Molson's gap in the prairies, and in 1962, the Newfoundland Brewery Limited changed hands from the O'Dea family to Molson's. Each acquisition involved delicate negotiations with the then family owners, and Hartland's skill and adroitness in having these companies become part of Molson's was crucial. All these companies and others were targets of the Canadian brewing industry's most aggressive consolidators, namely Canadian Breweries, Labatt's and Molson's. Molson's success in acquiring and expanding so successfully was to Hartland's credit; that he transformed the company in this way remains one of his enduring legacies.

Hartland's 21-year-old nephew Eric, Tom's oldest son, joined the family business in 1959, two years before Molson's celebrated its 175th anniversary. He had graduated after four years at Princeton University (with a degree in chemistry, specializing in the properties of yeast) and a course at the U.S. Brewers Academy in New York City. Transferred to the Vancouver brewery in 1960, he was recalled to Montreal a year later to become assistant brewmaster. Following an economics course at McGill he became assistant to the president in 1963, and travelled with Hartland to Newfoundland that summer to attend the opening ceremonies at their newly acquired brewery.

Eric was sixteen years younger than his cousins David and Pete, who had joined the brewery in 1948 and 1953, respectively. Pete, within five years of joining the company, had moved from secretary to assistant to the president, to assistant general manager and was about to be installed as vice president and general manager in Quebec. Hartland offered to hire David as his personal assistant and closely guide his career.

One thing David and Hartland had in common was their love of hockey. Like his older cousin, David had played the game in Europe, but he had also played in Molson's Brewery's commercial league. He began to move his way up the middle rungs of the brewery's corporate ladder, first appointed assistant manager of the Quebec division, where he worked with Pete, then promoted to vice president of the division. But as Pete was evidently the choice successor to lead the brewery, David made it clear to Hartland that his interests were drawn toward the hockey team. Hartland agreeably installed him as a director of the Canadian Arena Company, and in 1964 made him president of the Canadiens. Eric Molson then became Hartland's assistant.

Inasmuch as Pete's rise in the company may have caused some envy on his cousin's part, Pete was enduring some private torments that only Hartland and very few others knew about. For some years he had been admitted as an out-patient at the Allan Institute, a psychiatric hospital in Montreal, where he was treated for depression. To what proportion physiological predisposition, an unfulfilling career and an unhappy personal life played into Pete's disorder can only be speculated upon. Dr. Ewan Cameron's controversial treatments (experimental drugs and shock therapy) for depression and other psychiatric illnesses are still debated to this day, and whether he helped Pete or hastened his demise is still questionable.

In the summer of 1966, Pete was elected president of Molson's Breweries Limited. His wife Lucille had tried to talk him out of accepting the position, and said she thought it would be a mistake. They had been drifting apart over several months, and she had fallen in love with another man. That summer Pete moved into a room at the University Club of Montreal and began taking all his meals there. The weekend after Labour Day in September, he drove up to Ivry on his own. When he didn't show up for work on Monday morning, executive assistant Morgan McCammon telephoned Hartland, who was in his office preparing to leave for a meeting of the Canadian Paraplegic Association. He told McCammon to contact the guardian at Ivry. The guardian found Pete's body in the solarium, where he had shot himself through the roof of the mouth with a .410 gauge shotgun.

Hartland wept when he heard the news. Dealing with the physical and emotional aftermath of the tragedy was something for which he had no preparation. Apart from his personal grief, there was the shock and horror of his cousin's action and the decisions to be made within the family and within the organization of the business. How to deal with the press was another matter: calling Pete's death "an accident" seemed to be the only palatable conclusion to offer the public.

In his heart Hartland held Pete's wife Lucille responsible for the tragedy, and many other family members took up his opinion. In retrospect Hartland's uncharitable and even harsh treatment of her can only be viewed as an example of how ill-tuned he was to psychological complexities in people. He struggled with issues that weren't black and white and reduced behaviour to terms of good or bad and actions as right or wrong. So to consider Pete as a victim of difficult cumulative circumstances, to wonder about his depressive psyche, or even to speculate about which prompted which, was beyond his conscious reach. Part of Hartland's anguish was doubtlessly generated by regret that he had not recognized his cousin's serious emotional trouble. To allow his feelings of guilt to surface – the looming spectre that his own actions over the years might have played a part in Pete's state of mind – was inconceivable. When Lucille came to see Hartland at the brewery, instead of recognizing that she too was suffering, she recalls he was so angry and agitated that he verbally attacked her and then physically pushed her out of his office.

After Pete's death, vice-president David Chenoweth became president at Molson's Brewery. Chenoweth, who had formerly been president of Pepsi-Cola Canada Ltd., would be the first non-family member to take this position at Molson's: by tacit agreement, no family member would ever be installed as president again. At the time, Tom and Hartland felt that Chenoweth was better equipped to take care of all the financial correspondence with the trust company responsible for Pete's four young children's trust accounts and educational arrangements. A lump sum death benefit, allowed as an expense to the company, consisted of three months' salary.

A letter that Hartland wrote Lucille on October 12 conspicuously left out a salutation. "I am," he began, "enclosing a copy of a letter … which went forward with a cheque … for the credit of your account with the Trust Company. This is an ex gratia payment from the company which, under the tax law, attracts the minimum amount of taxation … It is our hope that you will find this a convenient nest egg to provide for unforeseen needs of the children, which are bound to arise from time to time."

CHAPTER THIRTEEN

I N 1967, WHILE Canada celebrated her 100th confederated birthday with special projects and events, including the world fair in Montreal, the separatist movement in Quebec was gaining momentum. Pearson, who'd come through another election in 1965 with a second minority government, had tried to give Quebec stronger representation and appointed a royal commission on bilingualism and biculturalism. The provincial government (headed by Quebec nationalist Daniel Johnson), while opposed to the FLQ's actions, nevertheless recognized the issue of independence for Quebec.

Meanwhile, Montreal's Mayor Jean Drapeau – who was committed to a bilingual, united country and was widely seen as an advocate for the province – found himself in a volatile situation one afternoon in July at City Hall. French President Charles de Gaulle, who was the guest of honour at a civic luncheon, delivered a speech from the outside balcony at City Hall to a responsive crowd below, and closed his address with some unscripted encouragement to the separatists: *"Vive Montréal! Vive le Québec! Vive le Québec libre!"* His words inflamed his listeners and caused shock waves across the nation.

Drapeau was appalled at the French president's breach of protocol and immediately rebuked him in a strongly worded speech. Pearson heard about the incident minutes later in Ottawa and called a television press conference where he stated that "certain statements of the President tend to encourage the small minority of our population whose aim is to destroy Canada; and as such, they are unacceptable to the Canadian people." General de Gaulle had planned to go to Ottawa the next day to meet Pearson; instead he cancelled the rest of his trip and returned to France. Later that day Hartland wrote a supportive letter to Mayor Drapeau. To Pearson, he drafted another:

> *May I, as one Canadian very deeply conscious and somewhat involved in the evolution of French Canadians in this country, congratulate you on your most statesmanlike handling of the De Gaulle incident.*
>
> *I thought your statement said all that was necessary, firmly enough, but with good manners and tact. I only regret that the General could not have found it possible to finish his trip, so that a little restraint on his part combined with the way I feel sure you would have received him, might perhaps have removed a few of the scars from which we are at the moment bleeding so profusely.*

By the end of the summer of 1967, Walter Gordon and others observed that Mike Pearson had aged noticeably. Gordon concluded that the prime minister was "disillusioned by his inability to obtain an overall majority, and seemed to have lost the interest he once had in policy issues and political strategy." Pearson was, in fact, exhausted. In December he announced that he wanted to retire as leader of the party and called for a leadership convention to choose a successor.

Pearson and his wife Maryon left for a holiday after Christmas, but had to return to Ottawa shortly after to attend the state funeral of Vincent Massey, where they once again encountered Hartland and Magda. The PM had been invited to Jamaica the following month to receive an Honorary Doctorate of Letters at the University of the West Indies and to deliver a graduation address to the students; the Molsons urged the Pearsons to join them at their Jamaican house afterwards.

Five years earlier, tired of the touristy milieu of Montego Bay and Ocho Rios, Hartland had started to develop his secluded two-acre property, a narrow promontory called Alligator Head on the north coast of the island, which he had bought in 1949. He hired Bahamian architect Henry Melick, and together they designed a 4,600 square-foot house and separate staff residence. The "tropical" style of the villa incorporated an open-plan design with tile flooring; high, wood-panelled "tray" ceilings and a roof of Canadian cedar shingles. Glass doors opened on every side giving all-around views of the sea and the magnificent vista of San San Bay. A verdant backdrop to the property at the west of the house was provided by a collection of bell lilies, palm trees and bougainvillea.

This part of the island was known for its spectacular panoramic views, lush vegetation and its solitude and tranquillity. The "White House" and property on the east side had been bought by one of the richest men in Europe, German steel magnate Baron Hans Heinrich Von Thyssen. On the west side, across the bay was Frenchman's Cove, owned by the Westons, where in 1963 the movie *Lord of the Flies* was filmed, and in later years would be the setting for more movies including *Club Paradise*, *The Mighty Quinn* and *Treasure Island*.

Mike and Maryon Pearson had been at the Molsons' for less than twenty-four hours and the four friends were playing a game of bridge when the telephone rang. It was minister of Trade and

Commerce (and acting PM in Pearson's absence) Robert Winters, calling from Ottawa to tell Pearson that a "routine" third reading of a bill in the House of Commons had been defeated. The minority government had been trapped; the House was in an uproar of confusion. An adjournment then an emergency cabinet meeting had followed, and Diefenbaker had demanded that the government resign. It was the most serious crisis faced by Pearson since he first took office. Arrangements were made for the Pearsons to fly home early the following morning.

The Molsons' telephone kept ringing throughout the evening, and Hartland fielded calls from reporters investigating and monitoring the story. He would not give them any information or let them speak to Pearson, though he was unerringly polite. "I can't reach him now," he said. Asked how Mr. Pearson had received the news of the government defeat, Hartland replied, "I'm sorry, I wouldn't know."

Maryon Pearson wrote from Ottawa to Magda and Hartland on February 22.

> *Chaos reigns up here & we think with great envy and nostalgia of our lovely visit to San San Bay! It was a brief glimpse of Heaven. It is hard to believe that all this Hell would break out because of missing a vote by 2 or 3 on a 3rd reading of a bill but such is the case.*
>
> *The Opposition won't allow parl't to operate at all and are refusing to allow a vote of confidence to be produced in the house. Constitutionally it is possible to bring it before the house tomorrow but Stanfield says they will not allow even the test of a vote to be proposed – what we do now is anybody's guess but an election seems to be inevitable.*
>
> *Anyhow this is to say thank you very much for all your kindness to us & to apologize for causing such a furor on Monday night – love to you both.*

And Mike Pearson wrote to Hartland the following day:

> *I don't have to tell you how bitterly disappointed we were to be obliged to leave your haven of beauty and repose almost as soon as we got there, and how distressed we were to put you to so much trouble Monday and Tuesday.*
>
> *I won't even mention the situation in the House. I must wish to express Maryon's and my own warm thanks to you both for wanting to take us "away from it all" for a few days. We had a very quick trip back, over the mountains, and on by Jet Star reaching Ottawa by 12:15. Since then, words can't be found.*

A caricature was published in the newspaper depicting Pearson reclining in a beach chair with a drink near his hand and Diefenbaker standing in front of him clad in an overcoat, earmuffs and scarf, lifting Pearson's sunglasses, and saying "Guess What?"

"GUESS WHAT?"

The problem in Ottawa was complicated by negative implications for the government as well as the opposition, given the various possible courses of action. House Leader Allan MacEachen pondered alternatives and by the end of the week came up with an answer to the crisis. A motion was carefully worded that tied a confidence vote to the one issue rather than the government's total record, and on the last day of February the motion was voted on; the Liberals emerged victorious with 129 votes. Hartland sent a telegram with his best wishes to Pearson the next day: "Delighted things back on rails."

Hartland and Magda attended Pearson's retirement party in Ottawa on April 4, the first day of the national leadership convention. Two days later, Pierre Trudeau was chosen as the leader of the Liberal party and became prime minister. Soon after leaving public life, Pearson accepted chairmanships of three successive groups concerned with the problems of developing countries. He continued to see the Molsons in Montreal and Ottawa. Hartland invited Trudeau and Pearson to the final playoff game at the Forum in April 1968; a photo of the three men sitting together was published on the front page of the *Gazette* the next morning.

Molson continued to support Pearson's interests and involvements, and at his request joined the national advisory committee for the Canadian Institute of International Affairs. The former prime minister invited Hartland to luncheon meetings at the Rideau Club in Ottawa to discuss committee matters. Their paths continued to cross over the next three years while Pearson was travelling, lecturing and working on his memoirs.

The year 1967 marked a turning point for Molson's Brewery, the beginning of its venture into diversification. This decision was made for several reasons. The Sick's Brewery acquisition in the early 1960s had included a 42 percent share of this company's Rainier Brewery in Seattle, to be managed separately from Molson's other plants. Molson directors then decided to look at other breweries in the United States and soon began negotiations with a western chain, the Hamm Brewing Company of Minneapolis–St. Paul. As the American senior executives were ready to retire and the Hamm family wanted to sell, the timing seemed perfect. Molson's lawyers in Washington advised that there would be no antitrust problem. However, after a formal offer was made to Hamm, the deal was abruptly halted – U.S. antitrust laws "stymied" the agreement, and the opportunity for Molson's to expand across North America was lost.

This failed transaction was a seminal event in Molson's history. The directors, seeking investment strategies for surplus cash in the business, knew further expansions were unrealistic and American acquisitions not immediately possible. At the same time, a trend to build conglomerates – later termed "merger mania" – was beginning to be *de rigueur* for breweries. Research was conducted that resulted in Molson's purchase of Vilas Furniture in July, a move followed less than a year later by the acquisition of Deluxe Upholstering.

That fall Molson's merged with Anthes Imperial Limited (a conglomerate of companies manufacturing pipes, scaffolds, furnaces, water heaters, boilers and radiators), issued new shares and changed the company name to Molson Industries Limited. Donald Gilpin "Bud" Willmot, former president of Anthes, became the president of the newly merged company; Tom retired from the brewery and Hartland was appointed the new chairman of the board. Willmot proceeded to diversify the company further by acquiring Aikenhead Hardware, Beaver Lumber, Willson Office Specialty and Diversey Corporation, an American chemicals firm.

By 1970, Molson Industries Limited had metamorphosed into much more than a brewery, being responsible for making things from petrol pumps to pressure pipes, hot water tanks, household furnaces, stainless steel barrels and construction equipment. They controlled three plants in the United States and had affiliations in Mexico and Italy. Gross sales came to $310 million. The directors and management team believed they were on their way to becoming a major world conglomerate, and projected that more acquisitions and even higher profits lay ahead.

Meanwhile, in 1968 Hartland and Tom Molson agreed to sell their controlling shares in the Canadian Arena Company and the hockey team to David Molson and his two brothers, Peter and William. David had been president of the hockey team since 1964, and although he still maintained office space at the brewery, the bulk of his time in and out of the hockey season was spent on sports administration. As early as 1966 he had written a letter to Hartland with an offer to buy the franchise for $2.5 million, a sum that he and his two brothers – Billy, a stock broker, and Peter, an insurance broker – would have been able to raise by selling the Molson company shares they'd inherited from their uncle Bert Molson in 1955. David knew that in January 1966 the Forum building, including its equipment and land, had been assessed at $2.8 million, and that the whole franchise – the team and the arena – had been evaluated in 1965 at $5 million. His proposal to Tom and Hartland, that they would sell the team for 25 percent more than they had paid for it nine years earlier, was turned down. But Hartland's reasons for refusing the offer at that time were not financial, as later events will attest. He was simply not ready to relinquish control of his beloved team.

The possibility of building a new Forum had first been raised at the end of 1965 as a means to resolve a combination of structural and accommodation problems. The forty-year-old building, though still in good shape, could have benefited from upgrades and modifications, as well as more seating capacity: season after season, sold-out games had left hundreds of fans waiting for years to get tickets. David began researching alternate building sites, but he was unable to find an ideal place with the right price. Another option, to demolish and rebuild the old Forum, was considered by the board of directors, but it too was discarded for financial reasons. A third option was to undertake extensive renovations on the existing Forum. With an estimate of between $8 million and $10 million, or two-thirds of the cost of rebuilding, the third option was clearly the most appealing.

Renovations, at first estimated to cost $8 million and to span three years (five off-season months per year), in the end were condensed into five months (or 118 days) of one year, entailing a cost rise of $2 million. Work began just hours after the final game of the 1968 playoff series, the game to which Hartland had invited Pearson and Trudeau to join him in the owner's box. David, who sat with them, described the renovation plans to Trudeau and invited the prime minister to attend the opening ceremonies of the "new Forum" five months later. That summer, phases of structural and interior modifications included the removal of all interior pillars (which had been obstructing the views of the fans), installation of elevators and air conditioning and replacement of wiring and lighting. A new lobby, box office and restaurants were constructed, and 2,000 more seats were installed in space that had previously been used for standing room. The new facilities now accommodated 16,500 fans, making the new Forum the largest arena in the NHL. So extensive were the changes that when the work was finally completed, only the furnace and ice refrigeration systems remained from the original building.

The renovations did not proceed without problems, but whether about cost overruns or worker incompetence, David confronted the general contractors each time. Another potential hassle developed that summer when some members of the press in British

Columbia began speculating that the Canadiens were going to block entry of the Vancouver team into the NHL. Hartland called a press conference, conducted by speakerphone between sportscasters in Vancouver and his brewery office. During the conversation, Molson hinted that David had initiated talks with other owners about expanding the league from six to twelve teams. One of the sportscasters wrote afterwards, "In all honesty, we were no match for the senator, who was all charm and sincerity and experience and didn't duck a question." The other sportscaster added, "The man's unfair. You come to one of these things prepared to be mad, and he disarms you."

Frank Mahovlich, a hockey player who later became a fellow senator, later said of Molson, "Never in my life have I met a person so passionate about the game of hockey." As Hartland explained to one of the sportscasters during the press conference, given how he felt about hockey and the Canadiens, he could not have let them go to anyone other than family members. But his action was also an example of how his altruistic impulses showed themselves inside the family as well as outside.

The legal transaction transferring ownership took place in August, for a payment (in brewery shares) of $5 million. Given the assessed value of the club three years earlier, the cost of the renovations, the increased real estate value, earnings potential and the increased value of the team resulting from the league's expansion, the worth was grossly undervalued; that it represented a gift on the part of Hartland and Tom to their younger cousins was clear from the start. When pressed to explain this decision, Hartland replied, "I believe that this approach, which places exciting colourful hockey ahead of financial return on investment, has been the main factor in creating the unique sports position that Les Canadiens enjoy with their fans in this city and province." David added, "We are conscious of the heritage and the trust that we undertake in assuming the majority interest in the Canadian Arena Company and the hockey club." In a private letter to Hartland, he admitted that he felt it was impossible to express his "sincere thanks and appreciation for every-thing that you have done for me since I first became your assistant in 1960 … I can only hope that your new role as an "ordinary fan" will not diminish your enthusiasm and support which have been for me in the past a great source of inspiration."

Over the nine years that Hartland and Tom had owned the team, the Canadiens had won the Stanley Cup six times and had finished first in the league eight times. After the sale, Hartland and his brother resigned as directors of the arena company and David became chairman of the board, president and CEO. Billy and Peter were made vice presidents of the company. On the evening of November 2, at the opening ceremonies of the new Forum, Pierre Trudeau arrived as promised to cut the symbolic ribbon, and he and Premier Daniel Johnson stayed to watch the first game of the season.

David and his brothers managed the hockey team competently and enjoyed their new status in the owners' circle of the NHL. The team continued to do well, winning two more Stanley Cups in the next three years. But Hartland's shoes were hard to fill: he had set a precedent of leadership marked by dedicated action on behalf of the team. As a member of the League's finance committee he had also played a vital role in strengthening owner-player relations and he had contributed to the cost of constructing the Hockey Hall of Fame building. Hartland's business background had been crucial during the establishment of the players' pension fund. Moreover, during and after his ownership of the team, Hartland fostered individual rela-tionships with team members, most particularly with Jean Beliveau, with whom he shared a mutual affection and respect.

Hartland's actions on behalf of preserving the integrity of the game of hockey in Canada had also been commendable, given that his was one of the few voices raised against the trend of growing roughness and violence on the ice. Boarding, charging and spear-ing, he said, irritated him beyond bounds. Even as a rookie among five veteran owners, as early as 1960 Hartland had begun writing

letters admonishing the other owners that refereeing was unsatis-
factory and there were too many injuries. To the press, he had said
"My fellow owners probably think I'm a panty-waist. But I still
believe that hockey is a rough game when played strictly according
to the rules; it could not be otherwise. But in the absence of strict
observance of the rules I cannot see any argument against criticism
of unnecessary roughness."

Molson had observed and pointed out that at least twenty rules
were constantly violated every game, with the full approval of all the
administrators. Either enforce the rules, he argued, or change them.
"The game is a great spectacle when played with the skill available.
It loses something every time some indifferent player makes up for
his lack of skill by breaking the rules." Managing director Frank
Selke, though he agreed with Hartland, said that coach Hector
"Toe" Blake pointed out "that while practically all the observations
are correct, he fears that if you make the objection official, the
Canadiens will be accused of being cry-babies because the objection
came on the heels of our first loss in recent years." When Hartland
had suggested that the rules of the game be printed in every program,
Selke argued that it would make for "very dull reading."

"I would be less than honest if I did not confess to a feeling of
regret," Hartland told reporters on the verge of the sale. The years
of owning the team, he added, had been the happiest of his life. But
operating the club had become more complicated each year and he
was unable to devote his full-time attention to its management.

Now, though Hartland would miss the close association he had valued with the players and the hockey club, he was able to channel all his
energies into the Senate and the brewery. At the same time that he
relinquished control of the arena company, he resigned his place on the
board of McGill University, a position he had exercised for twenty years.

In October 1970 Molson was honoured with a Human Relations
Award from the Canadian Council of Christians & Jews, "for his
personal qualities and character as well as contribution to Canada

as a public man." He was congratulated by senators Alan MacNaughton and Paul Martin Sr., who said his award "brought great honour to the Senate."

Lazarus Phillips, fellow senator, vice-president of the Royal Bank and another recipient of the Human Relations Award, had been sponsored by Hartland in 1966 to be admitted as a member of the Mount Royal Club. In this case and others, judgments Hartland made about people and situations were always concluded on the basis of intrinsic merit and never on that of being the right social, professional or political attitude. He was well aware of the passive but endemic anti-Semitism prevalent at the time in the circles in which he moved. In some respects the attitude of Canadians was changing, but there was still a strong residue of discrimination, particularly in Quebec, reflected in industries, professions, universities and clubs. Though quotas and restrictions imposed before the war had been lifted years earlier, a palpable sense of uneasy relations still pervaded the interiors of Anglophone and Francophone establishments.

Having been raised to respect the traditions of Anglo-centric men's clubs, Hartland would not take the aggressive step of boycotting them, nor draw attention to himself by boisterous agitation. He appreciated the benefits of club membership while at the same time reasoned that his efforts towards change could best be affected quietly from the inside. Beginning in the late 1940s he had been quietly challenging prejudicial admittance policies at Montreal's Canadian Club and Dorval's Forest and Stream Club. At the Mount Royal Club, where he had been a member since 1938, more than once he had spoken up for and sponsored Jewish and Francophone members: his first efforts had met with more surprise than resistance. After the 1950s when the focus of Anglo distrust had shifted from ethnicity to politics (communists had become regarded as the more serious threat to social order) the 1960s had readied the establishment to become more broad-minded, though there was still a long way to go toward cultural integration and equality.

Meanwhile the volatile political climate in Quebec had been steadily heating up. In June 1968, a riot at the St. Jean Baptiste parade culminated in the arrest of nearly 300 people. Santa Claus parades were cancelled that winter, and revolutionary slogans were painted on exterior walls. A strike of the Montreal city police was followed by armed attacks, arson and looting; radio communication was sabotaged; the tension was felt in all strata of city life.

The socio-political disturbances seemed to be beating a path that came closer and closer to the Molsons' door. In February 1969, a bomb destroyed the interior of the Stock Exchange building, where Billy Molson had a seat. The RCMP began conducting security searches through public and private premises. A rambling manifesto, broadcast by the FLQ on CBC radio in October 1970, singled out Molson beer: "*Oui, il y en a des raison pour que vous, M. Lachance de la rue Ste-Marguerite, vous allez noyer votre désespoir, votre rancoeur et votre rage dans la bière du chien à Molson.*" The kidnappings of James Cross and Pierre Laporte, followed by Laporte's murder, were interpreted by the federal government as a possible developing trend foreshadowing copycat crimes from other FLQ cells. A list of potential or likely people to be targeted by terrorists was compiled by the RCMP, and bodyguards were offered to those on the list, which included prominent Anglophones and federal-supporting Francophones. Hartland, David, Billy and Peter Molson's names were on the list, as were many of their friends and associates.

It was a very emotional time, and Hartland struggled to keep his composure as he delivered his speech in the Senate on the evening of December 1, 1970. His points were timely and appropriate. He claimed that though historically the English had come in and brought great developments to Montreal, there had never been any deliberate attempt to exclude qualified French-speaking individuals from positions of authority. He urged his fellow English and French Quebecers to "leave the past, with its recriminations and differences which evoke response from the heart instead of from the head" and to "tone down our emotions in order to admit recognition of the progress and allow fair chance to aspirations and promises of tomorrow."

Hartland further pointed out that the Quiet Revolution had begun ten years earlier, when economic opportunities for the French majority were poorer than for the English minority, "largely because of the inability to obtain an adequate education," but added that education had since been taken away from church influence to be completely revitalized and reorganized. Thus opportunities had been extended, and now large business establishments in Quebec welcomed graduates of the French system, Francophones were becoming leaders in businesses and taking senior management roles. He lamented the impatience for change, which was "bringing to light revolutionary symptoms." Why now, he asked, was there such an outcry, when there were finally such great changes underway? The economic wellbeing of the province was rising, opportunities were increasing and competition welcomed all those of skill and ability. In his view, it was simply impatience for faster change that had wrought the separatist movement.

Hiding under that politically respectable cloak we have the anarchists, the nihilists, even gangsters, who have brought us to the sorry situation where we require special legislation to cope with violence disguised as political action.

Do not listen to those trying to make political capital. Do not listen to those columnists, commentators or professors well known for their pink backgrounds. Proof was provided by the ballot box, when Jean Drapeau received an unprecedented 92 per cent of the vote, by two by-elections, and by the overwhelming support shown in public opinion polls. I think you can believe me when I say that the overwhelming majority of the people of Quebec want a situation of peace and quiet in order to get on with the vital task of improving economic and social conditions in the province.

During the years his grandsons were growing up in Montreal, Hartland made many opportunities to spend time with them. In January 1969, Zoë's third son Max was born; Hartland directed the chauffeur of his new Bentley to take him to the hospital to visit his daughter and new grandson. Andrew, who had just had lunch with his Hardinge grandparents, was not permitted in the obstetrical ward so was told to wait in the car with the driver for the hour that Hartland stayed with Zoë. When his grandfather returned to the car, Andrew recalled, he was horrified to find that his Bentley smelled of garlic rather than leather.

Hartland now had three grandsons, whom he doted on and adored. Andrew remembers that "he had a very soft heart and would always welcome us with open arms when we came to see him, and would always have several bottles of ginger ale reserved for us. It was a big treat for us as we would not get this at home." Andrew's older brother Charles remembered their weekends at Ivry, spending "magical evenings fishing with Grandad, with the lake clear as glass." Charles also remembered their "favourite but forbidden fishing hole, known more commonly as Grandad's Dock." Andrew concurs: "He would always get annoyed with us when he would catch us fishing off his dock as he would say the fish were reserved for his guests."

Hartland was indulgent with his grandsons, as he had been with Zoë. Max would remember "we as grandchildren looked up to him in awe." At Ivry at one time the Hardinge family kept horses, including two riding horses and a Clydesdale called Mirabelle, used for hauling logs. One morning Mirabelle "walked right through the fencing," recalled Charles, to graze the greener pastures of Hartland's "most prized and ... perfect lawn," and the other horses followed. Hartland telephoned the Hardinges at eight o'clock. "Do you know your horses are breakfasting on my lawn, and can you do something about it?" The boys ran out to find their grandfather "firmly attached to Mirabelle and neither was giving ground." To the annoyance of the groundskeeper, the lawn was badly damaged, but Hartland never spoke a word in anger about it.

Max maintains that their grandfather never forgot birthdays and Christmas, and always sent money so the children could choose their own toys and clothes. "This freedom of choice was always echoed by his comments that accompanied the gift. My fondest one was, 'Go buy yourself an oil well.' The gift was not in the monetary value but in his belief in our ability to make the right decision with it."

The year 1971 was a particularly busy year for Hartland. He and Magda left for Jamaica after Christmas and stayed through the first three weeks of January. After returning home, he left for France at the request of Pierre Trudeau, where he participated in a debate on cooperation in international development aid. In Strasbourg, Molson gave an address to the meeting of the Consultative Assembly of the Council of Europe and returned to Montreal at the end of the month. He resumed his routine of spending three weekdays in Ottawa, two in Montreal, and weekends at Ivry. In the Senate he participated in discussions about the Opportunities for Youth program, salmon conservation and corporal punishment.

Hartland and Magda joined David and his brothers at the hockey playoffs through the late winter and early spring, and saw the Canadiens win the Stanley Cup again. In June, rumours surfaced and circled through meetings of the NHL that negotiations were underway for a sale of the team. When the speculation reached Hartland's ears he questioned David, who denied it outright. He also refuted the story to the press, but added, "Anything, a hockey club or a house, is for sale … if the price is right."

In the summer, Hartland was irritated by an article published in *Canadian Magazine* by Tom Alderman, David Cobb and Paul Grescoe, that blazoned his name with nine others reputed to be the ten wealthiest men in Canada. The bold print on the page read: "Support your local Millionaire. He's the stuff your dreams are made of. Give him aid and comfort. Make him feel wanted. Really get to know him. Start here." The article estimated Hartland's personal net worth at $125 million, below Charles and Edgar Bronfman, whose collective worth was estimated at $400 million. Under Hartland's photo were the words: "Money doesn't come much older than this in Canada."

Hartland and Tom spent much of the spring finalizing, clearing out and preparing to sell the house on Ontario Avenue in which they'd been raised. After Bessie's death in 1969 the family had begun distributing her furniture and possessions, and once they'd decided the house would be sold, hired a real estate broker. The Soviet government made an offer, and following brief negotiations, purchased it to become their consulate.

In September Molson's Brewery introduced Brador Malt Liquor to Quebec and Lethbridge Malt to Alberta. Recent provincial legislation allowing for higher alcohol content, and a desire to stay ahead of the competition, prompted the move. Brador was 30 percent stronger than Export Ale; it was marketed at a "premium price" and heavily promoted. An article written by Dave Chenoweth explained that the new brew required a longer fermenting and aging process, and included a quotation from John Rogers, Molson's Quebec president: "We think of them (Quebecers) as being sophisticated in their purchasing practices – which is what led us to a premium beer." It was the first time the expression "premium beer" was used, and Chenoweth, who felt he had to explain what he meant, added "high quality." The first stock, estimated to last three weeks, sold out in three days.

Again, rumours were sweeping the city in mid-November that the Montreal Canadiens were going to be sold. This time, sports writer Pat Curran announced that the club was on the point of changing hands, and mentioned J. Louis Levesque as the buyer. This "gossip" was vehemently denied by David Molson, who became so irate that he threatened legal action against Curran. Again Hartland questioned David, who assured him there was no truth to the story. Reassured, Hartland left for Jamaica in December.

On December 31, Hartland received a telegram from David.

> *Tried unsuccessfully to reach you by telephone to inform you of sale of controlling interest in Canadian Arena Company stop Group headed by Jacques Courtois, Peter & Edward Bronfman stop Transaction completed 11 am today stop Regret this manner of connection stop Events moved very rapidly stop Letter follows with details stop Sincere regards to you and Magda stop.*

David's letter, dated December 29, read:

> *Last evening, I attempted to reach you by phone unsuccessfully. A cable was out of the question as you will appreciate. I had hoped that I could have informed you personally about the subject of this letter. Rapidly moving events and your absence made this impossible.*
>
> *On Thursday morning of this week, an agreement will be signed whereby Billy, Peter and I will sell our controlling interest in the Arena Company to a group headed by Jacques Courtois and Peter Bronfman. This decision was not arrived at easily, and I write to you with very deep and mixed emotions.*
>
> *There are many reasons which led to our decision. My first consideration naturally was Claire and the children who, over the past year and a half, have been subjected to various threats which*

resulted in police searches in the middle of the night, etc. Secondly, the fact that our investment is an immovable one representing for each of us a very large percentage of our total worth becomes more and more precarious in view of the political situation here and probably Government legislation with regard to professional sport.

Although I have not said this to anyone else, I have become more and more disenchanted with the internal policies of the N.H.L. as they relate to its future. The increasing American influence, planned expansion, and of prime importance the attitude of the new breed of hockey player and his demands make it no longer an enjoyment, and I see many storm clouds on the horizon. Those whose advice I have sought, including my father fully support the decision to sell as being both prudent and timely.

The group to whom we are selling first approached me some months ago and negotiations have been on and off until this week when they expressed the desire to close immediately. They are totally Canadian and have good French Canadian representation. The principals are Jacques Courtois and Peter Bronfman with minority financing from the Bank of Nova Scotia. I believe we are fortunate in having this calibre of purchaser, and are confident they will operate the club in a manner consistent with its traditions and in the best interest of hockey. Courtois will replace me as President and Governor of the N.H.L. The only changes in the overall organization will be the departure of Billy, Peter, and myself.

For obvious reasons, I wanted you to be the first to know outside of those involved, and only regret we were unable to meet personally. I can only hope that you will understand and accept the reasons for what has been done as you were the one who initially made it all possible. It has been a way of life for me over the past twelve years – the decision was not an easy one to make.

Please call me when you return. My love to Magda.

On receiving the telegram and letter, Hartland was stunned and

furious. He refused to believe that David had attempted to telephone him and interpreted his cousin's purpose and actions as
deceitful. Tom Molson was also very angry, as he had remained a
member of the Canadian Arena Club board; he read about the
transaction through the story in the *Montreal Star* the following day,
and telephoned his brother immediately. His name and reputation
were still so closely associated with the team that when Hartland
spoke to a sportswriter soon after, his words were chosen to deflect
any misunderstanding that he had been responsible for the sale.

> *Since 1968, my brother Tom and I have had nothing to do with
> the operation of the Canadiens hockey club. At that time we sold
> all our interests in the team to our three cousins … because we
> were sure that they would uphold the great tradition that had
> grown up around the club … I had promised the late Senator
> Donat Raymond to maintain this tradition, because the
> Canadiens hockey club has become an integral part of the life of
> French Canada and should continue to be so … [In 1968] we felt
> confident in turning over operations to [David] and his brothers.*

On January 5 Hartland issued a press release through the brewery.

> *It was with great surprise, and not until 24 hours after the official
> announcement, that Senator Hartland Molson learned of the sale
> of the Montreal Canadiens to a group of financiers. Senator
> Molson … did not attempt to hide his disappointment at the news
> of the sale … Surprised by the news while he was travelling out-
> side the country, Senator Molson could not understand the reason
> for the sale and was bitterly disappointed by this move on the part
> of David Molson and his brothers.*

Hartland continued to be most anxious to correct any misappre-
hension on the part of the public that he and the Molson brewery

had had anything to do with the sale. The press release emphasized that all connections between the brewery and the hockey club had been severed in 1968, with the exception of "an advertising involvement." Flatly, he added, "It has been nine years since David Molson has performed any administrative function at the brewery, and his brothers William and Peter have never worked for our company."

Hartland then wrote a brief note to David, which read: "This is to inform you that your name will not be resubmitted for election to the board at Molson's next annual meeting." When he returned from Jamaica, he quietly removed a framed photo from his office depicting Hartland with his three cousins on the day he had originally transferred ownership to them.

The English and French press speculated wildly about the reasons that David and his brothers sold the team when they did. One journalist suggested that David's brothers had exerted pressure on him to sell. Another wondered if it had something to do with brewery sales, that perhaps owning the Canadiens had had some adverse effect on beer sales, so that the connection had to be severed. A third demanded that David apologize to Pat Curran, saying, "It's the least he can do." Yet another wished him well, extended good luck to him in all his enterprises, and added that he hoped David would not forget those who guided him so well toward becoming a millionaire. *"La reconnaissance du ventre, a mon avis, c'est très important."* (Acknowledging who's feeding you is, in my opinion, very important.) For David and his brothers, the $13 million transaction represented a net profit of $8 million: the *Montreal Gazette* pointed out that they had saved an estimated $1 million by closing the sale when they did, forty-eight hours before the new capital gains tax came into effect.

None of the new owners – the Bronfman brothers, Jacques Courtois or John Bassett – commented to the press following the sale. One of the first actions of the new ownership syndicate came as a further blow to the brewery: John Bassett increased the price to Molson's Brewery for television sponsorship of *Hockey Night in Canada* by half a million dollars.

Feeling the wrath of his older cousin, David asked Hartland MacDougall to meet with him, and showed him the copy of the note Molson had sent dismissing him from the board. David asked his cousin if he would speak to Hartland on his behalf. MacDougall agreed to see Hartland and outlined David's reasons for selling the team. First, David feared that the formation of the World Hockey Association would diminish the value of the franchise. Secondly, the activities of the FLQ made the brothers feel that the longer they were in the public eye, the higher was the threat to their families. Before he could continue, Hartland interjected. "The third reason was greed," he said. "And those are three reasons why a Molson wouldn't sell."

In dismissing the possible validity of any of David's reasons, Hartland was revealing something that had always been fundamentally true about himself. Though not exactly naïve, Hartland had been an undeniably trusting person, and in spite of holding attendant earnestness in check and presenting a reserved exterior, his guilelessness had nevertheless been characteristic. He had always believed in the wholesomeness of the surface world, but doing so required maintaining illusions and repressing negative truths. One never mentioned anything unseemly. In such a world, something as simple as a handshake – such as the one that sealed his contract with Jean Beliveau – had been a typical symbol of that valuable confidence.

Throughout his life Hartland had believed in what he called "good faith," by which he meant that giving the best of himself, he expected the same of those around him. And one of the things he took for granted was that his friends and family members shared the same moral code, which lauded truth, honour and duty. That members of another generation were defying these values was deeply insulting and hurtful to him.

Trust – one of Hartland's great strengths – had suddenly become a tactical limitation. In the past he had been unable to separate moral from intellectual qualities in others: the "right" people had both, and were those who stood for the same principles as he did. In Hartland's mind, society had been made up of two elements: the respectable, hard-working people on one side, and a few scoundrels and hooligans on the other. Now he had to face the knowledge that there was an invisible and amorphous grey area he knew nothing about. For the first time, his sense of trust was deeply violated. The experience would change him irrevocably.

CHAPTER FOURTEEN

LESTER (MIKE) PEARSON died of cancer in December 1972, at the age of 75. Hartland and Magda attended his funeral in January, where Hartland was an honorary pallbearer. During his lifetime, Pearson had discussed with Hartland and former Liberal party president John Nichol his hope to one day sponsor a Canadian branch of the United World College foundation somewhere on the Pacific Coast. Not long after Pearson's death, Molson and Nichol held a meeting with Roland Michener and John Yarnell to discuss how to expand and develop their friend's idea into becoming a reality. The four men formed a board of trustees to establish the Lester Pearson College of the Pacific, to be erected outside Victoria, British Columbia. Nichol, who'd had a successful career as an investor and power broker, led a fundraising campaign to build the college; Hartland gave the fund a head start by donating $250,000.00. Government and other private sector support followed, a construction program began, teaching staff was assembled, and by

1975 the first students were enrolled.

The college, described as "an educational experiment to foster international understanding among students of differing racial and cultural backgrounds," offered full scholarship support for all students, who competed from all over the world for places. To cover the expenses, the trustees had to raise $1.4 million annually for the first several years; the funds were subscribed by governments of Canada and other countries, international foundations, business corporations and individuals.

Hartland's participation in the founding of the Lester Pearson College of the Pacific was not only a tribute to his great friend but was also in keeping with his many years of advocacy for young people. During his public career he spoke out often in the Senate in support of youth sports programs, while his private charities included the B'Nai B'rith association and the Boy Scouts of Canada. He also contributed generously to Bishop's College School, McGill University and the Royal Military College. For the last, Hartland established an endowment fund to help, with interest-free loans, those cadets who needed financial assistance to complete their courses. During the 100th anniversary celebrations of the founding of RMC in 1974, Hartland was thanked for his role as benefactor of the college and given an honorary Doctorate of Law in recognition of his support and distinguished career.

A second honorary degree was conferred on Hartland by Bishop's University that year, and a third distinction was bestowed through his election to the Aviation Hall of Fame. But no accolade could have been more appreciated or respected by him than his nomination and election to the Hockey Hall of Fame in 1973. Frank Selke had contacted Magda and Dorothy MacDougall and enlisted their support to help make the election a surprise for Hartland. The announcement in June was followed by induction ceremonies in Toronto at the end of August. Selke wrote Hartland,

Since the inception of Hockey the game has gone through several critical periods. One of these came during your presidency of Les Canadiens. Just think back to the danger of collapse of the Bruins, Black Hawks and Rangers. When you and Connie Smythe allowed your team managers to provide players for these teams, the NHL could easily have fallen apart at that time. Also Ted Lindsay's and Doug Harvey's ill advised formation of a players union, by which they planned to put the NHL teams at the mercy of two sharp-shooting New York lawyers, gave you and Jim Norris – supported by Ken Reardon in personal approach to Harvey – a chance to develop your diplomatic skills.

All of these fine attributes are as nothing compared to your personal worth as a truly great Canadian. I must tell you also that I am greatly concerned about the future of hockey in Canada. The trend is definitely pro-American – when Clarence Campbell goes the Canadian image will suffer … It was fun working for you; we had a great team and many pleasurable experiences.

Hartland's love of hockey, and the pride and empathy he felt for the team had not diminished in spite of the bad feelings engendered over the sale of the Canadian Arena Company in 1971. He never spoke about his innermost thoughts on the subject, but he now made an effort to avoid his younger cousins in social situations, going so far as to telephone clubs and ask if they were expected that day, before making reservations, to be assured that he would not encounter them there. He still attended many main-season and playoff hockey games, and kept in regular contact with several players including his friend Jean Beliveau. People still associated Molson's name with hockey and would continue to do so for many years. And although he no longer seemed to regard the world around him with characteristically reserved amusement, he still expressed his opinions with as much authority as he'd ever had.

During one Senate committee session in 1975, the members

were discussing proposed legislation respecting the Combines Investigation Act (now called the Competition Act). Having agreed there was a need for provision in the legislation covering professional sport (defined as an economic activity and an entertainment service), the senators began to discuss the connection between the profit-making motives of the players and owners and the related effect on the public. One senator suggested that competition had greatly improved the level of players' contracts, but Hartland disagreed that the increase was necessarily an improvement, as it made the tickets for the public double in price. He claimed that failure to amend the act (that is, to not address the segment of the population affected by rising costs in professional sport) prevented these people from benefiting from the legislation, and was therefore a form of discrimination. He also pointed out that the provisions didn't apply to organized labour such as the Hockey Players' Association.

> With the present competition, this particular entertainment has never been in worse shape. The thing has got out of balance. The public is paying too much money for seats, the players are getting too much money, and the cost of a franchise is getting too high … The quality of hockey has fallen off … These players are organized. This whole thing will do nothing to protect the public. The public can stay away in droves and they can kill hockey. As a matter of fact, the attendance is off a little bit. This will not improve the public's position vis-à-vis hockey, but it will give more strength to a group that is already, at the moment, a little bit overpaid and over–privileged. That is all it will accomplish.

Molson noted that during the history of the NHL, many owners had "suffered enormous losses" in order to keep the sport going. This, he believed, was a preferable situation to the one that had developed in modern times.

I cannot speak for the National Hockey League now because I am not closely associated with it, but the element of support always took precedence in the NHL in the years I was involved in it, and that went for all the teams I knew. There were dozens and dozens of examples of it. I am afraid that element may have changed somewhat. I am afraid that today ... the almighty dollar seems to take precedence, and that is highly undesirable.

One point of view for which Hartland became well known was his stance against abolishing the death penalty. He spoke out on this subject in the Senate in the first week of November 1973, and suggested that Canada needed to find a painless means of execution such as injection of a drug. Molson maintained that the death penalty was a more effective deterrent to crime than was imprisonment. There was, he said, a prevalence of crime because "society has accepted the cult of permissiveness." Three years later he was again arguing his point, referring to a "universally disturbing trend of disrespect for the law ... [which] starts at the top and naturally works its way down."

There has been a lack of emphasis on a firm deterrent punishment in the last few years ... a tendency to play down the seriousness of crime ... If, for example, we infer that murder is no longer as serious an offence as we thought it was, because we are not going to use the extreme punishment, at the same time we say that we put the other serious crimes on a slightly lower level. We push the whole list down a notch. Armed holdup becomes a little less serious; rape, robbery, theft and so on become less serious ... That is what I believe has been happening and to me it is extremely disturbing.

He expressed his cynicism about the philosophy of offender reform:

Organized crime has been playing a bigger and bigger role in my part of the world, Montreal … With the removal of capital punishment it will be even easier to … enforce the will of organized crime … [In Montreal there have been] vicious, planned murders committed by people … with regard to whom it is useless to talk about the bad breaks they had as children, or to suggest that if we took better care of them they could be rehabilitated. The people who commit that sort of crime are beyond hope, and … they are people we can well do without, and which society would feel better for eliminating.

Finally, Molson crafted his argument to appeal for the need for capital punishment laws to be in place to protect at least a certain part of the population: those involved in the police force and penitentiary services.

I think that if we are going to enlist good people to carry out functions in even greater danger, functions that require great integrity … I do not know how we can take away from them the greatest possible protection.

What is the effect of a twenty-five-year sentence of imprisonment? Will the prisoner be happy and say, "Thank God I was not hanged?" Is he going to go into this new hygienic penitentiary saying, "What a lucky fellow I am; where is my steak and colour television" and live there twenty-five years happily thereafter? It is reasonable to suppose that in spite of the aberrations or, in some cases, the viciousness of these characters, they are human beings. They are going to look forward to twenty-five years in a beautiful new pen with absolute horror … Will they think of the beauties of a country in which capital punishment has been abolished … or will they think of killing a guard or committing any crime to escape …? I suggest to you that we will produce a new type of criminal.

If Hartland's passion and cynicism were becoming sharpened in the Senate chamber, so was his wit. His 1976 comments on conflict of interest, though not reprinted in the newspapers, were characteristically reproachful and dismissive. Given the rule stating that "a senator who has any pecuniary interest whatsoever" should not sit on any committee related to that interest, it had been suggested by another senator that Molson resign from the Senate's Banking, Trade, and Commerce Committee because he was a shareholder and director of the Bank of Montreal. When a reporter had telephoned him to ask if he was planning to resign from the committee, he replied that he did not yet know. Hartland related part of his conversation with the reporter, who had asked, "What options do you have?" "Well," I said, "not many, but I think I have two – one is to resign and the other is not to resign."

To the senator accused of first demanding Hartland's resignation from the committee, Molson retorted, "This is a matter of my own pride, my own self-respect, and I am not prepared to come in here and have anybody, any more in this chamber than outside, cast any sort of aspersion on my integrity." To the other senators, he elucidated:

When I think of the Bank Act and banking in Canada and the size of the banks, and when I think of the trust companies in Canada and the size of the many trust companies, and when I think of the Caisses Populaires and credit unions, and when I think of the pecuniary interest that I or one of my colleagues here might have in something done to change the Bank Act … it occurs to me that the possibility of either pecuniary benefit or pecuniary damage is fairly remote.

If I may say so, I am a little concerned at the trend of the popular view of conflict of interest, because I think it is going a little too far. In looking at our various committees I am really concerned about who should sit on any of them. I have a valued colleague, whom I respect, who is the chairman of the Standing

Senate Committee on Agriculture. He is a farmer. There is no doubt in my mind that, in some way at least, he has a conflict of interest on occasion, but I do not say that he should not serve on the Agriculture Committee. I wonder whether medical people should sit on matters of health. I wonder if lawyers should take part in debates on capital punishment. Do they want to have their clients alive or do they want them dead? It is a fact that there is a conflict of interest.

Hartland never allowed anyone to forget that he took his independent point of view very seriously. Pragmatic and idealistic, he never violated his moral code. More than once he defended independence as intrinsic to the purpose of the Senate, and as the years went by he often denounced what he interpreted as a trend of partisanship pervading the upper chamber. In June of 1977 he said,

Today it often appears that the relative importance of some measure to the country and to the political party is distorted. The party in the Senate has become too important and I have made speeches about it. Sir John A Macdonald and other outstanding fig-ures have said the Senate shouldn't be a reflection of the House of Commons but rather a house of elder statesmen who think in terms of only what is best for the country.

Four years later, he was still expounding on the same theme, when he reminded senators that he always believed that they should forget their party duty and always vote for what was best for Canada:

At times I have found it very disturbing ... that there is such sub-servience, and a great sense of gratitude, to the party leader who appointed the lady or the gentleman to the chamber. I view the matter quite differently. When we are appointed to this chamber, we are called upon to do a job and the outlines of that job are made clear to us. While we may feel honoured and pleased that we have been selected for appointments, I do not think we should go around for the rest of our lives bowing and saying how grateful we are to somebody who was good enough to give us this nice job. If that is what the Senate is, I don't like it. I do not really want to be part of that kind of a setup. When an issue concerning the whole country comes up … the only duty we have here is to vote as we think the whole country would like to see that issue resolved.

Molson's independent status allowed him both to criticize and defend the Senate as he saw fit. While disparaging its tendency to be the "rubber stamp" for political parties, he defended its right to retain its place against voices advocating its abolition. When in 1973 a *Gazette* editorial asserted that "The Senate of Canada stinks of patronage. It reeks of special interest. It is crammed with political fat cats … It merely serves to consolidate an institution that is a farce and a scandal in the Canadian constitutional set-up," Hartland's response was simultaneously forceful and humorous. "I object particularly to the words "stinks" and "reeks." We may be redundant, we may be old, we may be tired, we may be useless, but I very much object to this chamber, this part of Parliament, being alluded to as a farce and a scandal."

On another occasion two years later, as an aside to the context of a debate on a proposed bill to control inflation, Hartland remarked: "If the Senate is no longer necessary, and if a bill to abolish the Senate were put forward, I would probably vote for it … [but] I would have to know that a substantial majority of the people of Canada felt that the Senate was no longer necessary." He pointed out in 1977 that members of the press were misguided when they reported on the number of empty seats in the chamber and questioned the attendance records of the senators. The members were often absent, Hartland stated, attending to other duties in committees. "One can question the purpose of the allegations made by the press. Is it just to pick on the Senate, or to attempt to destroy it? Whatever the objective, I say the press is doing a very poor job in reporting in that fashion."

Again in 1978 Molson criticized the press: "Why do the media go to such pains to downgrade everything we do? Why do they not give any credit for tasks, useful tasks, well carried out?" Hartland acknowledged that some reform was in order, but that it would be foolish to abolish the Senate in the absence of a better model. In conclusion, he maintained that the Senate was indeed serving a vital role and fulfilling the purpose in Parliament for which it was designed.

During the national unity debate in the early summer of 1977, Hartland announced that he would support the Parti Québécois as long as it provided "good government." His words were controversial, particularly as the PQ had just announced its objective to separate Quebec from the rest of Canada. Trudeau had recently acknowledged that the party had the right to restrict English schooling in the province. On the subjects of language and separation, Hartland spoke at length in English and French. It would be one of the most eloquent and important speeches of his career, and one in which his grasp of both sides of the debate proved to be mature, perceptive and widely sympathetic.

> These days a dark cloud is hanging over our heads, and it is reflected in the sombre views of many Canadians when thinking of the future of their country … Divisive forces are at work in different regions of Canada, to which we must respond vigorously.
>
> I am speaking as one who is an English Canadian, whose family has become completely immersed in its homeland of Quebec. I am Quebecois. I am in complete sympathy with the objective of preserving the French culture and language, and making the French language the prime language throughout Quebec. However there is evidence of concern on the part of both Anglo- and Franco-

Quebecois over the means proposed to accomplish this goal.

As a Quebecois, I have the right to express my feelings, and my comments are, therefore, of a personal nature.

(Translation) Why do I claim to be Quebecois? The answer is obvious. It is just on 200 years ago that my family gave up all other allegiance and made its home there. In the years since, six generations with the seventh approaching maturity, have participated in the development of Quebec, including some of the original ventures in steam navigation, railways, banking, manufacturing, water and light services, schools, hospitals, universities, the arts and research. This recital is not to seek recognition, but to substantiate the claim that our roots are very deep indeed in the soil of Quebec.

In addition, two generations, with their contemporaries, have backed their faith and affection for this land with their lives. We too have some French blood in our veins, going back through the Taschereau, de la Bruère and de la Gorgendière families to Louis Jolliet. Today it seems that in spite of this history, we Anglophones are to be treated as strangers who have had all the privileges over the years, but are now to be deprived of fundamental rights.

It is true that the prime minister said in Matane last week that the government was not abandoning the Anglo-Quebecois. I accept his word, naturally, but how do you think Anglo-Quebecois feel at this moment? How would you feel if some of your pre-Confederation rights – not new rights or greater freedom, but rights you had historically – were to be deferred?

Our concern stems from the moves to downgrade the Anglophone community and to reduce or restrict its numbers as a means to protect the French language and culture. Some of the legislative proposals are unnecessary and undesirable because in the long run the whole population of Quebec, French as well as English, will be the losers.

My greatest concern is caused by the serious misunderstandings between the English and French communities. Neither group really understands the inner feelings of the other, and, more importantly, neither wants to admit that there is any fault on its part ... Anglophones have been guilty, without doubt, of not trying very hard to become fluent in the French language. They have not shown the proper interest, sympathy or understanding for the normal and healthy aspirations of the French community. We should have done a lot more over the years ... English Canadians should realize how serious the issues are to the Quebec population. If Anglophones want Francophones to remain as partners, they must understand how vital and deep-rooted are the feelings of Francophones over their right to full self-expression and acceptance. Many would rather be poorer in their own country than continue to feel like second-class citizens in a greater one. Somehow this message must be more widely and more clearly understood.

On the French side, there should be recognition of the fact that historically, business was the least respected occupation in which their people wanted to become involved. The church, the professions, government and politics all took precedence, and the education system was limited by this point of view until a few years ago, although the realization of essential economic facts had led to the founding of higher schools of commerce several years ago.

One thing must be understood by the people of Quebec. Anglophones do believe in their identity, their destiny and their homeland, from sea to sea, including Quebec. It should be fully accepted that the reason Canadians of all backgrounds made such great sacrifices in two world wars was because of that proud loyalty.

If one looks back with an open mind it is obvious that the greatest achievements in our province have been as a result of the combination of the best talents from English and French stock. When we reflect on the exploration and development of our country, the great feats of construction, Expo '67, the Olympics, the Montreal Metro and other outstanding accomplishments, we realize that success has been due to the combination of qualities of our two cultures.

In February 1978 Molson spoke out in the Senate about unemployment and inflation. Of the two problems, Hartland thought unemployment was the more serious, "the one we should be trying to solve." He said that the private sector was "the only useful place where jobs are created," and criticized the government for spending money to create jobs, calling their actions "absolutely useless." It was Hartland's view that Canadians should not expect government to solve all their problems, but that it would be more appropriate for government to create an atmosphere in which problems could be solved, for example, he offered, by encouraging cooperation between employers and employees. He claimed that the government itself was recently responsible for creating the increase in unemployment, adding his observation that unemployment insurance was subject to abuse, as some were drawing on unemployment benefits at the same time as their pensions.

In June of 1974 Hartland resigned as chairman of the board at Molson Industries Limited and became honorary chairman, replacing Tom who was retiring. At the same time Bud Wilmott, former company president, became chairman. Since Pete Molson's death it had been tacitly understood that the position of president would no longer be assumed by a Molson family member, but would always be held by a professional brought in from outside.

The brewery's acquisitions continued to mount, with regard to both the brewing operations and adding to its diversified interests. By the end of 1974 Molson's had acquired another brewing plant in Barrie (originally built in 1970 for an expansion of Formosa Spring Brewery) for $27.5 million, outbidding Labatt; Molson's became Ontario's largest brewer for the first time. By this time the company had also bid for and purchased such retail mainstays as Beaver Lumber and Willson Office Specialty.

In 1975, Hartland and Magda moved to Rosemount Avenue, in Westmount. Their new home was smaller and therefore easier to maintain, but Magda, who had loved their Redpath Street house, was unhappy about moving. (The Redpath Street house later became a Swiss Bank, and many years after that the director reported to Zoë that many unbidden "extraordinary happenings" such as machines turning off and lights coming on, led him to believe there was a ghost. Zoë speculated that the "ghost" was Magda.)

By 1976 Zoë and her family were also preparing to move; Nick Hardinge had been transferred by the Royal Bank to work in London, England. In spite of the miles that would soon be between them, however, Hartland and Zoë would always make opportunities to see each other several times each year, whether in Montreal, London, Jamaica or Ivry. They continued to be very affectionate with each other in "an old fashioned, reserved, daughter-father kind of way."

Before the Hardinges moved to London, Hartland made a point of arranging a tour of the family brewery for his grandsons. He felt, Max recalled, that it was time for them "to get a better understanding of beer and what he did when he went to the office."

> He introduced us to the corporate office, with family saying "Hi" at each door. He showed us his office, which to me seemed immaculate, with items of familiar interest all around the room. He took us across the road and I was introduced to the wonderful smells of brewing – from the ingredients, to the kettles, he explained the process and showed us the stables and the cellars. He wanted to show us what was in our blood, and as a child it was very impressive.

Montreal was readying to host the Olympic Games in 1976. In January of that year, Hartland and Magda were among 900 guests invited to Walter Gordon's seventieth birthday party, held at the

Royal York Hotel in Toronto. The gala affair entertained present and past cabinet ministers, members of parliament and senators, and representatives from the arts.

In April 1978 Tom died at the age of 76. He had been suffering badly from arthritis for some years, but the final illness that claimed him, lung cancer, was diagnosed just a month before his death. Until 1971, when the media had first reported a link between smoking and lung cancer, Hartland had also been a smoker. Though he had indulged in the popular habit for four decades, he abruptly quit that year, and never smoked again.

Not long after Tom's death, the Bronfman brothers made an over-ture to Hartland to determine whether he would be interested in buying back the Montreal Canadiens. The price this time was $20 million, plus a thirty-year lease for the Forum. In spite of his fervent belief that the costs of professional sports were grossly inflated, Hartland seriously considered the proposal. He was reluctant to let the opportunity go by to once again be close to and in control of his beloved team. A few weeks later a rumour reached him that Labatt was about to make an offer to the Bronfmans. Such a sale would mean that Molson's would certainly lose the advertising contract for *Hockey Night in Canada,* and corresponding market share points. Hartland contacted the principals and confirmed his intentions, stating that he would be willing to top any rival bid by increments of $50,000.00, up to a limit. This time it wouldn't be his personal investment, but that of Molson's Breweries.

The decision to keep the Canadiens out of their rival brewery's hands turned out to be a double-edged sword. It is unclear whether Hartland realized it at the time, but his purchase of the hockey team in 1978 would be the linchpin to help the Bronfman broth-ers buy Brascan, the syndicate that controlled Labatt Breweries. On the other hand, Hartland's nephew, Hartland MacDougall, would personally benefit from Molson's association with the Bronfmans, becoming – upon their strong recommendation – vice chairman of the Bank of Montreal. (In 1984, MacDougall would leave the Bank of Montreal and become chairman of Royal Trustco, also part of the Bronfman "empire.")

In late 1979 Hartland made a decision to hire someone to handle and control his personal affairs. Several candidates were recommended to him and he took a long time to consider their qualifications and suitability. Finally, one person was introduced to him who he felt instinctively would be the best man for the job. This was Rolland Peloquin, who recalls that his first meeting with the senator was on Remembrance Day, November 11, 1980, in his brewery office. The meeting was made more memorable when precisely at 11 a.m. the power went out, and Rolland joined Hartland in a minute of respectful silence that was observed throughout the brewery. This long-standing tradition at Molson's was forgotten only once during Peloquin's twenty-two year tenure, but it was an oversight that incensed Hartland.

Rolland Peloquin began working as Hartland's principal private secretary in January 1981. Hartland left for Jamaica at that time, and as a measure of the trust he already felt for his new associate, invited Rolland to familiarize himself with all the records in his office. Thus began a long professional relationship in which Rolland handled Hartland's accounting, sorted his correspondence, arranged interviews, meetings and reservations and dealt with a variety of problems that Hartland brought to his attention.

A close bond of friendship also formed between the two men. When Molson first invited Peloquin to join his party for salmon fishing on the Bonaventure River in 1981, the senator was gratified to catch a 21-pound and a 24-pound salmon on the same morning. One year later, Rolland caught a 32-pound salmon the day after Hartland had left to return to his Montreal office. Hartland received a phone call from another member of the fishing party to tell him the news. When Rolland walked into the office the following day, Hartland, his eyes shining with amusement, said,

"You're fired!" In view of the fact that the senator fished for over fifty years, he never did catch a salmon over 30 pounds.

Between 1979 and 1981, Hartland participated in the twentieth, twenty-first and twenty-second annual meetings of the Canada–U.S. Interparliamentary Group, held in rotation in different cities in the two countries. He represented the Senate at each of these week-long symposiums and reported back to the chamber on proceedings upon his return. During the second and third year meetings Molson co-chaired the Canadian delegation, and in addition, chaired three related meetings with American congressmen. The issues (some of which Hartland referred to as "hardy perennials" because they were on the agenda each year) were vital to the times, including bilateral trade, defence matters, fisheries treaties and the management of energy supplies.

In December 1981 Hartland spoke out on his province's ambivalence about repatriating Canada's constitution. The constitution was then still under the control of the British parliament, and Prime Minister Trudeau wanted to make it a Canadian statute. Molson began by referring to Ontario's support of the French language, noting that one of the reasons (an upcoming provincial election) pointed toward cynicism and hypocrisy. Then he made some memorable comments about Bill 101, the Quebec language law.

> As one of the vanishing Protestant representatives of the province of Quebec ... I have been deeply concerned with the lot of Quebec minorities. Our position there, since the passage of Bill 101 ... has become affected to a degree of which I do not think the majority of the people in Canada have the slightest idea.
>
> Bill 101 was introduced in Quebec for the very laudable purpose of preserving the French culture and language. That is an aim which non-Francophones can understand, appreciate and support. It suggests that the language of work and of matters of culture should be clearly established as French, and that all public

information and communication should be so formed that French is in the dominant position. It also establishes control over the language of education.

Hartland also had serious reservations about the language law. In his opinion there was "an element of revenge" in the legislation, "of hatred, of excess in the application of this law which is reminiscent of dictatorship." He condemned "excessively restrictive educational rules, curtailment of social services, and the elimination of any English word from any public sign," and pointed out that there were "practically no Anglophones" in the Quebec civil service.

In 1982 Bruce McNiven, an acquaintance and neighbour of Hartland's at Ivry, brought him some information about the newly formed English rights group, Alliance Quebec. McNiven invited Hartland to be co-chairman of the association, with Justice Louis de Grandpré. Hartland responded with a letter that was "circumspect in tone, and supportive of the general objectives," in which he explained that he had to consider such requests most carefully given that his name was tied to a market brand. McNiven, fully expecting the letter to conclude with Molson's regrets, was pleased and surprised when he reached the end of the letter. Hartland was "sufficiently confident of the moderation of the objectives" and the positive spin of Alliance Quebec's approach to conclude that it would be a worthwhile endorsement. (One of the first efforts made by the Alliance in defence of English minority rights was to lobby against Quebec's language law, Bill 101.)

In May of 1982 Hartland was 75 years old, the age at which, thanks to a 1965 parliamentary ruling, he could have voluntarily retired from the Senate. But as long as he felt he was making a worthwhile contribution he did not want to leave his colleagues or his work on Parliament Hill. Asked in 1977 when he planned to retire, he had replied, "I don't know how long I'm going to stay but

I'll tell you one thing, I don't want to be carried to Ottawa in a basket." His contact with the brewery was lessening, although he was always consulted for major decisions. He retained his old office on the third floor of the administration building, next door to his nephew Eric Molson, who became deputy chairman of the board in 1983.

Hartland was devastated in the fall of 1982 when Magda died. For some months leading up to her death, bizarre symptoms such as intermittent confusion, sudden temper flare-ups and failing memory indicated that her mind wasn't functioning properly. A visit to the doctor when they returned to Montreal was followed by a series of tests, for which she spent some time in hospital. Her death came suddenly, and an autopsy revealed she had been suffering from a low-grade meningeal (meninges being the membrane enclosing the brain) tumour. For Hartland, Magda's death was a major emotional setback. Grief seemed to hasten his aging, and, losing interest in many of his commitments, he began to relinquish directorships and sever ties with companies with which he had long been associated. Family members showed their concern by going to see Hartland whenever they could, and offered to have him visit them for extended periods of time; a round of friends provided frequent contact and stimulation. His niece Lorna (MacDougall) Bethel and her husband Tony joined Hartland in Jamaica during his first winter holiday there without Magda. Lorna and Tony insisted that Hartland purchase a television set for Belmont and install a satellite dish so that he could watch all the Montreal hockey games.

During the years after Magda's death, Hartland cherished his links with Zoë and his grandsons. Following a divorce between Zoë and Nicholas Hardinge, Hartland's emotional support of his daughter and her sons became even more essential. He kept up a regular correspondence with Max, who was a pupil at the boarding school Milton Abbey, in Dorset, England. After Nicholas died of cancer in 1984 Hartland's letters became even more important to his grandson, easing the boy's grief and homesickness and providing a tether to his home in Canada. "[Grandad] always asked how I was enjoying school and sports, gently persuading me to see the value of studies and sports as a way of sharpening the mind and building on my competitive social skills. His letters and notes would take me away from the rain of England to his world of the Senate, the brewery, and Ivry. He was the glue that helped to keep our family together."

Zoë was introduced by a friend to British business entrepreneur Christopher Murray at a dinner party she gave in London. Murray, born in a village near Malmesbury in Wiltshire, was then living in the Channel Islands. Their London friend's instincts were sound; the couple's attraction was mutual. Zoë took Chris to Ivry to meet Hartland, who liked him and instantly formed a bond. The couple married in December 1983. Hartland always referred to his new son-in-law in an affectionate way, as "C Murray." Hartland's three grandsons continued to be a source of pride, delighting and gratifying him.

In 1983 a documentary was released by the National Film Board of Canada called *The Kid Who Couldn't Miss*. The film, directed by Paul Cowan, was an interpretation of the life of Billy Bishop and raised doubts about the former First World War flyer's record. Suggesting that Bishop had inflated the reports of his victories, the film specifically questioned the validity of his having been awarded the Victoria Cross for a certain dawn aerodrome raid to which there had been no witnesses. According to Cowan, the purpose of the film was to show how Bishop and others were used by generals and politicians for propaganda purposes, to further the idealization of war. The film's narration closed with the words "Heroism, like war itself, is neither as simple nor as glorious as we would like."

When veterans were invited to a screening of the film in cities across Canada, there was little reaction. A campaign against the film started slowly, led by some members of Bishop's family and interest groups such as the Canadian Legion and the War Amps of Canada. By the time the controversy reached the Senate, the momentum was unstoppable and brought great political pressure upon the Film Board.

A hastily formed Subcommittee on Veterans Affairs, chaired by Senator Jack Marshall and of which Hartland was a member, brought Cowan, his co-director and producers to attend hearings during which they were cross-examined for weeks. Many of the members of the subcommittee were war veterans, ferociously critical of the film, taking great personal offence to its content and form. Jack Marshall argued for censorship; he wanted the NFB to withdraw the film or have certain portions deleted and replaced. For months, tedious, repetitive arguments circled over details ranging from whether Bishop as a boy had shot squirrels or birds with his .22 rifle, to measuring the validity of each claim of every witness quoted in the film. Canadian historians were invited to express their opinions. Seemingly endless discussions endeavoured to reach consensus on the definitions of truth, reality and drama.

Billy Bishop had been Canada's most decorated serviceman and, in the eyes of many of the senators, his memory was inviolable. They regarded Paul Cowan as someone out to ruin the reputation of a Canadian hero. Molson, the only senator who had known Bishop personally, spoke at length and with much emotion in his friend's defence. During the years he had known him, said Hartland, he had seen "no objectionable characteristics such as have been suggested by the film," and added that no one had ever intimated, within his hearing, that Bishop was anything other than honourable and truthful. Molson said he found it very difficult, having known him for so many years, "knowing his character, to accept the charges laid in this film."

No one has denied that there can be those who doubt that Bishop did all that he said ... but to rewrite history, there must be a convincing weight of supporting evidence ... In this film creative and artistic effort were used to advance a personal theme at the expense of truth ... We do question very seriously the use of public funds ... and particularly the use of the prestigious label of the National Film Board of Canada to destroy the reputation of a hero ... We in Parliament cannot condone the dishonesty of any government agency. In this case the known history of Billy Bishop has been distorted and he has been shown falsely as a fraud and a cheat. The film is simply and totally a mistake.

The report of the Senate committee clearly indicates that damage has been done by the film The Kid Who Couldn't Miss. Damage has been done to our national image, to our pride, to all those who served to protect our liberty and our way of life, to the families who gave their lives and, last but not least, to the members of Billy Bishop's family ... I honestly believe that this film should not be allowed to circulate in its present form. I believe the film is dishonest, and not in the national interest.

Four years after the crusade began, a compromise was reached, and the producers agreed to withdraw the film as a documentary, relabel it as a "docu-drama," and to add a detailed disclaimer before the credits. Senate committee member Jack LeMoyne, though he would continue to give Bishop the benefit of the doubt, concluded that it was not the place of the Senate to restrict artistic integrity of filmmakers.

Whether we like it or not there is a hole in Bishop's story as an air force ace. In the admirable succession of the established details of his service over there one encounters a problem of continuity. None of the witnesses we heard could deny it: the famous solo raid which gained him the Victoria Cross cannot be substantiated, historically proved, or scientifically established. Great was my dismay when finally I had to admit the damned and damning hole could not be plugged with any concrete fact.

Though the majority of Senate members would never abandon their image of Bishop as "the greatest Canadian ace, as a real hero for his time, for our time and for ever," historical evidence in the intervening years has affirmed Paul Cowan's suspicion that Billy Bishop was less than wholly honest about many of his aerial exploits – including the aerodrome raid that won him the Victoria Cross. Independent research compiled and documented in books such as *The Making of Billy Bishop* (2002) by Department of National Defence historian Brereton Greenhous, leaves little with which to quarrel today. It leads one to wonder whether, had Hartland been confronted during his lifetime with this overwhelming historical evidence, his defence of Bishop would have been as strong, or whether he would have continued to hold fast to his belief in the integrity and honour of his close friend, to his dying day.

CHAPTER FIFTEEN

URING THE LATTER half of the 1980s it seemed that Hartland had settled most comfortably into the roles he'd defined for himself as elder statesman, family patriarch, hockey team owner and philanthropist. His life had been extraordinary, if not unconventional, and most responsibilities he had undertaken were not the kind he could choose to retire from: his public life, though separate, had never been alienated from his private life. One journalist summed up his social persona by describing him as "a man with half the letters in the alphabet after his name but still the grace to be listed in the phone book."

Although he limited his social engagements to a minimum, some events had priority, such as a Battle of Britain commemorative ceremony held at the British High Commission in Ottawa in September 1986, to which all surviving Canadian members of the RCAF and the RAF were invited. At the end of the first week of October, Hartland delivered a speech to the Conference Board of

Canada (a non-profit research institute) upon his acceptance of an honorary associate award, granted in recognition of his distinguished career. During this speech he revealed his observation that there were two current trends which made him "a trifle sleepless": the enormous concentration of power in very few hands and the change in structure of financial empires.

We have always kept a lid on the control of banks, with successful results, but today we find that Trust companies are being changed from their traditional role and being used as building blocks in developing great "one stop" financial groups, incorporating several functions such as investment, insurance, mortgage and real estate ... My own feeling is that the law should provide stricter limitations over Trust companies in their Trust role, certainly not less control than presently exists over banks.

At the same occasion Hartland commented upon the role of media in communications:

In a democracy such as ours, public opinion is vital both to business and to government. However, I question the way major events of the day are often compressed into one minute capsules on the evening news, or into headlines which at times bear no resemblance to the story they convey. At one time, we trusted the role of the media in reporting the news, but it seems to me that today some of the media see their responsibility as creating the news. A crisis occurs and minutes later political leaders are asked what, precisely, they are going to do about it, even before they have had a chance to learn any of the details of the situation. Apparently it is not considered necessary to think before acting ... the public is left to judge the issues on the basis of superficiality and bias.

The editorials of newspapers were at one time respected as conveyors of the papers' editorial opinion. Today, too many newspa-

pers, it seems to me, use the entire paper to convey the bias of the reporters or editors. There are really very few countries in the world which permit the freedom of the press that we enjoy in Canada, but I question whether such freedom is resulting in the development of an alert and informed electorate so necessary to the survival of democratic society.

Molson had long been an advocate of WASP establishment values, including the importance of hard work, the supremacy of family and the need for personal integrity and responsibility. In 1988 he found himself engaging in issues such as Canada's free trade agreement with the United States (which he supported but with reservations), and in 1989 he was once again arguing for the protection of Anglophone minority rights in Quebec, this time in the context of the Meech Lake accord. As always, whenever he found others' ideals and principles lacking he would promptly speak up, such as in October 1990 when he observed actions in the Senate that he considered rude. "When a person of charm and grace such as Senator Martha Bielish makes a farewell speech on the occasion of her retirement and the leaders of the opposition party refuse to stand with every other senator in the chamber to applaud, I think this demonstrates a singular lack of civility and courtesy."

One of Hartland's grievances about modern changes was that there was, in his view, no such thing as "society" any more. "The days of coming-out parties and calling on people are over," he grumbled. "People had a social pattern then. Fashion used to be set by a man or a woman. Today, somebody gets on TV looking a certain way and everybody copies them. Taste and background mean nothing." He was quoted by another journalist as having stated that "practically everything is a dirty word nowadays. Free enterprise takes a beating; so do all the other -isms. It's common practice to knock everything."

Molson became a bit of a curmudgeon in his later years, letting impatience slip into his manner more often, an attitude he represented by swinging his eyeglasses by the arm between his thumb and index finger, or turning the signet ring (the one left to him by his Uncle Percy in 1917), which he still wore, on his little finger. At times his habitual amiability would switch to irritability; his benevolence would give way to scorn. On one occasion, his colleagues in the Senate thought he had become seriously out of touch with matters of everyday social reality, and tried to call him to account for his erroneous perceptions. While attempting to make a point in 1990 about how the Senate traditionally dealt with amendments to legislation, Hartland claimed that the price of prescription drugs had not risen dramatically. Three members leapt up to contradict him. "Where do you live, on another planet?" one shouted. "Shame on you!" said another. "They're not expensive for you; you get them free!" Other voices were raised: "What a statement to make!" "Totally incorrect!" At first Hartland would not let himself be provoked by their outbursts and quickly defended himself with his usual humorous flair, retorting "You have a lovely voice, please keep it to yourself!" But as the interruptions persisted, his ire rose. "Aren't you ashamed of interjecting all the time?" Insults were followed by more insults, until Hartland finally lost his temper, shouting "Oh, shut up! Do shut up!"

In 1990, Brian Mulroney's Progressive Conservative government proposed the creation of a national Goods and Services Tax in an attempt to cure the problems of a poor economy and massive deficits. The controversial proposal was unpopular among the vast majority of constituents across the country and was attacked by the Liberals and New Democrats in Parliament. Senator Roch Bolduc remembered that during this "tumultuous period" throughout which it was difficult to rise and speak, Hartland "waited his turn until 3:30 a.m. For 40 minutes, he spoke about the importance of this tax and the fact that although it was not popular, it was necessary for Canada."

After the Liberal-dominated Senate refused to pass the tax into law, Mulroney resorted to an unfamiliar constitutional provision and temporarily increased the number of senators in order to give his party a majority in that chamber. Though Molson supported the tax measure, he was "dismayed and disgusted" by Mulroney's action, which had "made history – unfortunately, history of the wrong sort."

These days there seemed to be more events that annoyed Hartland during Senate proceedings and fewer issues that challenged him in a positive way. Age had isolated him even here, where he was the last of the group appointed in 1955, and while his attendant wisdom was respected and the rigorous independence of his thinking continued to be appreciated, his views had become all too often regarded as quaint and outmoded. Though he had not lost his gift of eloquent logic, nor his effectual combination of gravity and charm, these qualities had somehow ceased to be as relevant as they once had been, and he felt the transformation keenly.

Hartland was now spending three months of every year in Jamaica. At Belmont he was his most relaxed self, where he could dress casually, stay barefoot in his bathing suit and not have to keep an eye on the clock. Here he would pour rum drinks – his own "delicious concoction," which he called "Purple People Eaters" – for himself and guests before lunch. His local household staff (whom he called "helpers") was made up of the same people he'd hired in the early 1960s, and who felt a great deal of affection and respect for him. While maintaining all the traditional proprieties that defined their relationships, he went to "untold lengths" to ensure that they were well looked after, arranging that their medical needs were always attended to and that their pensions were in place.

In 1988 Hartland's cousin Pat Molson, who worked with the

Canadian High Commission in Kingston, dropped in to bring Hartland the sad news that Pete Molson's eldest son Peter had been killed in a car accident in Spain. It was a tragic note that marred an otherwise positive season, for that year Hartland was supervising the construction of an addition to the house, with another spare bedroom to accommodate more guests. Zoë, her family, and his nieces and nephews and their families often stayed with Hartland, as had friends like the Meighens. Teddy Meighen, the son of former Prime Minister Arthur Meighen, was another RMC graduate, a successful lawyer and a great friend of Tommy MacDougall's. Teddy and his wife Peggy (née Robinson) had become regular guests of Hartland's in Jamaica during the 1970s, and in the years after Teddy's death in 1979, Peggy, who was also a good friend of Dorothy's, continued to go to Belmont with her sister and brother-in-law, Helen and John Starnes.

Hartland faithfully flew back to Montreal every January for the annual meeting of the Bank of Montreal. He continued to follow the progress of the Canadiens through satellite TV during the winter months he spent in Jamaica and flew to Montreal occasionally to root for them at the more important games. His lifelong interest in hockey was mirrored by Peggy Meighen, who had loved the game since her girlhood days; it was said that Peggy knew as much about hockey as did the coaches. Over the years after Teddy's and Magda's deaths, she and Hartland grew closer, and, to the satisfaction and delight of their friends and all the members of their respective families, fell in love. They were married in May 1990.

As Peggy's son Michael Meighen later said, "Hockey is probably the reason I became Senator Molson's stepson. My mother and he had known each other all their lives, but after the deaths of their respective spouses, it was hockey that brought them together. Senator Molson … had no lack of admirers among the widows of Montreal, but I have no doubt that my mother's love and knowledge of the game … gave her a competitive edge."

Through Peggy, Hartland found new joy in life. She was a fun, charming person, who enjoyed good health, still played tennis and golf, and also loved travelling. She encouraged Hartland to be "in touch with his impulsive side." One friend noticed that he "loosened up" after marrying Peggy – as though he "didn't have to keep up a front any more." Another called Peggy a "nifty dancer," and noted that the couple laughed a lot together. Peggy was determined, however, that others would not interpret or suspect there were any financial improprieties to their relationship. Making it clear that she "didn't want to have anything to do with" his money, she refused at first to let him buy her a ring, leaving Hartland "surprised and slightly hurt," but later on he did give her a ring, which she adored and wore every day of her life.

In 1990 Hartland invited John and Geills Turner to stay with them in Jamaica, and Michael Meighen, who was by then also a senator, joined the party on a fishing expedition. The newlyweds would frequently visit Port Antonio's Musgrave Market, where Hartland got to know many of the vendors by name. There he would haggle over the price of tomatoes or bananas, and always provoke laughter. One local entrepreneur who ran a business out of Montego Bay flying small planes over the island for tourists took Hartland and Peggy with the latter's sister Helen Starnes and her husband John on a flight one day. During the flight the pilot offered Hartland the controls, which he operated for a few minutes and thoroughly enjoyed. Molson also loved to drive Peggy's Audi car, which he "flew like a fighter plane" over the countryside's windy roads. His passengers described the experience as a "terrifying affair." One time, to their amazement, he depressed the accelerator to bring the car to 80 mph, and shouted "Wheeee!"

Speaking to a reporter from Jamaica's *Skywritings* magazine in December 1991, Hartland described how he loved to watch the sun rise over Monkey Island every morning. "Here in Jamaica," he added, "I do most of the things I don't do at home. I'll fix things and I go shopping … I particularly enjoy sitting by my pool, talking to the board of directors in Montreal on my portable phone … they get so envious!"

Hartland's role with respect to the family brewery was, to all intents and purposes, by now a minor one. He had resigned as honorary chairman of the board in 1988 and accepted the lesser position of honorary director. Although he was still consulted on major decisions and the younger family members deferred to him out of respect, he stayed very much in the background of the corporation, trying to neither influence nor intervene, but trusting his nephews and the active members of the board to do what they considered best for the company.

Molson continued to keep in touch with his oldest friends, who included the only other two surviving pilots from the original No. 401 Squadron RCAF, Dal Russel and Paul Pitcher. When the latter wrote to Hartland to congratulate him upon his marriage, his reply included a few words describing how he felt about the Senate: "I feel that the Senate's role has been so changed and distorted that it has lost sight of its real responsibility. As it stands, I feel it would be better to abolish it. Right at the moment, I am trying to see whether I can make any useful contribution to the present mess by throwing out some more of my deathless prose."

In January 1991, a throng of demonstrators protesting against the GST were "camped noisily" on Parliament Hill directly under Hartland's office window. Hartland described the situation to a friend, adding that a "deep antagonism has remained … partisan politics seems to be the principal preoccupation here." By May, he was already considering resigning: "Matters in Senate are very unpredictable and I don't know how long I'll be here." A few months later, he realized he had reached an age when he either couldn't or didn't want to take part in many activities. He sent more regrets than acceptances to invitations including dinner dances, fundraisers and receptions.

On Friday, January 24, 1992, Hartland slipped on some wet tile while climbing out of the pool at Belmont. Though the fall resulted in a crack fracture to his pelvis, he continued to walk for some days until the pain became worse and he made arrangements to cut his holiday short and return to Montreal. There, at the Montreal General Hospital, an X-ray revealed the fracture. Confined to his home on doctor's orders, "for an indefinite period of time," for several months he was unable to attend Senate sessions. Hip replacement surgery was scheduled for the end of September 1992.

Meanwhile, Hartland heard about a new made-for-television mini-series *The Valour and the Horror*, which had been released by the CBC, over which great controversy had arisen. This time, the subject of the "docu-drama" was a three-part examination of select Second World War campaigns. While the director and producer, brothers Brian and Terence McKenna, protested that the film did not attack war heroes but "cast doubts about strategy and leadership," war veterans and others saw it differently. They claimed that the film was "biased and bigoted" and that it unjustly denigrated the bomber pilots of the RCAF. Once again, furor rose in the Senate and another Subcommittee of Veterans Affairs was formed, for the second time chaired by Jack Marshall.

Public hearings were scheduled to begin in November 1992. Newspaper columnists, independent journalists and editorial writers unanimously took the view in favour of the veterans, but differed in opinion as to censorship or control. The film's production partner Arnie Gelbart protested: "The Senate is putting a considerable chill on creativity. Is it appropriate for any government organization to judge program content?"

Although Hartland was unable to attend chamber sessions or the public hearings, there was never any doubt about how he felt. On February 4, 1992, he composed a letter that he had copied and sent to all senators:

In common with a very large number of veterans who have served their country, I feel a strong objection to the use of our tax money for the production of radio or television programmes designed to apologize for what we have achieved in two World Wars in spite of the enormous sacrifices made.

In the case of the CBC's "The Valour and the Horror" and the NFB's effort on Billy Bishop, it appears that consultation with those who were involved at the time has been carefully avoided and the result certainly is one that can make every veteran ask "WHAT WERE WE FIGHTING FOR?"

When the public hearings were over, the CBC Ombudsman's report concluded that "The series as it stands is flawed and fails to measure up to CBC's demanding policies and standards." The recommendation that second (and any further) airings of the series were to be followed by discussion programs was, in the end, a compromise with which neither of the sides was completely comfortable.

On Wednesday, May 26, 1993, Molson announced his resignation from the Senate, to take effect May 31. He had made his decision privately and gave the announcement with no prior warning for his listeners who might otherwise have prepared lengthy speeches of appreciation and farewell. Hartland took the opportunity to rebuke the members one last time with regard to partisanship.

You will understand that, after 38 years in this chamber, it is with great regret that I bring this association to an end. I am the last of our list, which covered 13 appointments by Mr St Laurent in 1955 and was, on that day, the longest list ever appointed.

The years have gone pleasantly, and the association and friend-

ships I have made in parliament have left me with a deep sense of warmth and gratitude. The changes that have occurred in the Senate during this period are enormous. While some of these changes are effective and beneficial, others leave me with a sense, rather, of regret and disappointment.

Since its birth, the Senate has been pictured as the elder states-man's place in our parliament where, in the hackneyed phrase, "sober second thought prevails." There was a lot of merit in this role, but in some ways the purpose has been frustrated with a very obvious deterioration in the atmosphere of the house, and with a substantial, almost catastrophic, decrease in public respect and support.

The last thing I want to do today is criticize, but I must observe that some of the problem has been created by the great increase in petty partisanship which has gone beyond party loyalty. I hope that some day the group of independent senators will regain its num-ber, with the result that we have seen in the House of Lords of some leavening in their relationship. Of course, you would expect me to say that as the first independent appointee by Louis St Laurent when he made that different and distinctive move.

Honourable senators, I have said all that I intend to say, and it is quite enough – perhaps too much. In closing, I do want to express my appreciation of the many courtesies and friendships that I have enjoyed here over all these years. I also wish to thank most warmly the officers and staff of the Senate who, in perform-ing all sorts of different functions within the chamber and the com-mittees, from the front door to the restaurants, give such generous service. I shall miss this association greatly.

Lowell Murray, the leader of the government, followed Molson's remarks with an acknowledgement that he fully appreciated the "sincerity and the devotion to public service which motivates those comments," and added, "there is nobody in this place who has earned the right and who has established the credibility to make such comments to us more so than our friend, the Honourable Senator Molson."

Thirty-eight years is a long time. We are losing the dean of the Senate, the dean of Parliament ... [who, since 1955] has been an ornament to this chamber and to Parliament.

In bidding him farewell I want to express my entire personal satisfaction that he is leaving us pretty much at the peak of his form and in excellent health, and to wish him and his family good health and much happiness in the future, and in doing so to record, on behalf of the prime minister and the government, our profound appreciation to him for his services to Parliament and, indeed, his services to Canadians throughout his adult lifetime.

Senator Maurice Riel also had something to say, in addition to feeling very moved to hear that Molson was resigning.

You know, in Montreal, Molson is the most French Canadian name there is. Those who have been on Papineau Street in the east end near Delorimier or on Jacques-Cartier Bridge realize how important this company is for Montreal ... I can say that most of the employees of Molson's Brewery in Montreal are French Canadians or, if you prefer, Quebecois, as they like to be known today.

Every time we see the name Molson on television, we think of all he has done to give Montreal publicity that is unique in the world. Hockey is the favourite sport of French Canadians, now it has become a favourite sport in North America.

Senator Molson is leaving us. I am very sorry. We were great friends in this chamber and outside it. He is a little older than I but not by much. Until now, I was the second longest-serving senator from the province of Quebec. He was the longest-serving senator from that province. After he resigns, I become the dean of Quebec senators. That is a hard role to fill. He did it much more easily than I. I hope to do as well as he.

John Lynch-Staunton, the deputy leader of the government, rose next to add his remarks to the record.

There is no facet of the Montreal economy which has not been touched by the knowledge and the generosity of the Molson family. Today is an opportunity to underline their many contributions which have benefited the province and the country as a whole, whether it be in banking, transportation, business in general, hospitals, universities and many other activities. The Molsons have always been there. Senator Molson is just the latest, and certainly not the last, of that family to which we owe so much.

I know that as he leaves the front benches in this chamber, we will spot him behind the bench of his favourite hockey team on television. I can only hope that his fondest wish will be realized, and that in a couple of weeks we will see him share in the celebration of the great victory of the Montreal Canadiens as they win the Stanley Cup.

Jack Marshall, in his farewell address to Molson, reminded the chamber of his support during the defence of Billy Bishop's reputation: "He gave us guidance in defending that great Canadian." Finally, Senator Consiglio Di Nino said:

I know the gentleman is a man of high integrity and a man of ethical and moral substance; but what many may not know about him is his generosity and service to Canadians in a very quiet manner. In particular, his involvement with Scouts Canada is an example of the type of leadership our country desperately needs. I should like publicly to acknowledge his generous support of the Scouts and the hundreds of initiatives he has made possible though his exemplary leadership.

One of the first events that Hartland enjoyed as a retired public servant was his youngest grandson Max's marriage to Elizabeth Valleau, which took place in 1994. When the couple had announced their engagement the year before, Zoë offered to arrange the wedding ceremony at Ivry. Though Hartland was happy and "gave his blessing" to the union, Max remembers that he joked with Zoë, saying that she was "crazy" to take on the work that would be involved to accommodate a wedding there. "Where are you going to put all those people?" he kept on asking. The preparations started a year in advance of the wedding because it was necessary to build a short road and level the site and seed it, where the large tent would be at the edge of the lake. Max and Elizabeth's wedding day was perfect, with 140 guests mingling on the grounds and admiring the beautiful setting. After the ceremony and reception, the bride and groom left by boat to cross the lake where Hartland's car and chauffeur awaited them.

The following winter, Hartland and Peggy spent three last months at Belmont; they had decided the time had come to sell the property. In the summer of 1995, a family reunion in Montreal was organized, and Hartland presided as patriarch over the more than 200 family members there. Three days of activities and events were followed by a closing dinner held in the Reception Room at the brewery. Family artifacts had been collected and displayed around the room to mark the occasion and Hartland had prepared a speech, which he delivered after the dinner. "They asked me to bring the oldest thing I have," he began, "so I brought myself."

Billy Molson's son Ian, who had long enjoyed a friendly relationship with Hartland and "admired him enormously," came to

Montreal from his home in London to be there. Ian, an investment banker with Credit Suisse First Boston, had been in regular contact with Hartland since 1972, when he worked at Molson's over five summers as an intern. Over the years they spent more time together: Hartland mentored Ian, examining and evaluating the brewery's strengths, problems and potential future. Rolland Peloquin recalls Hartland expressing his hope that Ian would "get more involved in the brewery." Finally in the mid-1990s, Hartland offered to sell Ian a significant block of his Molson's Brewery shares, and a series of transactions took place. Hartland appreciated that Ian was seriously interested in and supportive of the welfare of the business, and suspected that he would soon be invited to join other family members on the board.

In 1995 Hartland was named an Officer of the Order of Canada and travelled to Ottawa in November to accept the award. Gildas Molgat, the Speaker of the Senate, wrote to congratulate him, calling it "a well-deserved and indeed overdue recognition of your great public service." He would have received the Order earlier, but under the rules Molson could not have been considered for it while he was a senator.

Another event that brought Hartland back to Ottawa the following year was the National War Museum's launching of a major fundraising campaign. Hartland had heard about the campaign and made arrangements to visit the museum and meet the director, Victor Suthren. Suthren took Hartland on a tour of the facilities and showed him some of the artifacts on display, before sitting down to lunch to discuss the museum's future. On behalf of the Molson Foundation Hartland not only became a key donor to the campaign but also offered to give his own collection of military books to the museum's new library. Two years later when the new library was opened and named after him, Hartland attended the dedication.

Those who were close to Hartland and Peggy first noticed in

1996 that she was exhibiting symptoms of Alzheimer's disease. Lapses of short-term memory were followed by periods of disorientation and obscurity. Hartland had some difficulty understanding what her symptoms were all about: he tended to regard any breakdowns of the mind as simple "weakness," or something one could overcome through application of will. But by this time Hartland himself was beginning to experience hearing problems and short-term memory loss as well.

Hartland's long-term memory remained excellent. One time when Max and Elizabeth were staying with him in Ivry, the conversation turned to the Battle of Britain. Max recalled that Hartland suddenly "stood up and once again became the young pilot in the cockpit. He recounted a time when he was behind an enemy plane and flipped 'the tits' (the safety catch) off his machine guns and gave them a 'squirt' of 30 calibre. He looked so electrified as if he were once again flying."

Peggy's disease progressed very quickly. Within a year of the first symptoms of Alzheimer's, it was evident she could no longer be left alone. Hartland and their family physician, Dr. Doug Kinnear, decided Peggy needed to be moved to a long-term care facility and booked her into the nearby Manoir Westmount. Soon after, a room became available on the first floor in Kensington Place, Montreal's more exclusive and fashionable residence for the elderly. Hartland would visit her every day before he moved to his own apartment in the residence, but often she failed to recognize him. Each time he saw her – until the end of her life three years later – he would ask hopefully, "Do you remember me now?"

Even after his ninetieth birthday Hartland still made a noticeable physical impression: he was described in 1998 by one journalist as "resplendent in a three-piece, pinstriped suit and military moustache." Molson continued regularly to lunch at the Mount Royal Club and also to spend time at his Montreal office, although as the months went by he grew to be physically unsteady. Because he had household staff, including a personal secretary in addition to a companion, Elmer "Michael" Tacuboy, who accompanied him everywhere, Hartland saw no need to curtail his usual routines and habits. However, though his mind was relatively clear, he was conspicuously frail, leading Zoë and Dr. Kinnear to believe he should not stay in his house any longer, drive his car nor travel up to Ivry. When they made arrangements to have his driver's licence taken away, Hartland was both furious and incredulous. "I used to fly Hurricanes, and now you're taking away my driver's licence?"

As Zoë remembers, "for a long time he refused to move out of Rosemount Avenue – which was causing concern to everyone." One day he caught his foot in the carpet near the bottom of the very steep stairs. He fell and broke his arm. The injury, an impacted fracture of the humerus, did not require surgery; however he was put in the hospital and had to wear a sling for several weeks. While he was recuperating in the hospital, the apartment that was waiting for him on the fourth floor at Kensington Place was decorated and his furniture moved there from Rosemount Avenue. Zoë describes it as "a very rushed job – the only way we thought he would be happy was to make it as close as possible – a mini copy of his house. We really just got it done on time – as the curtain maker was leaving by one door, Dad was being wheeled in by another!"

Hartland adjusted very gradually to Kensington Place. In the beginning he would often say "I don't live here." But Zoë and her husband Chris spent as much time as they could with him and made sure he was as comfortable as possible.

One of Hartland's continued pleasures was going to the Mount Royal Club every day for lunch. The staff and fellow members would greet him there as he, his chauffeur and his caretaker made their way to a special table in the corner, and if he felt cold, staff would bring in a heater for him and place it near his chair. There Hartland would order a Bloody Caesar and nine oysters "on the half-shell." At the end of his meal, he would shrug off well-meaning friends or staff who would be at his elbow to help, struggle to his feet on his own and leave in a slow but dignified manner.

Hartland's family organized a party for seventy people at the Mount Royal Club to celebrate his ninetieth birthday on May 29. His oldest grandson Charles spoke in tribute to his grandfather, "a great gentleman who is so difficult to give something to, and who has given so much to all of us." Calling Hartland "a great Canadian, and the bedrock upon which our family has flourished," Charles continued,

> My Grandfather is a remarkable man. He is a man who has deep love for this country and this province and who has instilled that love in all of us. He is a great businessman who proved you did-n't have to be the biggest to be the best. He is the builder of one of the most revered franchises in sports and its guardian during the time Les Canadiens enjoyed their greatest success. He has led this proud family with grace, dignity, wisdom and humility and has taught us the meaning of responsibility, honour, and our duty to our fellow man. I now watch Grandad develop the same loving relationship with my children that I myself have treasured for so long. It gives me such pleasure to see them reply in kind. They feel as I believe everyone in this room feels, very privileged to know you, to be with you, and to be a part of your life.

Hartland's grandsons always loved to ask him about his war experiences. He showed the young men his medals, "but never explained their importance." Max recalls, "He never wanted to be considered a hero, and downplayed his involvement." Andrew also remembers his "Grandpère" as "a very private man who would never dream of gloating about his achievements." Hartland had often admonished interviewers: "Don't make a ruddy hero of me. I am a survivor. I have had a good life and have no complaints." Asked once if he was planning to write his memoirs, Molson laughed. "Heavens, no! I haven't had what you would call an exciting life. Who would want to read about me?"

In the year 2000, Hartland made an unprecedented donation of $5 million to Bishop's College School. This gift (as described in the Introduction to this book) became "seed money" for a capital campaign to raise $15 million in three years, funds that were directed towards building improvements and initiatives as well as scholarships. A new building, designed to house a library and theatre and to be architecturally in keeping with the older buildings of the school complex, was named Hartland Molson Hall. The groundbreaking ceremony and dedication events were attended on Hartland's behalf by Max Hardinge, who to his grandfather's pride had attended Bishop's University.

Hartland's daughter, grandsons, nieces, nephews, cousins and friends continued to visit him in Kensington Place. But losing Peggy in December 2000 to the unrelenting, character- and memory-robbing disease was very distressing to Hartland. All who knew them had noted how close and loving the couple had been with one another, and remarked with awe on the romantic tone of their union. John and Helen Starnes recalled one of the last times they visited Hartland and Peggy at Ivry, when they walked into the living room to find the couple sitting on the sofa in front of the fireplace, holding hands. They and others observed that their relationship – to have had each other – provided a comforting end to both their lives.

Max and Elizabeth taught their sons (twin boys born in 1999), when they were 2½, to respond in unison to two questions posed by their parents: "What's good beer?" Boys: "Molson!" and "What's bad beer?" Boys: "We don't drink Labatt's!" Max remembered this performance would always "bring a smile to Hartland's face" during the time when his health was failing.

When asked how his grandfather had been an example to him, Max replied that he had learned from him how to keep events in his life in perspective. "You get from life what you put in. Work hard and hope for great things – never lose sight of your family, and help those who are in need." When Hartland's health and memory were both breaking down near the last months of his life, Max would end his telephone calls with one of his grandfather's favourite expressions, "Keep in the groove," and Hartland would reply, "That's right."

By Hartland's ninety-fifth birthday in May 2002, he was markedly enfeebled and shadowed by a recent diagnosis of lung cancer, the same disease that had claimed his father and older brother. Near the end, remembered Zoë, her father's "Air Force blue" eyes expressed everything. On September 28, 2002, Hartland passed away.

It fell to Zoë to make funeral arrangements befitting her father, meaningful of his role as a family man, public figure and statesman. When Archbishop of Montreal Andrew Hutchinson offered to arrange and plan the order of service, Zoë declined. "This is something I have to do," she told him. "I understand," he replied. With help from Archdeacon Peter Hannen, who made suggestions and saw that everything was in the right order, Zoë spent days at Ivry planning her "tribute to a wonderful father." The private funeral service, by invitation only for close family members and friends, took place on October 4 in the Molson Chapel at Christ Church Cathedral. The Archbishop officiated at the solemn communion service, at which were sung Hartland's favourite hymns, including "The Lord is My Shepherd" and "Abide With Me."

A service of thanksgiving held at Christ Church Cathedral in December was led by the Archbishop of Montreal, the Bishop of Quebec and six other members of clergy. It was a celebration of Hartland's life, with "good readings and marvellous music; a very good 'send-off,'" recalls Zoë. RMC cadets in ceremonial uniforms flanked both sides of the aisle, and a gathering of several hundred people came to pay their last respects. An anthem was sung by the members of the Cathedral Singers Choir, joined by the eldest son of Andrew Hardinge, Hartland's 9-year-old great-grandson Thomas de Montarville Hardinge. As the congregation left the cathedral, the organist was playing some of Hartland's favourite wartime music, including "The White Cliffs of Dover," "A Nightingale Sang in Berkeley Square," "Wish Me Luck (As You Wave Me Goodbye)" and "We'll Meet Again."

A tribute read at the service of thanksgiving by his eldest nephew and godson, Hartland MacDougall, touched upon Molson's wartime service with the RCAF. MacDougall remembered his uncle characteristically having said about his squadron, after the war, "I feel we represented the country not too badly."

At the end of Hartland's life, after all he had achieved in his ninety-five years, it was his brief but glorious wartime service about which he reminisced most vividly. Though he had led a remarkably full life, he kept few mementoes. In his office at the brewery were six miniature Stanley Cups lined up on a bookcase, and on a side table stood a photo of Princess Alexandra, Princess Marina, Aird Nesbitt and himself on the steps of the church in Ste. Agathe in 1954. But the image he gazed at more often than anything else was a painting that hung on the main wall opposite his desk, depicting Hurricanes engaged in a Battle of Britain dogfight, the blue sky in the background etched with trails of smoke.

Hartland would revisit the events encompassed by the summer and fall of 1940 many times in different ways during his lifetime. His last trip to England had taken place in September 1990, when he and Peggy travelled to London to attend the commemorative ceremony marking the fiftieth anniversary of the Battle of Britain. At a reception at Canada House, Hartland was ineffably moved when he saw many old faces that he recognized, and encountered bittersweet memories. In the company of other veterans and retired personnel, the couple took pleasure in attending a "glittering service" in Westminster Abbey attended by the Queen, members of the royal family, and Prime Minister Margaret Thatcher, where the Archbishop of Canterbury addressed the guests.

The day before, the party had been invited to Buckingham Palace where they were given seats of honour in the forecourt to view a parade of 2,500 men, women, massed cadets and military bands paying homage to Winston Churchill's famous "few." The veterans were saluted by an aerial show featuring sixty-three aircraft led by five reconditioned Spitfires and two restored Hurricanes, followed by a series of modern aircraft flying in precise formation. During a walkabout by Queen Elizabeth after the flypast, Hartland chanced upon a few moments to speak with Her Majesty. She remarked that the weather was marvellous. "Just like it was in 1940," he replied, smiling. "Yes," said the Queen, who had been a princess and an army officer at the time. "It was a lovely summer."

SELECT BIBLIOGRAPHY

Algarsson, Grettir. *A Selective Two-Pitch Airscrew*. Montreal: private publication, 1939.

Burpee, Lawrence. "The Trans-Canada Airway." *The Canadian Geographic Journal* Vol. VII no. 2 (August 1933): 65–74.

Carruthers, Richard. *Molson Family* (genealogy). Privately published,1995.

Casgrain, Therese. *A Woman in a Man's World*. Toronto: McClelland & Stewart, 1972.

Chadderton, Clifford. *Hanging a Legend*. Ottawa: War Amps of Canada, 1986.

Denison, Merrill. *The Barley and the Stream: The Molson Story*. Toronto: McClelland & Stewart, 1955.

English, John. *Shadow of Heaven: The Life of Lester Pearson*. London: Vintage, 1989.

Foster, J.A. *The Bush Pilots*. Toronto: McClelland & Stewart, 1990.

Fox, James. *Five Sisters*. New York: Simon & Schuster, 2000.

Francis, Diane. *Controlling Interest*. Toronto: Macmillan of Canada, 1986.

Gilbert, Martin. *The Holocaust: The Jewish Tragedy*. Glasgow: Collins, 1986.

Goldenberg, Susan. *Troubled Skies*. Toronto: McGraw Hill Ryerson, 1994.

Grandbois, Alain. *Born in Quebec*. Montreal: Palm Publishers, 1964.

Greenhous, Ben, and Alec Douglas. *An Interview with Senator Hartland de M. Molson*. (transcript) National Archives Collection, 10 December 1980.

Greenhous, Brereton, et al. *The Crucible of War, Official History of the RCAF Vol. III, 1939-45*. Toronto: University of Toronto Press, 1994.

Greenhous, Brereton. *The Making of Billy Bishop*. Toronto: Dundurn Press, 2002.

Harrison, Rosina. *Rose: My Life in Service*. London: Cassell, 1975.

Hoy, Claire. *Nice Work*. Toronto: McClelland & Stewart, 1999.

Kavaler, Lucy. *The Astors*. London: George G. Harrap, 1966.

Keith, Ronald A. *Bush Pilot with a Briefcase*. Toronto: Douglas & McIntyre, 1997.

Lacey, Robert. *Ford: The Men and the Machine*. Toronto: McClelland & Stewart, 1986.

Marks, Christopher. *Rackets in Canada and the Montreal Racket Club*. Montreal: Price-Patterson Ltd., 1990.

McQuaig, Linda. *Behind Closed Doors*. Markham, Ontario: Penguin Books, 1987.

Milberry, Larry. *Austin Airways*. Canav Books, 1985.

Molson, Kenneth Meredith. *Pioneering in Canadian Air Transport*. Winnipeg: D.W. Friesen & Sons, 1974.

Munro, John A., and Alex I. Inglis, eds. , *Mike: The Memoirs of the Right Honorable Lester B. Pearson*. Volume II 1948-1957. Toronto: University of Toronto Press, 1973.

Newman, Peter C. *Titans: How the New Canadian Establishment Seized Power*. Toronto: Penguin Books, 1998.

Ondaatje, Christopher. *The Prime Ministers of Canada*. Toronto: Pagurian Press, 1985.

Patriquin, Graham. *B.C.S.: From Little Forks to Moulton Hill*. Sherbrooke, Quebec: 1978.

Pigott, Peter. *National Treasure*. Madiera Park, British Columbia: Harbour Publishing, 2001.

Pigott, Peter. *Wing Walkers*. Madiera Park, British Columbia: Harbour Publishing, 1998.

Pigott, Peter. *Flying Colours*. Vancouver: Douglas & McIntyre, 1997.

Pigott, Peter. *Flying Canucks III – Famous Canadian Aviators*. Madiera Park, British Columbia: Harbour Publishing, 2000.

Preston, R.A. *Canada's RMC*. Toronto: University of Toronto Press, 1969.

Rawlings, John. *Fighter Squadrons of the RAF and Their Aircraft*. London: MacDonald Books, 1969.

Render, Shirley. *Double Cross: The Inside Story of James A Richardson & Canadian Airways*. Vancouver: Douglas & McIntyre, 1999.

Rohmer, Richard, *E.P. Taylor*. Toronto: McClelland & Stewart, 1978.

Saywell, John, ed. *Canadian Annual Review for 1968*. Toronto: University of Toronto Press, 1969.

Shaw, Margaret Mason. *Bush Pilots*. Toronto: Clarke, Irwin, 1962.

Shores, Christopher. *History of the Royal Canadian Air Force*. London: Bison Books, 1984.

Stikeman, H. Heward. *The Mount Royal Club 1899–1999*. Montreal: Price-Patterson Ltd., 1999.

Thomson, Dale C. *Louis St. Laurent, Canadian*. Toronto: Macmillan of Canada, 1967.

Thornton, Martin, ed. *Nancy Astor's Canadian Correspondence 1912–1962*. New York: Edwin Mellen Press, 1997.

Weintraub, William. *City Unique: Montreal Days and Nights in the 1940s and 50s*. Toronto: McClelland & Stewart, 1996.

Wheeler, William J. *Skippers of the Sky*. Calgary: Fifth House Publishers, 2000.

Woods, Shirley. *The Molson Saga*. Toronto: Doubleday, 1983.

Woollett, Babe. *Have a Banana!* North Battleford, Saskatchewan: Turner-Warwick Publications Ltd., 1989.

Wynn, Kenneth. *Men of the Battle of Britain*. Norwich, Norfolk, U.K.: Gliddon Books, 1992.

LIBRARY AND ARCHIVES CANADA, OTTAWA, ONTARIO

Debates of the Senate, Official Reports (Hansard), Government of Canada, 1955-2002

Molson Archives Collection

Peter Stursberg interviews

Walter Gordon papers

Lester Pearson papers, correspondence and diaries

Index

Note: "HM" indicates Hartland de Montarville Molson.

A

Alderman, Tom, 268
Alexandra of Kent, Princess, 228–9
Algarsson, Grettir, 121–3
Alice, Princess, Lady Athlone, 185, 191, 197
Allan, Anna, 53
Allan, Gwen, 53
Allan, Lady Montague, 53, 65
Allan, Montague, 45, 65
Alliance Quebec, 292
Anthes Imperial Limited, 257
Astor, Bill, 162
Astor, David, 203–4, 240
Astor, John Jacob, 203
Astor, Nancy, 160, 161–4, 165–6, 169, 173–4, 186, 191, 198–9, 203–6, 222–3, 230, 244
Astor, Waldorf, 160, 163, 165–6, 168–9, 186, 198–9, 203, 204
Athlone, Alexander Cambridge, Earl of, 184, 186, 191, 197, 207–8

B

Banque Adam, 89, 90–1
Barker, Billy, 107–8
Bassett, John, 272–3
Baxter, Clive, 239
Beardmore, Eric, 134, 138, 153, 166
Beaubien, Louis de Gaspé, 244
Belderberg Group, 240–1
Beliveau, Jean, 226, 261, 277
Bell, Bobby, 92
Bell, Russell, 197–8
Belmont (Jamaica home), 243, 253–4, 302–5, 311
Bernhard of the Netherlands, Prince, 240
Bethel, Lorna, 205, 293
Bethel, Tony, 293
Bielish, Martha, 300
Bishop, Margaret, 107
Bishop, William Avery, 107–10, 112, 150–1, 159, 169, 179, 230, 244, 295–6
Bishop's College School, 69, 200, 222, 316

Black Watch Regiment (42nd Highlanders), 50, 53–4, 55–6, 57, 59–60
Blaiklock, Jim, 146
Blake, Hector, 262
Bolduc, Roch, 301
Boucher, Pierre, 30
Boucher de la Bruère de Boucherville, Joseph, 30
Bourassa, Henri, 35
Bourdon, Claire, 245
Brascan, 290
Britnell, Robert, 86, 88–9
Brockwell, Dora, 36
Bronfman, Charles, 268
Bronfman, Edgar, 268
Bronfman, Edward, 269, 272–3, 289–90
Bronfman, Peter, 269, 270, 272–3, 289–90
Burchill, Percival, 223
Buttram, Marjorie, 112

C

Cameron, Ewan, 248
Campbell, Clarence, 92, 226, 277
Canadian Airways, 115, 118, 119, 120
Canadian Arena Company, 226, 232, 247–8, 258–9, 260, 269
Canadian Breweries Limited, 213–14, 217, 247
Canadian Vickers Ltd., 123
Cantlie, Beatrice, 45
Cantlie, George, 45, 53, 54
Charterhouse School, 68–9, 74–5
Cheese, Paul, 231
Chenoweth, David, 220, 249, 268
Christmas, Bev, 153
Churchill, Winston, 172
Cliveden (Astor home), 161–5, 185, 186
Cobb, David, 268
Corbett, Vaughan, 147
Council of Europe, 267
Courtois, Jacques, 269, 270, 272–3
Cowan, Paul, 294–7
Craig, George, 218

Creighton, Donald, 244
Cross, James, 25, 264
Curlew yachts, 37–8, 84, 187, 198
Curran, Pat, 269, 272
Currie, Arthur, 65
Cushing, Jack, 78

D
Davis, Weir, 69
Dawes, Norman, 67, 194, 213–14
Dawes Brewery, 42
de Gaulle, Charles, 251–2
Desloges, Jean-Paul, 143, 147
Desmerais, Marie, 245
Dickinson, Hunt, 99
Diefenbaker, John George, 234, 239, 254
Di Nino, Consiglio, 310–11
Diversey Corporation, 257
Dominion Skyways, 110–20, 124
Dominion Soya Industries, 99–101
Douglas, Charles, 99, 100
Dow Breweries, 42, 214
Dowding, Hugh, 137–8
Drapeau, Jean, 242, 251, 252
Duplessis, Maurice, 194

E
Eastwood, Geoffrey, 184, 197, 229
Eaton, John David, 112
Ekers Brewery, 42
Elizabeth, the Queen Mother, 130–1, 208
Elizabeth II, 206–7, 208, 319
l'Esperance, Zotique, 227

F
Fairchild, Sherman, 122
Falkenberg, Alfred, 31
Falkenberg, Elizabeth, 31
Les Fils de la Liberté, 27
Findlay, Robert, 46, 47
Findlayson, Jock, 244
Fleury de la Gordenière, Claire, 29
Fleury de la Gordenière, Joseph, 29
Ford, Henry, 98–9, 100, 163
Fort Garry Brewery, 246
Foss, Roy H., 140
Fraser, Blair, 185
Front de libération du Québec (FLQ), 25, 234, 264, 273

G
Gagnon, Wilfrid, 206
Gault, Dorothy, 90
Gault, Hamilton, 56, 90, 125
Gelbart, Arnie, 306
Genest, Edgar, 219
Gipsy Moth aircraft, 105, 108
Gordon, Eve, 229
Gordon, Walter, 78, 95, 208, 219, 240–1, 252, 289
Gouin, Jean-Lomer, 67
Grandbois, Alain, 244
Grandpré, Louis de, 292
Greenhous, Brereton, 297
Grescoe, Paul, 268

H
Halde, Henri, 42
Hamm Brewing Company, 257
Hannen, Peter, 317
Hardinge, Andrew, 239, 266, 315
Hardinge, Charles, 239, 266, 315
Hardinge, Charles (Lord Hardinge of Penshurst), 228
Hardinge, Elizabeth, 311, 316
Hardinge, Margaret, Viscountess, 230
Hardinge, Max, 228, 266, 288–9, 293-4, 311, 313, 315–17
Hardinge, Nicholas, 228, 288, 293
Hardinge, Thomas de Montarville, 318
Harvey, Doug, 277
Henderson, Betty, 81
hockey, 75, 78–9, 89–90, 91–3
  professional, 270, 278–9
Hockey Hall of Fame, 261, 276–7
Hogg, Annie, 103
Hogg, George, 103
Hogg, William, 103
Hollinger Gold Mines, 115–16
Holt, Andrew, 78
Holt, Herbert, 45–6, 109
Houde, Camillien, 131, 206, 208
Howe, C.D., 119–20
Huggins, John, 197–8
Hungary, 127–8, 129, 224–5
Hutchinson, Andrew, 317
Hyde, George, 147
Hyde, John, 66, 196
Hyde, William, 196

I

Imperial Brewery, 42
Ivry (Quebec), 55, 196–7, 227–8, 229, 242, 248, 266–7, 311

J

Johnson, Daniel, 251, 261
Johnson, Philip, 119–20
Jolliet, Claire-Françoise, 28
Jolliet, Louis, 28

K

Kelly, Mel, 218
Killam, Izaac Walton, 243
King, William Lyon Mackenzie, 119
Kinnear, Doug, 313, 314
Klemin, Alexander, 122, 123
Knowles, Stanley, 241

L

Labatt Breweries, 214, 247, 290
Laporte, Pierre, 25, 264
Laurier, Wilfrid, 35, 36, 51
Lawrence, Tommy, 180
Leary, Timothy, 237–8
Leckie, Robert, 183–4, 185
Lee, Edwin, 163
LeMoyne, Jack, 296
Leuchtenberg, Catherine, Duchess of, 205–6
Leuchtenberg, Dimitri, Duke of, 206
Lindbergh, Charles, 168
Lindsay, Ted, 277
Little, Tommy, 149
Lloyd, Jean, 166, 186
Lochnan, Pete, 149, 153
Lowther, James, 112
Lusitania, 53
Lynch-Staunton, John, 310

M

MacDougall, Bart, 244
MacDougall, Dorothy, 36, 40, 69, 82, 131
    and HM, 190, 276
MacDougall, Edith, 62
MacDougall, Hartland Brydges, 37, 64
MacDougall, Hartland M., 131, 190, 229, 244, 273, 289, 318
MacDougall, Hartland "Tommy," 78, 82, 183, 190, 200, 226, 244, 303

MacEachen, Allan, 256
MacLeod, Alistair, 204, 228
MacNaughton, Alan, 263
Mahovlich, Frank, 260
Marcuse, Don, 113
Marina of Kent, Princess, 228, 229
Marshall, Jack, 295, 306, 310
Martin, Paul, Sr., 263
Mary, Princess Royal, 229–30
Massey, Vincent, 140, 213, 232
Mather, Larry, 78, 82, 190
Mather, Naomi Elizabeth, 36, 40, 69, 82
McCammon, Morgan, 248
McColl Frontenac Oil Company, 107
McCulloch, Margaret, 39–40, 239
McDonald Currie, 95, 97
McGill, Frank, 132, 175
McGill University, 104, 200, 201, 244, 262
McGregor, Gordon, 139, 143, 152–3, 198
McKenna, Brian and Terence, 306
McMahon, Arthur, 175
McMurray, Ken, 244
McNab, Ernie, 137, 141, 143, 151, 152, 172
McNaughton, A.G.L., 163–5
McNiven, Bruce, 292
McRae, John, 45
Meighen, Margaret, 303–4, 311, 312–13, 316
Meighen, Michael, 303, 304
Meighen, Teddy, 303
Melick, Henry, 253
Michener, Roland, 75, 275
Mitchell, William, 69
Moffett, R.J., 123
Molgat, Gildas, 312
Molson, Anne, 32
Molson, Catherine, 39, 104
Molson, Celia, 99, 133, 190, 202
Molson, Claire, 269–70
Molson, Cynthia, 239
Molson, David, 196, 247–8, 258–9, 258–61, 267–8, 272
Molson, Doris Carington, 82
Molson, Elizabeth-Zoë, 31, 49, 54, 55 62–3, 70–1, 126, 129, 134, 244, 268
Molson, Eric, 244, 247, 248, 293
Molson, Frederick William "Fred," 34, 35–6, 37, 39, 41, 42–3, 44, 63, 66, 67,

68, 70, 83, 84, 103

Molson, Harry, 43

Molson, Hartland de Montarville (HM).
ancestry, 27–31, 285
as businessman, 193, 200, 246–7
accountancy career, 95, 97, 102, 104
banking career, 89, 90–1, 94–5
directorships, 197, 201, 262
investments, 95, 96–7, 105
ventures, 98–101, 110–20
education, 45, 69, 71–3, 74–5, 76–81
in England, 142–5, 149, 153–7, 204
in Europe, 85–95
family life, 190
as father, 124, 190, 288, 294
as grandfather, 239, 266–7, 288–9,
294, 315
homes, 129–30, 288
marriage to Babbie, 103, 123–4,
125–6, 128–9
marriage to Magda, 129, 132–3
marriage to Peggy, 303–4, 311, 316
and parents, 63–4, 71–3
during First World War, 54, 55, 61
and flying, 87, 105–7, 109, 189
as pilot, 108, 115–16, 131, 142–5,
149, 153–7
as French speaker, 87, 91, 92–3, 94–5
holidays, 75, 84, 102–3, 126–7, 204,
242–3
at Ivry, 196–7, 227–8, 242
in Jamaica, 197–8, 243, 302–5, 306
honours, 189, 242, 262–3, 276–7, 299,
312
life
birth, 37
childhood, 37–40, 44–6, 48–9, 63–4
death, 316–17
and Molson's Brewery, 82–3, 194
as chairman, 257
as executive secretary, 187–8, 192–6
honorary positions, 287–8, 293, 305
as president, 218–19, 221–2, 245–7
as vice-president, 196, 199–200
in old age, 298–301, 313–14, 316–17
health problems, 306, 313, 314
at Kensington Place, 313, 314, 316
opinions, 234, 237, 249, 300, 302
on banking, 281, 299
on business success, 235–6

on economics, 210
on hockey violence, 261–2
on media, 284, 299–300
on punishment, 238
on Senate role, 282–4, 305, 307–8
personal attributes, 25–7, 81, 239
appearance, 45, 85, 313
character, 72–3, 82, 85, 192–3, 199,
233, 263
reputation, 199–200, 222
values, 273–4, 282, 300
as philanthropist, 200–1, 222, 225, 244,
275–6, 316
amateur sport causes, 200, 222, 236
fundraising, 168, 200–1, 222, 229,
275–6
young people's causes, 236, 276,
310–11
public persona, 167–8, 233–9
as Quebecer, 26–7
in Second World War, 132, 134, 138,
186–7, 189
combat injury, 156–7, 159–60
as fighter pilot, 142–5, 149, 153–7
as group captain, 181–2, 183–7
in Ottawa, 168–9, 183–7
postings, 171–2, 175–8, 179–83
as squadron commander, 172–8
as wing commander, 178–81
as senator, 222–5, 234–9, 241–2, 245–6,
267, 277–81, 293, 300–2
on conflict of interest, 281–2
on constitution repatriation, 291
on crime and punishment, 279–81
and FLQ crisis, 25–7, 264–5
on Quebec language laws, 291–2, 300
resignation, 307–11
on separatism, 264–5, 284–7
and social change, 237–9
on unemployment, 287
Veterans Affairs subcommittees,
295–6, 306
social life, 84–5, 102–3, 191, 245,
298–9
friends, 228, 244–5, 305
and sports (see also Montreal
Canadiens)
as athlete, 75, 76, 78–80
as hockey coach, 93–4
as hockey fan, 189, 225–7, 258,

260–2, 267, 277–9, 303
as hockey player, 75, 76, 78–9, 89, 91–3
support for, 200, 222, 236
wealth, 84–5, 105, 235, 268
Molson, Helen Kerr, 103, 107, 123–4, 128, 129
Molson, Herbert (1875–1938), 36–40, 84, 124, 125, 227
business career
directorships, 104
Dominion Skyways interest, 111, 112
at Molson's, 35–6, 41, 42–3, 83, 103–4
and prohibition, 68, 69–70
family life, 36–7, 47–8, 64–5
as father, 40, 56–9, 63–4, 67, 85–6, 104–5, 124
homes, 39, 46–7, 48, 268
marriage, 31–2, 34
in First World War, 52–4, 55–65, 67–8
friends, 45–6, 164
travels, 44, 46, 75, 83
Molson, Herbert (1882–1955), 43, 66, 83, 210, 220–1
as Molson's president, 125, 187, 188–9, 194–6, 208–10, 221
retirement, 214, 218–19
Molson, Ian, 311–12
Molson, Isabel, 55
Molson, Jack, 38, 39, 82
Molson, Jennie Baker, 33–4, 39, 54, 61, 64, 83
Molson, John, Junior, 27–31
Molson, John, Senior, 28, 32–3
Molson, John Henry, 83, 196, 218, 219
Molson, John Henry Robinson, 33, 43
Molson, John Thomas, 32, 33–4, 35, 39, 42–3
Molson, Kenneth, 39, 54–5
Molson, Kenneth Meredith, 117–18, 239
Molson, Lily, 39, 61
Molson, Lucille, 215, 248, 249
Molson, Mabel, 39, 65, 239
Molson, Magda, 127, 132–4, 159, 169, 171–2, 178, 179, 191, 197, 198, 200, 201–2, 228, 229, 230, 245, 267, 276, 293–4
Molson, Markland, 33, 37, 39
Molson, Martha, 33
Molson, Naomi, 39, 44

Molson, Pat, 302–3
Molson, Percival, 37, 39, 54–5, 56, 57, 60–1, 63, 64
Molson, Percival Talbot "Pete," 212–13, 214–17, 219, 247, 248–50
Molson, Peter (b. 1935), 258, 261
Molson, Peter (son of "Pete"), 303
Molson, Sarah, 33
Molson, Stephen, 244
Molson, Stuart, 109, 196, 219
Molson, Thomas, 33
Molson, Thomas Henry Pentland, 36, 39, 44–5, 58, 61, 63–4, 67, 68–9, 75–6, 79, 83, 99, 111, 112, 129, 187, 190, 195, 196, 218, 219, 227, 244, 257, 271, 287, 289
Molson, Velina, 39
Molson, Verity, 202
Molson, Walter, 55, 64, 68, 84, 215
Molson, William, 214–15, 258, 261
Molson, Zoë, 123, 202, 229, 288, 303
children, 266, 303, 311
in Europe, 205–6
and HM, 124, 288, 294, 314, 317–18
at Ivry, 228, 311
and Magda, 134, 229, 230
marriage to Nicholas Hardinge, 229, 230, 239, 294
marriage to Christopher Murray, 294
in Second World War, 169, 172, 179
Molson Brewery Employees Association, 188, 230
J.H.R. Molson & Brothers Brewery, 32, 33, 34–5, 36, 41–3
Molson Foundation, 243–4, 312
Molson Industries Limited, 257–8, 268, 287–8, 289–90
Molson Prize, 244
Molson's Brewery Limited, 43, 219, 230–1
employees, 68, 188, 193, 195, 230
expansion, 193–4, 217–18, 221, 231–2, 246–7
growth, 84, 221, 246–7, 256–8
Montreal plant, 83, 189, 195, 208–9, 213, 220, 230–1
products, 66, 220, 268
during Second World War, 186–8, 194–5
shares, 189, 208, 231
structure, 43, 83, 125, 208–10

Toronto brewery, 217–18, 220–1, 229
and U.S. market, 232
in western Canada, 231–2, 246
Molson's (Ontario) Limited (MOL), 193–4, 220
Montreal Canadiens, 262
David Molson and, 247–8, 258, 259–60, 261, 267–8, 269–74
HM's love for, 258, 271–4, 303
Molson ownership of, 226–7, 258, 260–1, 262, 289–90
sale of, 267–8, 269–74
Stanley Cup victories, 232, 261, 267
Montreal Forum, 258–9, 289.
Montreal General Hospital, 201, 229–30
Montreal Light Aeroplane Club, 105–6, 108–10
Mount Royal Club, 314–15
Mulroney, Brian, 301, 302
Murray, Christopher, 294, 314
Murray, Lowell, 308–9

N
National Breweries Ltd., 42, 194, 213–14
National Film Board, 294–6
National Hockey League, 260, 261, 270, 277, 278–9
National Research Council, 99, 122, 164
Nesbitt, Deane, 134, 139, 143, 150, 244
Nesbitt, J. Aird, 228–9, 245
Netherwood School, 202
Newfoundland Brewery Limited, 246
Newfoundland Skyways, 117
Nichol, John, 275
Nodwell, John, 151–2
Norris, Jim, 277
Northern Skyways, 110

O
O'Brien, Andy, 175
O'Dea family, 246
Ogilvie, Archibald, 86
Ogilvie, Bartlett, 78, 86, 90, 129
Ogilvie, Grace, 62
Ogilvie, Margaret, 205–6
O'Keefe Brewing Company, 217–18
O'Leary, Grattan, 241

P
Papineau, Louis-Joseph, 27

Parent, Paul, 201
Paris, 88–9, 90–1, 94
Parti Québécois, 284–7
Patton, Rosie, 89
Paul, Betty Henderson, 133–4
Pearson, Lester Bowles, 75, 162, 207, 211–13, 215–16, 224, 234, 240–1, 245, 251, 252–6, 275
Pearson, Maryon, 207, 245, 254
Peloquin, Rolland, 290–1, 312
Pentland, Catherine-Zoë, 30
Pentland, Charles, 30
Pentland, Charles Andrew, 30–1
Pentland, Christine, 126
Pentland, Margaret, 126
Pentland, Mary, 31
Pepin, Jean-Luc, 241
Peterson, Otto, 150, 151
Philip, Duke of Edinburgh, 206–7
Phillips, Lazarus, 263
Pickersgill, Jack, 225
Pignatorre, Alice, 39
Pitcher, Paul, 134, 144, 153, 228, 244, 305
Princess Patricia's Canadian Light Infantry (PPCLI), 54, 57, 60
Pulitzer, Ralph, 118

Q
Quebec Brewers Association, 66–7
Quebec Liquor Commission, 194

R
Rae, Jackson Ogilvie, 122
Rainier Brewery, 257
Rankin, Donald, 151, 160, 162, 163, 166
Raymond, Donat, 226, 244
Reardon, Ken, 277
Reeve, Robert, 106–7
Reford, Elsie, 62
Reford, Robert, 62
Retty, Joe, 115
Richard, Maurice, 226
Richardson, James, 119, 120
Riel, Maurice, 309–10
Roebuck, Arthur, 225
Rogers, John, 268
Ross, Dwight, 78
Royal Air Force (RAF) Coastal Command, 175–8

Royal Canadian Air Force (RCAF), 108,
    132, 134–5, 136–58, 161, 165, 169,
    170–1, 172–82
Royal Canadian Regiment, 57
Royal Flying Corps, 107
Royal Military College, 76–7, 276
Russel, Colin, 38, 83
Russel, Colin, 38, 44, 49
Russel, Dalzell, 134, 170, 172, 305
    as fighter pilot, 138, 143, 150, 151, 152
Russel, Evelyn, 38, 39, 44, 49–50, 54, 55,
    63, 83
Russel, Margaret, 38, 44, 49

S
St. Andrew's Ball, 190–1
Saint-Exupéry, Antoine de, 106–7
St. Laurent, Louis, 222, 223, 234, 308
Savard, Anatole, 244
Sawyer, Reg, 79–80
Scott, Barbara Ann, 200
Selke, Frank, 227, 262, 276–7
separatism, 251–2, 264, 270, 284–7
Shaw, Bobby, 163
Sick's Breweries, 231, 246, 256–7
Sims, "Tim," 110–12, 118
Sinclair, Gordon, 176–7
Skaife, Adam, 35, 42–3
Skaife, Queenie, 38
Smart, Campbell, 219
Smart, Tommy, 79–80
Smith, Sydney, 241
Smither, Ross, 150
Smythe, Conn, 277
Starnes, Helen and John, 303, 304, 316
Stevens, Steve, 72
Stikeman, Harold, 244
Sully, Jack, 183, 184
Suthren, Victor, 312

T
Tacuboy, Elmer, 314
Taschereau, Elzéar-Alexandre, 30
Taschereau, Françoise, 30
Taschereau, Gabriel-Elzéar, 29
Taschereau, Louis-Alexandre, 30
Taschereau, Marie-Claire, 29
Taschereau, Marie-Louise-Elizabeth, 29
Taschereau, Thomas Jacques, 29
Taschereau, Thomas Pierre-Joseph, 29–30
Taylor, E.P., 201, 213–14, 217–18
Thyssen, Hans Heinrich von, 253
Timmins, Jules, 115–16
Trans-Canada Airlines, 119–20, 198
Troup, Peter, 110–12
Trudeau, Pierre Elliott, 25, 256, 259, 261,
    267, 284, 291
Turnbull, Wallace Rupert, 123
Turner, John and Geills, 304

U
Union Brewery, 42

V
Victoria Rifles, 50
Voss, Carl, 226

W
Weston family, 253
Whitbread's Brewery, 205
Wilkins, Hubert, 168
Williams, M. Lawson, 122
Willmott, Donald Gilpin, 257, 287
Winn, Alice, 166, 186
Winters, Robert, 253–4

Y
Yarnell, John, 275
Young, Frank, 117
Yuile, Ann, 202
Yuile, Arthur, 134, 172, 176